EXPLORING WALES

EXPLORING WALES

by

WILLIAM CONDRY

FABER AND FABER
London

First published in 1970
by Faber and Faber Limited
24 Russell Square London WC1
Printed in Great Britain by
Latimer Trend & Co Ltd Plymouth
All rights reserved

ISBN 0 571 09434 1

CONTENTS

'*Steal, if possible, my dear friend, one summer from the cold hurry of business, and come to Wales.*'

SHELLEY

ILLUSTRATIONS

9

Illustrations

PREFACE

For over twenty years I have enjoyed living in Caernarvonshire, Merioneth and Cardiganshire. Of course I had often visited other parts of Wales but it was not until I came to write this book that I explored them in detail. It has been a rewarding experience and I hope what I have written will help others to get as much delight as I have had. Wales is a tiny country on world standards. But how big or how small a land really is depends on the power of the lens under which you examine it. After all, whole books have been written about one parish. So in writing about all Wales in this one volume I have had to discard, very reluctantly, lots of fascinating detail. But I console myself that the discoveries which mean most to us are those we make for ourselves. So I would be happy to feel that the main achievement of this book will not be the information it imparts so much as the encouragement it may give people to go exploring for themselves. The truth is that the most unpromising places can be full of interest: each county has its personality if it is approached with a desire to understand something of its natural and human history. I pray that what I have written in this book is accurate. But guide books are marvellous hunting grounds for error-spotters and I shall be grateful if those readers who swoop hawk-like on my mistakes will let me know of them.

People who visit towns or the coast have no difficulty in amusing themselves. But often in the countryside it is less easy to know where to go or what to do. In Wales it is easier than it was now that there are three National Parks: Snowdonia, Brecon Beacons and Pembrokeshire (with another imminent in Mid-Wales). These parks have information centres that give every help and guidance to visitors. The Forestry Commission too has its National Forest Parks where people are allowed considerable freedom for walking, picnicking and camping and are encouraged to follow forest tracks and nature trails. Regarding access elsewhere, including the National Parks: not quite every place I have mentioned in this book has a public right of way to it. So if there seems any doubt on this point please ask first. The polite inquirer is rarely turned away. But do not expect to be welcomed if you let your dog go unleashed across sheep country.

I have not travelled through Wales without getting some vivid impressions about the appearance of the countryside. It is striking how much care is taken over the look of some towns, villages and farms; and how neglected others are. And alas, there are those increasing threats to rural beauty—power stations, masts and pylons, poles and wires, wrongly sited chalet and caravan developments, military installations, reservoir dams, the unnecessary petrol stations (often the pumps of two or three rival firms in a single village). Such blemishes offend the eye especially painfully in a land so small and fair as Wales. So I hope that all who love Wales and wish to see its beauty spoilt as little as possible will join the Council for the Protection of Rural Wales (address: Meifod, Montgomeryshire). The National Trust also has done much to save the Welsh countryside from ugly forms of development and needs more members. If your particular interest is wildlife conservation there are Naturalists' Trusts to support in every part of Wales. The Royal Society for the Protection of Birds also has important reserves in Wales.

The pleasures of exploration can be much increased by the use of one-inch and two-and-half-inch Ordnance Survey maps; and to help in locating the places mentioned in this book map-references are included in the index.

Many kind friends have helped me with information and comment about all parts of Wales and I gladly take this opportunity of thanking them all.

1

ANGLESEY[1]

(Môn or Sir Fôn)

Anglesey, the island county of Wales, is except for Flint-shire also the smallest. It is a place of wide skies and the light is often brilliant. Doubtless it used to be a part of the mainland but not during at least the last 5,000 years, the strait being produced by the subsidence of land that occurred on many parts of the Welsh coast in early post-glacial times. Anglesey takes pride in being the 'Mother of Wales' as the road-sign 'Môn Mam Cymru' assures you when you reach the suspension bridge. The title probably arose from the island's fertility compared with less productive mountain districts of North Wales whose people were formerly supplied with much grain from the Anglesey cornfields (which are now mostly cattle pastures). But it is possible that Anglesey's motherhood was a religious one, going back to the Iron Age when Celtic paganism had its deepest roots in this remotest corner of Wales. Here, according to Tacitus, were the headquarters of druidism until A.D. 61 when the Romans overran the island and expelled the druids from their sacred groves. But though the druids have gone Anglesey remains a Celtic bastion and speaks much Welsh.

The largest off-shore island in the British Isles, Anglesey has no real mountains but is crossed by several lines of parallel low hills only nine of which exceed five hundred feet. Their rocks are of many ages and types: besides a predominance of Pre-Cambrian there are also several Ordovician areas, just a touch of

[1] To the Romans Anglesey was Mona but 'Mona' on nineteenth-century milestones refers to a coaching station 12 miles from Holyhead along what is now A5.

Silurian, a streak of Old Red Sandstone and plenty of Carboniferous Limestone. Add the material brought by glaciers coming across the sea from the north; and the wide sand dunes in the south; and you have a remarkable assortment of soils for one small county. There are several fine natural lakes and reservoirs; a few small marshes; extensive lengths of sea cliff; numerous offshore islets; and many little muddy creeks and estuaries. In all a place of great variety and interest.

To get to Anglesey by road or rail you must cross the Menai Strait (Culfor Menai) which stretches for eighteen miles from Abermenai Point to Puffin Island. The strait is deep between rocks in some places, shallow over sand in others; but even the shallowest parts are never likely to silt up entirely because of the tides that come swishing through. On a calm summer day with yachts idling about and terns plopping in after fish the strait looks idyllic. But it can be a dangerous water when winds are high and tides are big; and there were frightful accidents in the pre-bridge days when everybody crossed by the various ferries.

The suspension bridge (1826) was the crowning glory of Telford's Holyhead road and as the first bridge ever to cross the strait its building caused great excitement. As one report put it: 'On the 26th of April, 1825, the first chain of this stupendous work was thrown over the Menai Strait in the presence of an immense concourse of persons.' The new route to Holyhead was an immediate success and for twenty-five years the Anglo-Irish traffic streamed across it. But then came the railway and Robert Stephenson. Like Telford, Stephenson and his advisers had to experiment with various bridge designs. Eventually they hit on the idea of two iron tubes, rectangular in cross-section, spanning the strait side by side. These not very beautiful tubes were slung across the water in 1850 a mile west of Telford's more elegant bridge; and still they carry the iron horses across. A problem both Telford and Stephenson had to face was that of keeping their bridges high enough above the water to clear the masts of tall sailing ships. This is why both are about a hundred feet above the level of high water.

The person to greet you once you have crossed either of the bridges is the first Marquis of Anglesey. He did well at Waterloo and as a reward now stands on top of a column of Moelfre limestone on a wooded hillock along A5 surveying his domains from a great height, a sort of nineteenth-century pole-squatter. For a small fee and by climbing a vast number of steps inside the column you can share his view of a really marvellous all-round panorama of Anglesey, the strait and Snowdonia. The column was built in 1816, the statue added in 1860. If you have no head for heights you had better do the walk to the island church instead. This path leaves A5 a little beyond the suspension bridge and takes you down past a windswept wood of Scots pines, then along a causeway to a tiny church (medieval but much altered) on an island. The walk then returns under the bridge to Menai Bridge town which under its original name of Porthaethwy had an ancient ferry and today is a calling place for pleasure steamers, is a yachting centre and has a very active marine biology station.

The village just beyond the marquis's column is Llanfair-pwllgwyngyll, usually shorted to Llanfairpwll or Llanfair P.G. But it is also often lengthened to become the world's longest place name which is, alas, not genuine. It was invented by some witty but now forgotten Welshman presumably to amuse the tourists towards the end of last century. Anyway Llanfairpwllgwyngyll ('the church of Mary by the white pool under the hazels') is long enough. The village's other claim to distinction is that here was founded Britain's first Women's Institute (1915). It also remembers the traffic of other days: a neat white toll-house still displays the dues chargeable at its former gate. For instance, if your wagon wheels had tyres 'fastened with nails projecting and not countersunk' you were a menace to the road surface and paid double toll.

The eastern corner of Anglesey, easily reached from Menai Bridge, is one of the most attractive and interesting parts of the county. In a few miles along the strait you come to Beaumaris, a place of yachts and famous for the splendid castle placed there by Edward I to command that end of the strait as well as all Anglesey. Today this many-towered castle which never saw military action stands quietly beautiful, enclosed by its reflecting water, and has rather the atmosphere of a moated manor-house, being almost surrounded by a parkland with trees and pleasant walks. A special external feature is its private dock once used by supply ships. The fourteenth-century church of Beaumaris is also worth seeing. It has early memorials, some glass and a brass of the sixteenth century and seats with well-carved misericords.

Its most conspicuous historical possession is the fifteenth-century tomb of William and Ellen Bulkeley on which vandals have cut their worthless names and initials in every succeeding century. The half-timbered house called Tudor Rose, now an antique shop and museum in the main street, is an interesting survival of medieval Wales. Also in the town there survives a seventeenth-century court house and a gaol that preserves its old treadmill. Beaumaris is almost unique in being a Welsh town with no Welsh[1] (nor English) name. It was christened in 1295 by Edward I himself. He looked across the lovely coastal lowland and said, no doubt in his best Norman French: 'This shall be Beau Marais' ('fair marsh'). Or as a chronicler put it in Latin: 'Bellummariscum voluit appellari.'

In Anglesey's easternmost tip is Penmon which has two major attractions: the priory ruins and the headland. Here in the sixth century came Seiriol, a holy man who probably established his cell near a spring which became a medieval holy well and still retains it covering masonry. The priory church has good twelfth-century work and a tenth-century font and cross. There are ruins of a thirteenth-century refectory and an almost perfect dovecote of the early seventeenth century. Eight hundred yards due west of the church a cross of about the year 1000 stands alone in a field. It is carved with faint patterns on all sides and looks across the sea to Penmaenmawr.

For a fee you may motor through a deerless deerpark to the headland opposite Puffin Island. The waters here have a bad name among sailors and there is a black-and-white lighthouse that tolls a mournful bell. They call this place Black Point (Trwyn Du) but in fact everything is shining white limestone, including the pebbles on the beach. Here are still active quarries that probably produced the stones for Caernarvon castle. There are many limestone flowers and nesting sea birds—gulls, fulmars and terns. And there really are puffins on Puffin Island, almost their only Anglesey home. 'Puffin' is only one of several names for this island which is also Priestholm or Ynys Seiriol, names which preserve the memory that Seiriol had a cell here as well as at Penmon and that later there was a monastery whose twelfth-century church tower still stands with earlier monastic remains.

The limestone of Penmon continues west along the coast to

[1] Unless you call 'Biwmares' Welsh!

1. Puffin Island, Anglesey, breeding place of seabirds and site of early Christian settlement

2. Celtic cross of about A.D. 1000 at Penmon, near Beaumaris, Anglesey

3. Caernarvon Castle, most celebrated of all medieval Welsh castles

4. Bardsey Island (Ynys Enlli), Caernarvonshire, had great prestige as a place of medieval pilgrimage

Anglesey

Bwrdd Arthur ('Arthur's table'), a flat-topped hill still partly defended by the thick bases of Iron Age walls built long before the time of the Arthurian legends. Bwrdd Arthur, also called Din Sylwy, is a delightful spot, with common and hoary rockroses on its south-facing crags and monkshood on the slopes below. From it you look west across the great sweep of Red Wharf Bay (Traeth Coch) to the growing holiday resort of Benllech. Five miles island from Benllech is Llangefni, which is at its best on Thursdays if you like busy little market towns with stalls in the streets. For peace escape along the lane past the parish church to what is rather rare in Anglesey—a streamside, woodland walk. The church is nineteenth century but has a Dark Ages memorial stone to one Culidorus (son of Secundus) and his wife Oruvita. North-west of the town is the Cefni reservoir, popular with anglers and bird-observers. And a good three miles east in the lonely church of Penmynydd is a tomb (1385) with effigies of two Tudor ancestors of Henry VII. Down the centuries people have broken off bits round the edge of the alabaster in the belief that a healing lotion could be concocted from them. The church is fourteenth century but in the outside east wall you will find three stones, decorated with chevrons, from some more ancient building. Geologists may like to visit the grave of A. C. Ramsay, a pioneer of North Wales rock study. It is in Llansadwrn churchyard between Penmynydd and Beaumaris, its headstone appropriately a glacial erratic.

Mecca for botanists in this part of Anglesey is Cors Goch, a wide, wet hollow in the limestone hills west of Red Wharf Bay. This quiet attractive fen, a reserve of the North Wales Naturalists' Trust, is rich in lime-loving plants such as sedges and marsh orchids. Yet the slight hill that forms its south-east flank is an acid ground covered with heather amongst which grows the rather rare pale heath violet. Devotees of George Borrow will remember the delicious account of his visit to the birthplace of Goronwy Owen (1723–69), one of Wales's most celebrated poets. The rockiness, sterility and desolation as well as the grunting, sniffing pigs of Llanfair Mathafarn Eithaf depress him at first. But when he finds the people generous and welcoming, his spirits revive and he goes on to give a characteristic description of finding first the poet's church, then his house called Ty Gronwy where he meets an eight-year-old girl who, to his delight, gives him her autograph: 'Ellen Jones yn perthyn o bell i gronow owen'. ('Ellen Jones belonging from afar to gronow owen.')

Moelfre, two miles north of Benllech, is a holiday and fishing village that looks along the coast to Puffin Island nine miles away. Close to busy shipping lanes Moelfre has a long and glorious history of lifeboat rescues. For a lovely cliff walk go past the lifeboat station (glimpse of efficient-looking boat) to the headland with views of Ynys Moelfre, a gull and cormorant island. Then round to the memorial to the *Royal Charter* (wrecked 1859) and so back inland to Moelfre; or for a longer ramble continue with the cliffs to Llugwy Bay.

Among trees and fields inland is the unique fourth-century site called Din Llugwy. This is a group of hut-circles within a former walled enclosure. But they are so much more elaborate than the hut-circles you normally find in hill forts that they are assumed to have been some important chieftain's headquarters. The foundations, some circular, some rectangular, are beautifully preserved; and herb robert and shining cranesbill now decorate them happily. Excavation showed that the hut in the north-east corner had been an iron-smelter's workshop. The footpath leading to Din Llugwy, passes near the remains of Capel Llugwy, a twelfth-century church alone on a hill that slopes gently seawards. It has an additional sixteenth-century chapel with a crypt reached down seven stone steps. Anglesey, with about fifty, has or has had more Neolithic tombs than any other Welsh county and there is one with a colossal capstone a few hundred yards south along the lane from Capel Llugwy. Like another close to Benllech this was a communal burial chamber where excavation has yielded remains of many human skeletons, various domestic animals and numerous shellfish.

This parish of Penrhosllugwy was the birthplace of Lewis Morris (1701–65), one of the most accomplished Welshmen of his century. Antiquary, poet, prose-writer, mineralogist, surveyor, engineer, he collected valuable Welsh manuscripts and wrote a large number of highly interesting letters many of which survive. Of value to the geographer is a survey of Welsh ports and harbours which he carried out for the government. A granite cross high above A5025 half a mile south-east of City Dulas commemorates him and his accomplished brothers

Richard and William. The Morris brothers were the founders of the Cymmrodorion Society in London, 1751.

From Llugwy Bay's wide red sands you look inland to one of Anglesey's most prominent hills, Mynydd Bodafon. Up there you are off the limestone and on to vastly more ancient rock—a quartzite of Pre-Cambrian time. Here Bronze Age man had his huts on the eastern slopes and here modern man comes for his picnics among the rocks and the heather. Four miles north, Mynydd Eilian, between Dulas Bay and Amlwch, is spiky with radio masts—the hub of post-office tele-communications for shipping. In the nineteenth century this same hill was used for semaphoring messages to Liverpool, advising shipowners there when their vessels had been sighted off Holyhead. The signals were sent from hill to hill and the name of a ship so semaphored took less than a minute to travel the seventy miles from Holyhead to Liverpool.

From Mynydd Eilian the land drops quickly northward to a rocky coast. Here until the eighteenth century pilgrims flocked to visit the well of St. Eilian, famous for miracle cures. It is half a mile north-west of Llaneilian church but is now in ruins. Curative wells were valuable money-raisers, it being made clear to the devoted that no benefit could come from drinking the holy water unless they also dropped an offering in the chest provided. At Llaneilian the old chest (cyff) still survives in the church which is unique in Anglesey in retaining its medieval loft and screen in anything like entirety. It is rather plain work but is enlivened by a gruesomely painted skeleton. There are also jolly-looking, colourful angels observing you from high up the walls. Dog tongs and two musical instruments are shown in a glass case. A curious chapel reached down a passage from the chancel is by tradition the site of Eilian's original sixth-century cell. The altar (or part of a shrine?) that it contains looks extremely ancient.

All along this coast on both sides of lighthouse-crowned Point Lynas are good cliffs, secluded coves and many fine walks. (Can we see 'Eilian' lurking in the name of Point Lynas?) From that headland you can follow a cliff path west until you come to the harbour at Amlwch, a town and port that developed after the discovery of a rich vein of copper on nearby Parys Mountain in 1768. Before the end of the century the biggest copper mine in Europe had developed there with 1,500 men on its pay-roll; and Amlwch had grown from a hamlet to a town, its harbour being built in 1793. But by 1815 the best of the ore was exhausted, foreign copper was undercutting the prices, Parys mine closed and though it reopened later it never fully recovered. Though Parys Mountain today lies derelict, its summit hollowed into a vast arid crater, it retains a certain grandeur and beauty in the naked rawness of its terraces and screes and the delicate pink colouring of the rocks, some of which are sheened with a coppery green. The ore here was known to the Romans: their circular cakes of copper about a foot across and three inches thick, some stamped in Latin, have been widely found in Anglesey. Today attempts are being made to open the mines again.

Amlwch port, which used to accommodate thirty vessels each of 200 tons, has long since reverted to being a harbour for small craft. It is also used by pilot boats waiting for ships approaching the Mersey. Westwards the headland is grossly disfigured by a factory that extracts bromine from sea water. But beyond that the prospect improves and a cliff path goes pleasantly on to Bull Bay (modern holiday village) and further west to the much wilder scenery of Dinas Gynfor. On this brackeny, chough-frequented promontory are the embankments of an Iron Age fort; and all about lies attractively wild and rocky country broken up by little wet-floored valleys.

Off Dinas Gynfor is the most northerly fragment of Wales, the islet of Middle Mouse. The Welsh named the island Ynys Badrig (Patrick's Island) and there is still a lonely church dedicated to him on the adjacent mainland cliffs. Why, you may wonder, site a church in isolation on the cliffs? Probably the answer is simply that Patrick first landed on the coast at the nearby cove and thankfully established his cell immediately above. The spot once sanctified, the power of tradition would be enough to maintain a church there ever since. Tradition also has it that this was the Patrick who went over to convert the Irish and that it was from Llanbadrig he set sail.

The two arms of Cemaes Bay might be called Beauty and the Beast. On the east side is Beauty in the form of unspoilt cliff-lands owned by the National Trust and occupied only by Patrick's church and one farm. On the west is the sinister-looking hulk of Wylfa Head nuclear power-station ('lady guides available'). And from Llanbadrig you see another contrast: straight across the bay you look at this most modern source of power but if your eye travels south you see on the skyline one of the most ancient sources of power—a windmill. But like all the many Anglesey windmills it is long since disused.

A couple of medieval churches inland are also worth seeing: at Llanfechell and Llanbabo. The one at Llanfechell (a best-kept village) has an odd-looking cone of stone upon its square tower. This excrescence, the locals will tell you, was put there as a sound-suppressor on the insistence of an eighteenth-century squire who claimed that the fermentation of his beer was upset by the vibration of the church bell! The church has a modern door in an ancient doorway: beside it stands a medieval grave-slab with floral decoration. Also in the porch are more recent gravestones, one in Latin to a nameless botanist or herbalist who died in 1709. From the north end of the village you can see a triangle of tall, slender stones. They stand on a rise close to a stile in the hedge at a meeting place of no doubt ancient foot-paths and have presumably been there since the Bronze Age. Three miles south at the isolated little church of Llanbabo three crude medieval faces greet you over the door. But inside is finer work—an ornate grave-slab of the fourteenth century that is probably a memorial to Pabo to whom this church is dedicated.

Close to Llanbabo is the long narrow reservoir called Llyn Alaw from which flows the Alaw stream, famous in story. For in the *Mabinogion* it is related how Branwen, a British princess whose marriage with an Irish king had caused war between Britain and Ireland, died of a broken heart. She was buried, says the tale, in a four-sided grave on the bank of the River Alaw. This grave by long tradition was a tumulus called Bedd Branwen ('Branwen's grave') a mile and a half south-west of Llanbabo. The tradition seemed confirmed when in 1813 the mound was opened to reveal in very truth a four-sided grave. Proper excavation, however, has revealed that this tumulus was in fact a multiple grave of the Bronze Age containing the remains of at least eight burial urns. Two miles south of Bedd Branwen the road skirts one of Anglesey's loveliest natural lakes, nearly all of which are rich in plant and animal life. This is Llyn Llywenan, a lake that has both extensive reed beds and plenty of open water and is a breeding place of many waterfowl. Two Neolithic burial chambers, visible down the lake's length, stand close to its southern end. Beyond are the woodlands of Treiorwerth which are interesting because planted in the eighteenth century to disprove the oft-stated assertion that trees would not flourish in that exposed part of Anglesey.

The north-eastern corner of Anglesey gets wilder and rockier the nearer you get to the sea. The path to Carmel Head takes you through heather, bracken and gorse and out to the cliffs. There you look across two miles of water to the Skerries and their red-and-white lighthouse whose powerful beam, like Bardsey's, sometimes brings mass destruction to migrant birds. The Skerries—the name is Viking—have breeding sea birds and seals. Their Welsh name, Ynysoedd y Moelrhoniaid, means 'seal islands'. Your best hope of getting there (calm weather only) is by boat from Holyhead. The Skerries light was one of those which made a vast income from shipping dues in the days when it was privately owned. It was sold to Trinity House in 1841 for about half a million pounds. For a sweeping view of Carmel Head and district go up gorse-topped Mynydd y Garn, easily reached from a high climbing lane on the west. From Carmel Head east the coast continues rocky and almost uninhabited for two miles to Cemlyn Bay which is a splendid curve of pebbled storm beach remarkable for the profusion of sea-kale growing all along it. Locked in behind this high beach is a lagoon of great beauty often visited by birds. Cemlyn, alas, looks across to Wylfa power-station less than two miles east.

South of Carmel Head the coast is cliffy for several miles but there are a few small coves and larger beaches, such as at Church Bay, which are popular bathing places. They are easily reached from villages along A5025 such as Llanfaethlu. If you want to see a windmill with fairly recent memories of its working days there is one at Llanddeusant with its arms still picturesque against the sky. Naturalists may find it worthwhile to look or listen at Llyn Garreg-lwyd, just north of Llanfaethlu. It is a complete reed swamp and a haunt for many water birds. On the coast here the botanist Samuel Brewer recorded in his diary on 27th March 1726, that near Trefadog he had come upon 'a large creek in the rocks about forty yards long, at the end of which is the finest cave I ever saw, adorned on the sides and crown, very thick set, with *Chamaefilix marina anglica*. The cave is so large that eight couples might dance in it'. The plant he means is the fern called sea spleenwort. I hope it is still there in such abundance.

That the pronunciation of Holyhead has slipped from 'Holy' into 'Holly' is historically unfortunate. It tends to obscure the probability that in the Dark Ages Holyhead was chiefly known as a religious centre. Very likely before that it was the holy of holies of druidism. The earliest Christian name surviving from there is that of Cybi (pronounced 'Kubby') who seems to have been a strong-shanked preacher of the sixth century, keeping the Christians on their toes in all parts of Anglesey. He is by tradition the sun-burnt missionary, 'the tawny saint', as Borrow calls him, translating his Welsh name Cybi Felyn. So it is from this holy fellow that we get Holyhead's Welsh name, Caer Gybi ('Cybi's fortress'). The 'fortress' is explained by the unusual site which Cybi chose for his church—a space within the lofty walls of a Roman fort. And there a church dedicated to him still stands within the Roman walls. It is partly medieval with a later tower. There is an admirable south porch with figures and shields above it. Along the battlemented parapets are carvings of various weird creatures. A little building by the churchyard gate is the much altered nave of a fourteenth-century chapel.

Holyhead, easily Anglesey's largest town, has developed entirely as a port for crossing to Ireland, a career it began centuries ago. Because of this it has become a real outpost of Ireland. But the many Irish who have settled there have been so well assimilated that many of the O'Reillys, O'Briens and Murphys speak Welsh with the rest. But they have not forgotten St. Patrick; and Holyhead, uniquely in Wales, celebrates 17th March with as much enthusiasm as St. David's day (1st March). Today Holyhead is more than a port. It is also a holiday place with a harbour full of yachts, a bathing beach and a promenade which runs right round the harbour and then for another mile and a half along Britain's longest breakwater. The harbour is a base for the Trinity House ship *Argus* which regularly services lighthouses along the Welsh coast. Its depot along the promenade displays a fascinating array of spare buoys. The county library has an attractive display of model ships and ship photographs.

For a viewpoint walk go on past the breakwater and the quartzite quarries that built most of it (there is also limestone in it from Red Wharf Bay and sandstone from Runcorn, Cheshire). Beyond the quarries with their raw white cliffs you can climb rough gorsy slopes to the cave-hollowed headland of North Stack. From there you can go up to the highest point in Anglesey (720 feet) and one of the great prospects of Wales. You look east right across Anglesey to all the Caernarvonshire mountains from the Carneddau to the end of Lleyn. And sometimes out in the western sea, especially against a sunset sky, you see many miles of the Irish mountains seventy and more miles distant. Immediately about you on this rocky summit are the walls of the Iron Age fort called Caer y Twr. Down the west side, and especially at South Stack, Holyhead Mountain plunges to spectacular cliffs where gulls, puffins, guillemots and razorbills breed. There are also fulmars gliding about and you may see a few of Anglesey's rare choughs here. The remarkable contortions in the South Stack rocks close to the lighthouse tell of enormous and ancient pressures in the crust of the earth.

If the hill fort on top of Holyhead Mountain contains no hut-circles it is because the ground was too rocky for regular habitation. This fort was probably a refuge for emergencies, its builders living in the village three-quarters of a mile south-west down the slope near the road to South Stack. Marked on the map by the traditional name Cytiau'r Gwyddelod ('Irishmen's huts'), though there is no particular reason to call them so, about twenty of these hut foundations remain in a remarkable state of preservation. Some are circular, some oblong; and when excavated they yielded tools and pottery of the second to fourth centuries. Today they lie among gorse and bracken but in their day were surrounded by fields. There are far earlier traces of man on Holy Island. A couple of miles south-east of South Stack two fine stones, presumed to be Bronze Age, are upright in a field behind the house called Plas Meilw. Two miles east we are back in the Stone Age with the communal burial chamber at Trefignath. It looks like three burial chambers end to end but was perhaps one large one. The erect stone just up the lane towards Holyhead is probably Bronze Age.

On the west side of Holy Island's narrow waist is Trearddur Bay, a rapidly growing holiday resort. It stands on what was the main road to Holyhead before the Stanley embankment was built. In pre-embankment days the coaches used Four Mile bridge (which is ancient) at high tide or went across the sands near the present embankment at low tide. Trearddur has lovely but often breezy bathing sands. Rhoscolyn beach, three miles south, is sheltered by a headland and an islet. It too is very popular for bathing, picnicking and yachting. There is a glorious northward walk along unspoilt cliffs past a look-out station to the ancient holy well called Ffynnon Gwenfaen, then on to Black Arch (Bwa Du) and the White Arch which are re-markable cliff formations. Along the shore east of Rhoscolyn you soon come to the end of Holy Island and look across the channel to Valley R.A.F. airfield, scene in 1943 of the richest find of Iron Age remains ever made in Wales. It was when a small lake called Cerrig Bach was being filled in to make the war-time airfield that a mechanical digger scooped up from the lake's peaty margin over a hundred miscellaneous objects such as spears, swords, scabbards, shields, chariot wheels and slave-gang chains. One of these chains was even used in 1943 to pull out a stranded lorry! The presence of such a collection of useful objects in a lake is usually explained by calling them votive offerings. The finds from Valley are in the National Museum at Cardiff.

Across Cymyran Bay from Rhoscolyn is another popular place, Rhosneigr, which has a large natural lake (yachting and angling) as well as a magnificent sweep of sands. For anyone wanting to alternate beach-lolling with plane-spotting this is the place, for behind stretches the busy Valley airfield. To see all the planes arriving and departing, station yourself in the lane close to the railway bridge at Llanfair-yn-neubwll. On a small head-land south of Rhosneigr at Porth Trecastell (also called Cable Bay) stands a burial chamber worth seeing, especially if you find it hard to visualize what these tombs originally looked like. For this one has had its dome reconstructed and fitted with a window on top to let the daylight in. It is called Barclodiad y Gawres ('the giantess's apronful'), a typical folk-lore place name of the type that explained all large stone antiquities as the work of giants. An important feature of this particular passage grave is the patterns carved on five of the stones, for prehistoric tomb art is rare in Britain.

Anglesey

Southwards the coast continues rocky to Aberffraw, the most interesting feature being the miniature church of Llangwyfan built on an islet to which you can walk at low tide. There can be little doubting the antiquity of a site so typical of early Celtic foundations. This church remained in regular use until fairly recent times but it must often have been touch and go whether the parson and his congregation got home with dry feet. Perhaps it was because of these special risks that the minister was granted the right to claim 'hay for his horse, two eggs for his breakfast, a penny loaf and half a pint of small beer' from the nearby farm of Plas Llangwyfan.

Aberffraw (accent on the 'ber' or call it simply Berffro) is a small, dune-neighbourhood village with a medieval church whose west wall has a noble twelfth-century arch. Though you would never guess it Aberffraw was, from the Dark Ages to the Edwardian conquest, a seat of government of the princes of North Wales. But if there was any splendour in the way they lived there is absolutely nothing to show for it now. No palace walls remain, no line of memory in the church. Before the railway age Aberffraw was a busy little port but today it sits quietly by its stream which is crossed by an ancient disused bridge and goes on down a little estuary to the sea. Note at two places on the map south of Aberffraw the name Cwningar. It is related to 'coney', a rabbit, and means a rabbit warren. It evidently goes back to the Middle Ages when the Normans introduced rabbits to Britain, liberated them in sandy places where they could burrow and multiply and become a source of cheap meat.

Though Aberffraw church lacks any memorial to the early princes you will find one in the church hidden behind houses and trees at Llangadwaladr a couple of miles east. Here there is an ancient stone that remembers 'Catamanus wisest and most illustrious of all kings' (to translate the oriental-flavoured Latin inscription). 'Catamanus' is a Latin form of Cadfan, a seventh-century king of Gwynedd. Formerly the estuary of the Cefni went inland a full twelve miles to Llangefni, nearly cutting Anglesey into two unequal parts, the southern portion being known as Sir Fôn Fach ('little Anglesey'). But near the end of the eighteenth century an embankment, or cob, was thrown across the estuary at Malltraeth (an ancient shipyard). This reduced

26

Anglesey

the estuary to three miles in length, the rest of it being turned
into difficult, sea-level pastures.

Newborough was new when Edward I, having settled on
Beaumaris as his Anglesey headquarters, moved the Welsh from
there and settled them at Rhos-hir, which he made into a chartered town called Newborough. It retained its importance until
Tudor times but then declined. Today from Newborough you
look seawards across a vast tract of duneland, some of it conifer-
covered. But in Newborough's early days this was a fertile
district; for there is historical and archaeological evidence for the
existence of medieval settlements that are now deep beneath
dunes that spread across mainly from the fourteenth to the
seventeenth centuries. In 1561 the government in London
ordered the mayor of Newborough to prevent the cutting or
uprooting of marram-grass (then used in mat-making) because
this grass was then, as it still is, being planted to stabilize the
dunes. Centuries earlier Abermenai Point had been a chief place
of departure of ships to Ireland but that anchorage also got
overwhelmed with sand.

Today, as in most British dune-systems, the spreading rate of
Newborough's dunes has slackened to a state of near-stability.
Between the sand hills, in places where there is no forestry, are
established the wide hollows usually called dune slacks where the
ground water is only just below the sand. In these wet slacks,
in sand that is lime-rich from powdered sea-shells, grow the
splendid wild flowers for which these dunes are well known. It
is because of this wealth of flora and for the highly interesting
ecology of the whole area that parts of Newborough Warren
were made into a National Nature Reserve. Marsh orchids,
marsh and dune helleborines, round-leaved wintergreen, grass
of Parnassus and felwort are among the dunes' attractive plants.
Formerly a fine tern colony, including the rare roseate tern, bred
annually along the Cefni estuary until increasing human distur-
bance drove the birds away. The hope is that the creation of
the nature reserve may some day induce them to come back.
Scenically these dunes are superb and artists and photographers
love the yellow sand and graceful, pale-green marram-grass
against a background of the distant blue mountains of Snowdonia.

A spine of Pre-Cambrian rock, partly quartzite, partly lime-

27

stone, goes right across Newborough Warren to culminate in
the little peninsula of Llanddwyn which at high tide is an island.
A road to Llanddwyn runs through the conifer forest to a car-
park near the shore which offers several miles of safe bathing.
The island has a few cottages at the southern tip, a former
lighthouse and the small ruined church of St. Dwynwen. On
slopes above the nearby shore grow patches of squills in spring
and on the rocks in summer you will find blood-red cranesbill,
rock samphire, rock sea-lavender and sea spleenwort. There are
countless shells on the beach. On off-shore islets are small
breeding groups of cormorants and terns. And the view south is
magnificent: across the sea to the majestic outlines of Yr Eifl and
sister mountains of Lleyn. It is a study in ancient rocks, for, like
those under your feet, the rocks of Lleyn are also of Pre-
Cambrian age. Incidentally Anglesey is the driest county of
Wales and this southern tip the driest part of Anglesey, having
a rainfall about the same as London's.

From Newborough whose church has a medieval tomb slab,
it is only a mile east to the old church at Llangeinwen which has
early stones and a saddle quern. For another interesting church
go north to Llangaffo where there is a finely ornate but broken
cross-head of about the ninth century. For one of several good
Neolithic tombs in this district go a mile east where you will see
three rough uprights supporting a capstone near the lane to
Bodowyr. But easily the finest burial chamber is that of Bryn-
celli-ddu which is a well-developed passage grave surrounded by
a stone circle and a ditch. There is a standing stone inside and
another (decorated) outside. The covering mound has been restored. Excavation revealed many burials and the whole place
has a temple-like atmosphere. As you come down the lane from
the farm notice the tall slim stone on a ridge away on your right.
It was presumably somehow linked with the rituals of the burial
chamber. This tomb and Barclodiad y Gawres are the best
specimens of passage graves in Wales. They belong to a type
well developed in the Boyne valley, eastern Ireland.

Llanidan old church, signposted on A4080 half a mile north-
east of Brynsiencyn, is well worth a visit. Long abandoned but
still cared for, this medieval building is full of the atmosphere of
other days. It stands in a quiet place among trees, partly ruined,
partly preserved. An arcade, its roof and walls gone from about

it, survives in the open air, its beauty enhanced by being seen against the sky. Within the church a reliquary displays the bones of an unknown woman. On the Menai Strait south-west of the tubular bridge is Plas Newydd, seat of the Marquis of Anglesey. The house has some well-known wall-paintings by Whistler; the grounds have two fine Neolithic tombs. Permission to view any of these should be sought from the Marquis's estate agent. So we are back to that first Marquis where he surveys the world from his column. And one of the things he sees in all that fine view is another hero on another column. For down at the edge of the strait below a small spired church near the railway stands Nelson, made to look very large and commanding in 1873 by his sculptor, Admiral Paget, son of the first Marquis. So, your bosom swelling with pride at our military and naval splendours, you take your departure from Anglesey. But do not go away with the belief that Anglesey was once the 'eye' or island of the Angles, as has often been claimed. In fact the name comes from that of some Viking chieftain and was originally 'Ongull's Eye'.

2

CAERNARVONSHIRE

(Caernarfon or Sir Gaernarfon)

Caernarvonshire is a long wedge of country that tapers all the way from its broad end on the Conwy river to where it finishes in the west on the high, windy, sea-stricken headland of Braich y Pwll. Its mountains, the highest in Wales, are of hard and ancient rocks. They stand up so high between Conway and Nantlle because of the resistant dolerites, rhyolites and other igneous rocks of which they are largely composed. West of Nantlle, where the wedge begins to narrow into the western sea to form the shapely peninsula of Lleyn, you come to mountains whose rocks are even nearer the origin of the earth, the rocks of the Pre-Cambrian period. They form the magnificent horizon you see north from Cardigan Bay or south from Anglesey, the jagged line of diminishing hills at the end of which Bardsey Island, also Pre-Cambrian, stands like a full stop at the end of a splendid sentence.

But suppose we begin at the thick end of the wedge in a splendour of white cliffs, sea birds and wildflowers on that fine headland, the Great Orme at Llandudno. To see the wildflowers of the Orme at their best go in spring when vernal squill, hoary rockrose, spring cinquefoil and Nottingham catchfly are all flowering together. Note also the wild cabbage on those calcareous cliffs and you will understand why your garden brassicas do best in limy ground. Among sea birds the fulmar is a Great Orme speciality. In fact even before you start round the Marine Drive you can see fulmars on their nesting ledges in a quarry just behind the public gardens. Over the years Llandudno has done its best to tame the wildness of this 679-foot Orme, a name that is a reminder of the Viking settlements of the ninth and tenth centuries. Yet the six miles of road cleverly engineered all round and the cable-railway straight to the top have not deprived the Orme of being a place belonging to the sea and the wind rather than to a town. The Orme enjoys superb views west along the coast to Anglesey. East the coast stretches far away into Lancashire. Inland you look at the massive shoulders of the Carneddau. Three miles east a twin limestone promontory stands into the sea—the Little Orme, a wilder headland with no marine drive. It is another good place for sea birds, plants and breezy walks along the edges of high white cliffs and above deep, abandoned quarries. Both Ormes, with Liverpool less than forty miles along the coast, are good perches for ship-watchers.

Llandudno must have begun as a settlement on top of the Great Orme for there its medieval church still stands, very likely on the site of the cell of its founder, Tudno, a Celtic saint of the sixth century. Besides the parish church which has two thirteenth-century cross slabs built into the south interior wall (they have attractive leaf designs), the Great Orme once had another ancient building, a fourteenth-century palace of the bishops of Bangor. Its scanty walls lie close to the cliff edge half-way along the south-west side. But though so ancient in its connections the town at the foot of the Orme is almost entirely post-1850, for it was designed in 1848 as a popular centre for holidays and retirement and remains a good example of Victorian town planning. The population, a mere 509 in 1821, is now about 17,000. There are all the popular holiday attractions as well as an open-air theatre, an interesting museum and picture gallery (Rapallo House) and a good library. It is a rather treeless town but there are woods with public walks at two historic estates, Gloddaith and Bodysgallen. Penrhyn Old Hall, near the Little Orme, is an old mansion whose attractions include sixteenth-century paintings on plaster. From near Llandudno the built-up zone is continued by Degannwy (meagre ruins of early Norman castle) and Llandudno Junction round to the Conway estuary, here crossed by three bridges: Telford's suspension bridge of 1826; Stephenson's tubular railway bridge of 1848; and a modern road bridge.

Conway (Conwy) was on the map before Edward I's time.

For the Cistercians had settled at Aberconwy, the site of present-day Conway, in 1186. The place was then remote from the world, secluded by dunes, marshes and estuary and exactly suiting the Cistercian taste for privacy. A hundred years later comes Edward I in his conquest of North Wales and sees the strategic possibilities of the site. Persuaded to move by a mixture of force and compensation the monks transplanted themselves to a riverside spot at Maenan, five miles upriver where they built again and continued for another two and a half centuries till Henry VIII dissolved them and had a lot of the abbey's stones carted off to do repairs on Caernarvon castle. The rest were sold for building local mansions. Today nothing structural is left of the abbey at Maenan except below ground. But at Conway parts of the original abbey church survive in the parish church.

So in 1284, in the place of the Cistercian abbey, rose the many towered castle and town walls that make Conway unique. For no other town in Britain has kept walls and castle so complete, nowhere can you more easily get the feel of a medieval bastide. 'It is like an illumination from the chronicles of Froissart,' was one visitor's comment. As for materials, both castle and town walls are mainly of the Silurian grit on which they stand; but the sandstone dressings on the castle were brought from Cheshire. A strong castle and, you might think, easy enough to guard. But who shall guard the guards themselves? In 1401 Owain Glyndŵr's men captured it while the garrison was attending Good Friday service in the parish church!

Conway's parish church of St. Mary shows building of many periods, the best stone work being the south transept. There is also a substantial portion surviving of a superb fifteenth-century rood screen on which note particularly the fan-vaulting under the floor of the loft, and carvings of roses, pomegranates, an eagle's claw grasping a fish, dragons, hounds and falcons—great stuff for heraldry enthusiasts. Stall ends of the same date are beautifully carved. The church also contains many memorials from the sixteenth century onwards. After castle and church Conway's best-known building is Plas Mawr, an Elizabethan town house now an art gallery. There is also the National Trust's sixteenth-century house called Aberconway. But even if it lacked all history Conway would still sit with charm along its

5. Snowdon, Caernarvonshire, from near Portmadoc

6. Maen-y-bardd, a Neolithic burial chamber near Ro-wen in the lower Conwy valley, Caernarvonshire

7. Remains of Valle Crucis, the Cistercian abbey near Llangollen, Denbighshire

8. Summer sheep sale, Ysbyty Ifan, Denbighshire

estuary and be visited by those who enjoy a waterfront with fishing boats and yachts (not forgetting Britain's smallest house) and who wish to explore a very interesting district. Good uphill walks from Conway, apart from those into the real mountain country, include the track west to the hill forts of Caer Leion (contains over fifty hut sites) and Dinas (views down Sychnant Pass); or follow the lanes south to the high-placed medieval church of Llangelynnin and its ancient healing well. A little south-west of Conway castle Gyffin church is worth visiting for its fifteenth-century painted ceiling and curious medieval carvings in the porch.

The Romans had also found it necessary to command the Conwy estuary. They chose a sheltered site down by the river at Caerhun (Canovium to them) where their rectangle of raised ground is still plain to see. In one quarter of it the Middle Ages added a church that still survives. Along the hills west of the estuary you can take in a whole sweep of local history. Megalithic man built his burial chamber at Maen y Bardd along the ancient track a mile west of Ro-wen, a village of gardens and charm near well wooded slopes. And there is a standing stone a little further on. Ancient field enclosures and hut remains in various places, east of Llyn Dulyn, for example, may be Bronze or Iron Age. Pen-y-gaer hill fort above Llanbedr-y-cennin is certainly Iron Age and has *chevaux de frise* almost unique in England and Wales. The track from Ro-wen is correctly marked on the map as Roman but may already have been in use a couple of thousand years before then. It goes over and down to the coast at Aber by way of Bwlch y Ddeufaen ('the pass of the two stones'). These prehistoric stones still stand by the track along with a hideous clutter of pylons. The Romans considered the route important enough to mark the distance with milestones, two of which survive—in the British Museum. Perhaps others await discovery. In the medieval period there developed now almost forgotten settlements such as Ardda whose site and fields are faintly traceable on the hills south-west of Dolgarrog. This was also the birth time of churches such as Llanrhychwyn, isolated on its upland shelf, a church of simplicity and appeal. Its roof-timbering as at Llangelynnin is of massive local oak.

Many streams drop in haste off these high lands, some into tree-shaded ravines such as Dulyn above Talybont. In their time they have turned the wheels of flour mills, fulling mills, woollen mills, now nearly all gone. But weaving continues at Trefriw where you can buy beautiful examples of local work. A tablet in the wall of the seventeenth-century cottage called Tan-yr-yw records in Welsh an early printing press. It began work in 1776, 58 years after the first press in Wales at Adpar in Cardiganshire. From Trefriw southwards conifer plantations begin to close in on you. But judging by the many fragments of deciduous woodland on both sides the Conwy valley must have been richly timbered until fairly recent times. Woods on the Caernarvonshire side are particularly plant-rich because the soils there are largely derived from the igneous rocks of the Ordovician period. Two of the woodlands, Gorswen, south of Ro-wen, and the steep tree-covered brow above Dolgarrog, are National Nature Reserves. In the Betws-y-coed area was the ancient Gwydir forest, centred on Gwydir castle which had a sizeable part in history. It is an Elizabethan house with peacock-enlivened grounds open to visitors. Up the nearby lane the seventeenth-century chapel of Gwydir Uchaf retains its original ceiling remarkable for the angels and cherubs painted all over it.

Just above the junction of the rivers Conwy and Llugwy (the latter has the famous Swallow Falls two miles upstream) is Betws-y-coed whose name, which means 'the oratory in the forest', is eloquent of its place in the medieval world. The church retains a fourteenth-century effigy. Today Betws-y-coed, strung out along A5, is traffic-cursed. But it is a good centre for a superb stretch of country and you can easily escape along many lovely walks. Up through oaks and beeches for instance to the islanded lake called Elsi, set amid conifers, bogs and glacier-smoothed rocks. From there the track goes on down the other side into the Lledr valley. Or there is the southward lane to the Fairy Glen and fine falls on the Conwy and Machno rivers. Two miles up the Machno the church of Penmachno has stones inscribed with Latin memorials of the fifth or sixth centuries and there is a cross slab almost as ancient. Two panels of oak, probably sixteenth-century Flemish, are painted on both sides with religious subjects. From Penmachno you can walk up through conifers and down into the Gwthernant valley two miles northwest where you will find Tŷ Mawr (National Trust), the sixteenth-century birthplace of Bishop Morgan, first translator of the Bible into Welsh (1588). From there you can go on down to A496.

With streams everywhere this is great country for bridges. Betws-y-coed offers a contrast between its iron Waterloo Bridge (1815) and its seventeenth-century stone bridges of Pont-y-pair (over the Llugwy) and Pont-ar-Ledr (over the Lledr). Pont-yr-afanc (over the Conwy) is more recent, dating from about 1800. The Miners' Bridge is a wooden curiosity built over the Llugwy to shortcut the route to the lead mines. Note also the castellated railway bridge crossing the main road about two miles up the Lledr valley—a memorial to the spaciousness of railway ideas a century ago. But it is always Telford's bridge that gets the most attention. As he said over 150 years ago: 'When you reach Waterloo Bridge I must insist that you leave your carriage and examine the work fully. It is the best cast-iron bridge yet constructed.'

Immediately north of Betws-y-coed the spruces and pines climb steeply to a region more attractive than the average conifer forest because broken up by small lakes and abandoned lead mines. The old mines have a fascination not only for the industrial archaeologist but also for the botanist. On some of their spoil heaps grow plants rare elsewhere in Wales such as forked spleenwort and alpine pennycress. As there is known to be quantities of lead-ore, though rather low-grade, still in these rocks, a government-sponsored lead mine at Parc has been modernized and could be quickly brought into production if the world price of lead rose high enough. This little world of lakelets and conifers is crossed by the steep lane up from Tŷ Hyll ('the ugly house') which is built of huge, unmortared blocks half a mile up the road from Swallow Falls. This lane eventually brings you down to Gwydir castle or you can turn off north-west about half-way and go by forest and field to Talyllyn at the head of Lyn Geirionydd, then over and down to Llyn Crafnant. The crags at the head of Crafnant are botanically rich and form the Cwm Glas National Nature Reserve.[1]

If you scramble up out of Crafnant you find yourself in bigger country. Now the high Carneddau are intimately before you. From the rocks of Creigiau Gleision (more good plants)

[1] The Council for the Promotion of Field Studies has a centre at Rhyd-y-Creuau, 3 miles south of Llanrwst.

you look across the deep Cowlyd reservoir at one of the most satisfying stretches of walking country in Wales. Here those best off are they who have no car nor hotel to return to. For the urge is to go on and find a way through the rocks and along the ridges from Penllithrig-y-wrach ('the witch's slide') to Craig yr Ysfa and on to Carnedd Llywelyn (3,485 feet), the highest of all these Carneddau. Once up there the rest of the hills are yours. You can do the superb ridge-walk north by way of Foel Grach, Garnedd Uchaf and Foel Fras to the Drum, which is pronounced 'Drim' and means simply 'the ridge'. From there you look down on a fair lake called Anafon and out on to a tremendous reach of the North Wales and Lancashire coast with Holyhead visible in the west and (through binoculars) Blackpool tower in the east. Or, from Carnedd Llywelyn you can find a way down under the dark, wet, plant-rich crags of Ysgolion Duon ('the black ladders') and down the Llafar to Bethesda. Or, keeping up, you can take in Carnedd Dafydd, look down on Ffynnon Lloer ('the well of the moon') and scramble down the long steep slope to Ogwen from Pen yr Ole Wen. But these are only a few routes among many, for the whole Carneddau region, its foothills and approaching valleys are full of delights. Llyn Eigiau, for instance, and wild Cwm Eigiau above; and the twin lakes Melynllyn and Dulyn whose cliffs go straight into the depths; and south of these lakes the strangely bare and stony little plateau called Gledrffordd.

Moel Siabod, well-shaped and rather apart, stands up to greet you in many Caernarvonshire views especially the one east from Snowdon across Llyn Llydaw. Pont Cyfyng ('the narrow bridge'), a mile down A5 from Capel Curig, is the best starting point from Siabod. On its eastern flank the mountain is hollowed into a splendid cirque of crags above a shallow, rocky lake. Keep to the ridge above this cirque if you want to ascend Siabod least arduously. But if you want to find mountain plants, hear songs of ring ouzels or see a cross section of slaty and igneous rocks, then scramble up the direct route from the lake. Either way the summit will give you unsurpassed views of the Lledr valley in the south-east and the Snowdon Horseshoe to the west. You can continue towards Snowdon along the ridge down to Cefnycerrig (good photographic point) and down again to Penygwryd. By coincidence there are the banks of

Caernarvonshire

Roman forts visible near the start and finish of this walk: the Caer Llugwy site in a loop of the river was no doubt sheltered in its day by thick woodland; but the Penygwryd camp was probably as bleak as it is today and therefore not used for long. As a site decidedly high and exposed for Roman tastes it can be compared with Cae Gaer on Pumlumon and Y Pigwn near Brecon.

The Lledr valley is one of the few valleys of Snowdonia viewable from the windows of a broad-gauge railway carriage. If you board the train at Llandudno Junction you follow miles of the lower Conwy then climb up almost the entire length of the Lledr. Then you dive out of Caernarvonshire under two miles of mountain and emerge with sudden drama amid the vast slate quarries of Blaenau Ffestiniog. While the railway burrows under a vast depth of Ordovician slate, the main road climbs over Crimea Pass which is a starting point for exploring the lonely region of rock, lake and grass that stretches along the county boundary to Cnicht and down to the Nanmor valley; or northwards to Siabod and Penygwryd. In base-rich bogs on the southern slopes of Siabod grows, but very sparingly, the charming grass of Parnassus at its most southern locality in Wales.

Prominent in the Lledr valley are the ruins of Dolwyddelan castle built by the Welsh before Edward I put on his display of castle building. The medieval track that went west from this castle through the moors to Nant Gwynant still exists. So does a pack-horse trail which went from Dolwyddelan to Penmachno. And there is the Roman road, important enough to be paved at least here and there, that came from Caerhun up the Conwy, then the Lledr, but not fancying what is now Crimea Pass, slanted away to top the moorland just east of Manod Mawr. It is unfortunate that forestry now obscures part of this road. The church of Dolwyddelan is early sixteenth century and possesses a rare but very battered bell of tenth-century Celtic design. There is also a brass of a kneeling armoured figure; and a large painted memorial with heraldic shields of the early seventeenth century.

Nearly every Snowdonian visitor arrives sooner or later at Capel Curig, for this small upland village is at the centre of all things. From there you command the whole Carneddau uplands or can set off on less ambitious walks like the popular one over to Crafnant. West you look along the skirts of Glyder to

37

the most photographed and painted view of Snowdon which does wonderful things with clouds and light at all seasons, helped by the Mymbyr lakes in the foreground. Novice mountaineers flock to Capel Curig for instruction at Plas y Brenin where courses are organized by the Central Council of Physical Recreation. But the two historic centres of Snowdon mountaineering were the hotels at Pen-y-pass and Penygwryd where the pioneers gathered from the 1860's onwards. At first they came mainly in the summer but by 1877 we find the comment: 'Of late, travelling in the winter up these mountains appears to be a favourite idea.' The idea has remained popular, to the astonishment of passing motorists who see the little tents of climbers along the high passes in midwinter. Since the early days other climbing centres have grown up, notably in the Ogwen area; and all-year-round adventure schools have multiplied throughout Snowdonia.

The Glyder range, best-loved Welsh upland after Snowdon itself, is a magnificent arc of mountains rising westwards from Capel Curig and curving into the north towards Bethesda: a total of only about ten crow-miles but vastly more if you follow the ups and downs of the whole ridge. It is a superb walk, with the Pass of Llanberis always deep below on your left and beyond it the Snowdon Horseshoe. On your right you look down into one great cwm after another where the forces of erosion have taken savage bites out of the north-east flank of the ridge. Along the top are some of the famous peaks of Wales: Glyder Fawr, reaching 3,279 feet; Glyder Fach, less by only 17 feet; and Tryfan, best known of all because beckoning so high and rugged above the Capel–Ogwen road. All give you tremendous views across North Wales; and all are more satisfying than Snowdon if you have to share its summit with train-borne crowds. Lovers of mountain solitudes should avoid the top of Snowdon until winter when the train is not running.

Glyder is often walked over from Penygwryd to Ogwen and vice-versa. Or you can do a satisfying scramble up from Ogwen by way of Cwm Idwal, then along the summit ridge and back again to Ogwen down the slopes of Cwm Bochlwyd. It all brings great rewards whether you want far views, appealing camera shots, or are earnest about geology, botany or some related science, or simply want to tone up your lungs and ankles.

And the heaps of great rocks scattered along a mile of summit plateau are quite unlike anything else in Wales—'the skeleton of the hill, exposed to open view by rain, snow, &c.' as Edward Lhuyd described them in 1695.

Llyn Ogwen, beautiful shallow lake alongside the highest part of A5, is poised above Nant Ffrancon into which its stream cascades down the Falls of Benglog. Not until the early nineteenth century was a vehicular road built through this pass. Before then walkers and riders climbed out of Nant Ffrancon up crude steps which Pennant reckoned 'the most dreadful horse-path in Wales'. You can find some of these steps not far from the falls. You can also see a pack-horse bridge still in position under the present bridge at the head of the falls.

Of all the hollows gouged into Glyder's flanks the greatest is Cwm Idwal which opens before you after twenty minutes' walk up a stony path from Ogwen. Idwal's are, I suppose, the most famous inland cliffs in Wales. They rise high above a waste of block scree around the south end of a shallow, shapely lake. Thousands have followed the rough track up through the screes to the top of the cliffs to look back into the cwm and take photographs through the great crack of the Devil's Kitchen which in Welsh is Twll Du ('the black chasm'). Cwm Idwal, Wales's first National Nature Reserve, is known for the luxuriance of its alpine plants and for the rarity of some of them, the most distinguished being a tiny white lily called Lloydia in honour of Edward Lhuyd (or Lloyd) who first discovered it in the late seventeenth century. Though now rarer than in Lhuyd's time this June-flowering Snowdon lily still grows on high, lime-rich ledges. It is found nowhere else in Britain.

So to Snowdon whose Welsh name is Y Wyddfa, which means 'the burial place' (probably of a legendary giant). It is climbed along five main routes: from Nant Gwynant up the Watkin Path; from Beddgelert by way of Llechog ridge; from Snowdon Ranger youth hostel (probably the oldest route); from Llanberis by foot or rail; or from Pen-y-pass along the Pig Track. From Pen-y-pass there is also the Horseshoe route which is pretty tough going because it involves you straight into a scramble up the narrow rocks of Crib Goch, then another one down between fangs and pinnacles to the saddle called Bwlch Coch. Here many people pause for a breather, looking down to

Llyn Llydaw on the south or into the deep, botanically rich cirque of Cwm Glas on the north. From Bwlch Coch you climb up and over Crib y Ddysgl. Then up and over Snowdon to descend to another saddle and climb another slope to Lli-wedd's thin ridge poised over east-facing crags. From there the path, perhaps your strength also, declines all the way back to Pen-y-pass. This is the classic mountain walk of Wales but not one to be attempted by the novice when snow and ice coat the rocks and the simplest slopes are streaked with treachery.

The Snowdonia National Park was instituted in 1951 but Snowdon itself became a playground for the many in 1896 when, despite protests against the desecration of upland soli-tudes, the rack-railway to the summit was opened. It began badly with a fatal accident on its first day. Since then from Easter to the end of September it has carried thousands up those steep four and a half miles from Llanberis to the top without mishap. The ascent takes one hour so if you feel surcharged with energy you can compete with the train on foot. A long-popular tourist centre under Snowdon's southern flank is Beddgelert, a village at a junction of streams and ancient roads. When Pennant called Beddgelert a place 'to inspire religious meditation amid lofty mountains, woods and murmuring streams' he had in mind its Augustinian priory burnt down as long ago as 1283. St. Mary's church, built on the same site, probably incorporates fragments of the priory church. For sparse castle remains go just over a mile along the Nant Gwynant road and climb the wooded hill that rises on your left just before you reach Llyn Dinas whose name used to be Llyn Dinas Emrys ('the lake of the fortress of Emrys'). A path winds up through the trees to an open space at the top where you see the basement walls of Dinas Emrys, a castle of much legend but little documented history. The legends relate to Emrys (also called Merlin) and Vortigern, a three-quarters-legendary British king of the fifth century whose misfortune it was to have to cope with the mess the de-parting Romans left behind. He it was who invited Hengist and the Saxons into Britain and then could not get rid of them. His story soon clouds into fiction: he retires into Wales and leads a fugitive existence in various places including this fort of Dinas Emrys. The site dates back to times that might accord with that of Vortigern, for it was an Iron Age hill fort which continued in use into the Dark Ages. The present stonework is the remains of a tower-keep built against the Normans by the Welsh in the twelfth century.

The name Beddgelert means 'the grave of Gelert (or Celert)' who was probably a now forgotten, early Celtic holy man buried there at a site now lost. The famous story of the faithful hound is a romance of the Middle Ages told in several European and Asiatic countries. 'Gelert's grave' was the invention of an eighteenth-century inn-keeper cashing in on tourism. So it is high time Beddgelert stopped trading in nonsense and relied upon its genuine attractions: streams, picturesque bridge, fine situation and lovely walks to mountains all around: Snowdon, Hebog and Cnicht. Or there are shorter strolls to Aberglaslyn Pass, Nantmor, Llyn Gwynant or Moel y Dyniewyd which is a superb local viewpoint. Railway enthusiasts can follow the trackway of the abandoned Welsh Highland Railway. Mineralogists can inspect old copper mines in Aberglaslyn Pass.

From Beddgelert the main road goes north-west for Caernarvon past the Beddgelert National Forest Park (camp site, woodland walks and nature trail). At Rhyd-ddu a path goes to the right for Snowdon and a road forks back left for Nantlle through a fine pass between high, crag-topped slopes. Cwm Silyn with its cirque of high cliffs looks especially inviting. A mile or so north of Rhyd-ddu is Cwellyn, a deep cold lake which reflects the shapely height of Mynydd Mawr. In Cwellyn are many trout and some of the trout's rarer cousin, the char, a beautiful deep-water fish which comes into the shallows only when breeding in late autumn and early winter. At that season it used to be netted but is now rarely fished for. Here is Snowdon Ranger youth hostel on the site of what in early tourist days was the place to hire a guide for the then perilous and trackless journey up Snowdon. On some maps Castell Cidwm at the north end of Llyn Cwellyn is marked in archaic lettering as if it were an ancient monument. So is Maen Bras, two miles east. But both are natural features.

North from Cwellyn the road goes through Betws Garmon, passing a charming garden and torrent open to the public at Nant Mill. It is famous for elver-watching. From there you can go on to Caernarvon or turn east at Waunfawr along minor roads to Llanberis where you will see what is claimed to be the best slate in the world being got from the biggest slate quarry in the world. In most of Snowdonia the Cambrian rocks lie deep beneath those of the Ordovician Period. But between Llanberis and Bethesda they outcrop hugely to form Elidir Fawr (3,030 feet) and Carnedd y Filiast (2,695 feet) and it is these mountains that contain the slate veins. The Dinorwic quarry extends from Llyn Peris (340 feet above sea level) up the slopes of Elidir in a series of 70-foot high terraces to a height of 2,300 feet. Slate is of ancient use: it formed the floors and roofs of Roman Segontium (Caernarvon). Port Dinorwic has a name from out of the Dark Ages: 'din' means a fort and 'orwic' comes from the name of the Celtic tribe called Ordovices by the Romans. Port Dinorwic, which formerly exported vast quantities of slate, is now a yachting centre.

The deep Llanberis lakes, the larger Padarn and the smaller and even deeper Peris, are long, narrow and dammed back by glacial deposits. Like Cwellyn they contain char as well as trout. Originally one lake (their water levels are the same) they have become separated by silt and stones brought down by a mountain stream. Above the lakes is the splendid Pass of Llanberis, a deep cut through the mountains with the crags of Glyder on the north and the shoulders of Snowdon on the south. It still bears all the signs of the glaciers that melted from it some twelve thousand years ago: the U-profile, the smoothed rocks, the perched blocks and the hanging valleys (Cwm Glas for instance). With industrialization Llanberis moved down the valley a couple of miles leaving Old Llanberis (now Nant Peris) and the original parish church behind. This church is medieval and retains a primitive, local type of screen like the one at Dolwyddelan. The round keep of a thirteenth-century Welsh castle, probably built by Llywelyn the Great, survives at Dolbadarn overlooking Llyn Peris. And don't miss the waterfall of Ceunant Mawr half a mile south-west.

I have so far said nothing of the coast westwards of Conway. As you slide smoothly along the well-built and tunnelled highway towards the resorts of Penmaenmawr and Llanfairfechan (promenades, good sands and bathing at both places), spare a memory for the anguished travellers and horses who formerly struggled this way to get to the Irish boat: up through the rocks of Sychnant Pass, then along the terrifying slopes of the great headland of Penmaenmawr. There was one rough stretch where carriages had to be taken to pieces and carried for some distance. Not until 1722 was a proper road constructed and, to quote a commentator of the time: 'what had been deemed impracticable was accomplished and a road formed on the most sublime terrace of the British Isles which will be the admiration of future ages'. You can still trace parts of this eighteenth-century marvel along the slopes above the present road.

Penmaenmawr mountain gets smaller year by year. Its tough igneous rock is in demand as roadstone, and quarries have reduced its once rounded summit to a table-top, removing what was a particularly interesting Iron Age fort containing scores of hut circles. But the mountain's Neolithic connections remain: on its inland slopes between five hundred and a thousand feet great numbers of hand-axes were manufactured about 3,000–2,000 B.C. These Graig Lwyd stone axes, made of Penmaenmawr's distinctive hard, pale, blue-grey granophyre, have been found in many parts of Britain. Remains of this axe-making—flakes, chips and other rejects—are scattered not only on Craig Lwyd but also at Dinas, two miles south-west and across the valley on Garreg-fawr. Perhaps this tool making was still in progress when in the early Bronze Age the ring of stones called the Druids' Circle was set up half a mile away. In an urn at the centre of this circle archaeologists discovered the cremated remains of a child, together with a bronze knife: finds hinting at blood and sacrifice deemed necessary for the circle's consecration.

The attractive little village of Aber, in the mouth of a wooded glen, has been a touristy spot ever since eighteenth-century travellers included it in their round of Welsh waterfalls. The falls, two miles south of the main road, occur where the Afon Goch drops over a terrace of igneous rock hard enough to have resisted the erosive forces that have cut into the softer shales downstream. Traces of Bronze Age settlements are numerous in the vicinity of the falls and on the nearby slopes of the Carneddau. Aber itself (the name is short for Abergwyngregyn) has distinguished historical connections, the castle mound, formerly moated, having been a seat of Llywelyn the Great (died 1240), most prominent of medieval Welsh princes.

If you want to bathe along this coast you must catch the tide at its peak for it quickly recedes across several miles of the Lavan Sands. Before Menai Strait was bridged much Anglesey traffic went across these sands and then by ferry to Beaumaris—a perilous passage. In fog and darkness a bell used to be rung at Aber for the guidance of incoming travellers. West of Aber the Strait begins. At low tide there is good mud for birds and bird-watchers off Penrhyn castle; and a couple of long fish-weirs that filter fish from the ebbing tides and which are the successors of medieval weirs. The castle, a National Trust property with extensive grounds, is a nineteenth-century product of the vast profits of the Bethesda slate quarries. It has medieval fragments and is open to visitors. Its exhibits include a collection of dolls from many lands and a small railway museum. The nearby church of Llandegai has an elaborate fifteenth-century tomb in alabaster. Along a lane a mile south of Llandegai is a medieval hall called Cochwillan.

Bangor, ancient centre of Celtic christianity (St. Deiniol had his church here in the sixth century), is a prosperous university and cathedral city. But though so old a settlement it has retained little in the way of historic buildings. The cathedral, containing fragments of past centuries back to the fourteenth, is substantially nineteenth century. The nearby, much altered Bishop's Palace is largely sixteenth to eighteenth century and is now the town hall. Fragments of Bangor's past can be seen in the Museum of Welsh Antiquities in College Road. Near the cathedral you will find a unique garden of Bible-mentioned flowers. From the pier you can take motor boat trips round Puffin Island or down the Strait to see the famous suspension and railway bridges. And if you find the sea too cold there is an indoor swimming pool.

Bangor's rival at the other end of the strait is Caernarvon which is smaller, more work-a-day, less genteel; but in the past a place of great strategic importance. Here at the water's edge Edward I built his great thirteen-towered castle which after seven centuries still stands tall and outwardly perfect, one of the great castles of Britain. It looks good from any viewpoint but especially so from downstream along the other side of the Seiont river with the Snowdonian heights as a background. It is easy to forget, until you get inside and find it a hollow shell, that this fine structure is in fact a ruin. Built in 1283 it went through various fortunes of decay and repair and was heavily involved in the Civil War until finally captured by the Cromwellians. In 1660 an order made for its demolition was for some reason not carried out. (Did some castle-enthusiast of those days 'forget' to deliver the message?) Since then the castle has been repaired (after long neglect), Edward VII being one of its keenest renovators. 13th July 1911, saw the investiture of the Prince of Wales, later Duke of Windsor; and on 1st July 1969, the investiture of Prince Charles took place. Samuel Johnson in 1774 was most impressed by this castle and rightly remarked that 'to survey this place would take much time'. But if you, like him, are short of time, at least be sure to inspect the King's Gate with its high archway and statue of either Edward I or Edward II; the great Eagle Tower; and the town walls within which was built a Norman-style bastide whose street pattern still survives. Some of the stones for the castle no doubt came from the ruins of Segontium, an important Roman stronghold less than half a mile up A487 which cuts the Roman fort in two. Segontium has been partly excavated, is open to visitors and its finds are on show in an excellent museum on the site. If you wish to see what use was made of the great oaks of the Middle Ages you should inspect the fine roof-timbers of the nearby church of Llanbeblig.

South-west from Caernarvon the peninsula of Lleyn stretches its rugged and muscular arm thirty-two miles into the Irish Sea. It is an arm that quickly bulges into the triple peaks of Yr Eifl, long since Anglicized as 'the rivals' though Yr Eifl really means 'the fork'. A coastal lane goes south-west from Caernarvon, winding round the edge of the Strait, and is a picnickers' and sea-anglers' road. Birdwatchers go on round to Foryd Bay, especially to south of the mouth of the Gwyrfai. Church-viewers can see the unrestored medieval church of Llanfaglan a mile inland. Sea-bathers carry on to the coast at Morfa Dinlleu and its long stretch of sands. Botanists will find many shore plants, among them a variety of kidney vetch (lady's fingers) with red flowers instead of the usual yellow. It would be cheering if some plant-seeker more serendipitous than the rest could re-discover the oyster-plant, a rare shingle species formerly found here. Dinas Dinlleu, the conspicuous earth-worked hill on the shore and described in some guide books as a Roman fort, is a defence work of the Iron Age.

St. Beuno is a name to remember as you go to Clynnog Fawr. In the early Celtic church what St. David was to South Wales St. Beuno was to the north, and many churches and some wells are named after him. His greatest foundation was the church at Clynnog Fawr, one of the mother-churches of Wales (the others in Caernarvonshire being Bangor and Aberdaron). The present large church is sixteenth century, 'the fayrest chirch in al Cairnarvonshire', said Leland who saw it brand new. A separate chapel, but connected to the church by a vaulted passage, marks the traditional site of Beuno's grave. Treasures in this church include an Anglo-Saxon sundial, an oak chest whose years are beyond all knowledge and a pair of iron dog tongs. Close to the shore half a mile west of the church is a Stone Age burial chamber on whose capstone some subsequent age, believed to be the Bronze, has chipped out over a hundred cup marks.

After Clynnog the coastal strip narrows under great slopes and the deeply quarried flanks of Yr Eifl are before you. Here, above the village of Trevor, a beautiful pink granite is won. Yr Eifl forces the road inland to Llanaelhaearn (ancient church with inscribed stones and a medieval screen). About a mile from there up the road to Llithfaen a footpath sign points you up the slope of Yr Eifl. This is the path to Tre'r Ceiri, in legend 'the town of the giants', in fact an Iron Age hill fort. But no ordinary one. For the path zigzags you up through heather to shattered walls that enclose dozens of Iron Age house foundations. Hut remains exist on many hills though you often need the eye of faith to see them. But at Tre'r Ceiri they are so elaborate that Iron Age life is more tangible there than anywhere else in Wales. This remarkable town was built round a big Bronze Age cairn. Another such cairn crowns the hill called Carnguwch a mile south.

An easier approach to the top of Yr Eifl is to motor up the hill north from Llithfaen to the cross-roads at Mount Pleasant and then walk up by gentle gradients to one of the great viewpoints of Wales. Or you can walk down a zigzag road into the depths of Nant Gwrtheyrn, a shut-in valley opening only to the sea. Here we are back again with Vortigern of wretched memory (see Dinas Emrys) for Gwrtheyrn is the Welsh form of his name. Traditionally he died in this shadowy cwm. Long after his day a castle mound was built in the mouth of the valley, a castle about as bereft of history as Vortigern himself. Given sunshine, a summer's day and a bright sea curling along the shore then Vortigern's valley is far from being 'the gloomy hollow' nearly all past guide books (repeating Pennant) have called it. But our time has added one melancholy touch—the rotting piers, decaying machinery and window-gaping buildings left by abandoned quarries.

As you go along the road down the north side of Lleyn you follow one of the great medieval pilgrim routes on which lay the churches at Clynnog, Pistyll, Nevin, Llangwnnadl and Aberdaron. Then the final desire—Bardsey abbey. Pistyll church crouches low between road and sea. It is small and dark within and has a symbolically inscribed font that may be early Celtic. About 500 yards west of the T-junction in Pistyll you will find at the foot of some recent walling on the south side of the road a little carved medieval cross such as were once common on waysides.

Nevin (Nefyn) a little holiday town with a golden shore and a sea safe for bathing, is sheltered from the prevailing wind. It has cliff and hill walks and boating trips along the coast to Bird Rock (Carreg y Llam), breeding place for auks, kittiwakes, gulls, cormorants and fulmars. A safe anchorage, the bay here has always been a place of ships and Nefyn is ancient. Welsh nationalists recall without joy that in 1284 Edward I held a great festival here to celebrate his conquest of Wales. A mile or so west Morfa Nefyn also sits above a fine sweep of sheltered sands. Here are more cliff walks, shore walks and a lofty, sea-viewing golf course. A good walk from Nefyn is up Carn Boduan, the bold hill fort on the south. South-west from Porth Dinllaen the coast goes away in small cliffs and stony shores which break up here and there into sandy bays such as Tudweiliog's beach, Porth Ysgadan ('herring harbour'), a name that is a memory of when herring fishing was a summer industry before these fish mysteriously forsook Welsh waters.

A double-headed hill of igneous rock, treeless and far seeing, becomes dominant from all sides as you near the end of Lleyn. It is Carn Fadrun, whose rocky 1,217-foot top has a view from sea to sea. Its steep sides and copious scatter of stones made it ideal for Iron Age settlement. There are still the ruins of walls and hut-circles. Ancient trackways zigzag up the east and western slopes. Llaniestyn, under Fadrun's southern flank, has a partly medieval church, double-aisled in the Lleyn tradition. It has an elaborate sixteenth-century font and a pair of eighteenth-century dog tongs. If you go west towards the coast there is a Stone Age burial chamber called Coetan Arthur ('Arthur's quoit') in a sloping field above a lane at the north end of Mynydd Cefnamwlch. From there it is a mile and a half south-west to the light and airy church of Llangwnnadl, an unusual building because three-aisled and therefore square within. Bold Latin lettering on the pillars tells you it was built in 1520.

All along the north coast from Tudweiliog to the end is a wild and unspoilt cliff land with occasional sandy beaches such as Porth Golmon and Porth Oer. There is lounging for beach lizards, cliff walking for the energetic and delight for all who love seas and wide skies. Porth Oer, signposted 'Whistling Sands', has the additional novelty of sand that squeaks as you run across it. Such sands sing because their quartz grains, rounded and uniform in size, produce a note of uniform pitch when vibrated underfoot. After Porth Oer the last massive fist of cliffs thrusts into the south-west gales. There is nothing now before you but the ocean, the sky, passing birds and the beckoning island of saints, called in Welsh, Ynys Enlli, but known more widely by its Norse name of Bardsey, which is presumed to mean the Island of Bardr, a Viking leader. But Ynys Enlli ('tide-race island') is a better name as all who have gone there know well. And they have been many, ever since pilgrims began to pour down Lleyn in the early Middle Ages. They gathered at Aberdaron's church on the shore (the present one is twelfth century) then across they sailed to Enlli which in the many years since Cadfan, its first holy man, settled there in the sixth century, had gained an immense reputation for sanctity, many leaders of the early church having been carried there for burial.

In the thirteenth century an abbey, independent of any order, was built on Ynys Enlli. But only a part of a tower remains today and nothing is known of the former extent of the abbey, so thoroughly have its walls, even below ground, been plundered for later building. There remains a monastic well; the lower half of a tenth-century cross slab kept in the island's chapel; another cross slab, perhaps as early as the seventh century, now built over a barn entrance; and faint hut-circles in the bracken of the mountain where early monks probably lived. Ynys Enlli in the nineteenth century had a large population of crofters. Today it is an island of very few fishermen-farmers, three lighthouse-keepers and a summer population of naturalists and holiday-makers. There is a thriving observatory where you can stay and take part in birdwatching and other natural history activities. Bardsey can often be visited for a couple of hours in summer by trips from Aberdaron. That way you see the auks, shags, ful-mars, choughs and kittiwakes along the cliffs. But stay a night there if you want to hear the weird caterwauling of thousands of shearwaters flying about in the darkness to and from their underground nests. For a distant view of puffins, walk along the shore from Aberdaron to the headland called Trwyn y Penrhyn. Through binoculars you can see them flying to their nests on the Gwylan islands.

On the headland opposite Bardsey was a simple church (faint remains) and a holy well. Perhaps this church of St. Mary met the needs of those pilgrims who were thwarted from crossing to Bardsey by bad weather. From it they looked longingly across to St. Mary's abbey on the island and that had to suffice. In the shelter of the great headland the village of Aberdaron with its medieval church (fine twelfth-century doorway) at the sea's edge. From there the flowery, boulder-clay cliffs continue east to Rhiw where the road climbs high above the sea to give a wonderful prospect along the sweep of Hell's Mouth (Porth Neigwl) with the Merioneth mountains far beyond. Plas-yn-rhiw, a charming house and garden, is a National Trust property frequently open to visitors. The wave-swept strand of Hell's Mouth looks a likely landing place for ancient curraghs and in-evitably the traces of early man are to be seen on the slopes of Rhiw. There are two burial chambers, one in ruins; traces of a Stone Age axe-factory at the north end of Mynydd Rhiw; and a hill fort on rocks above the sea immediately south of the village.

South Lleyn's other great windy headland is Cilan, the lower jaw of Hell's Mouth. Cilan has cliff walks, a sea bird colony (including fulmars) and views east to the mountains. St. Tud-wal's Bay in the lee of Cilan, is a fine natural harbour and was described in the official survey (1748) by Lewis Morris as 'one of the best and safest in Great Britain and so extensive that it could contain the whole navy of England'. For this reason Abersoch has grown since World War II from a hamlet into a most popular yachting centre and holiday place for those who want a sandy shore, safe bathing and dunes. Of the two islands in the bay the west one is topped by an automatic lighthouse. The east island had the sixth-century cell of St. Tudwal and in the Middle Ages a priory of Augustinian canons. After the Reformation pirates took over for a while. Today the only building is an eighteenth-century barn; and the only inhabitants are kittiwakes, herring gulls and auks. Former colonies of puffins and shearwaters are believed to have been wiped out by rats.

Two villages inland are worth a visit: Llanengan for its sixteenth-century rood loft, screen and stalls; and Llangian for its neat cottages clustered in a quiet dell, one of the most attractive villages of Wales, a mile and two centuries away from modern Abersoch. The excellent woodwork of the church roof is fifteenth century. And note in the churchyard a stone of the fifth or sixth century commemorating a Doctor Melus, a rare example of a profession being mentioned on a tombstone of such early date. The oldest Nonconformist chapel in North Wales (built 1769, restored 1958) is Capel Newydd, one and a half miles north-west of Llangian. Around the headland from Abersoch is Llanbedrog where you can enjoy another sheltered beach, go cliff walks, photograph the seventeenth-century Foxhole Cottage and see a medieval screen in a tree-shadowed church.

When in 1356 the Black Prince had won the battle of Poitiers his reward to Nigel de Loryng who had helped him, was the gift of Pwllheli and Nefyn which had just been made into free boroughs. Since then these two towns, best harbours on their respective coasts, have remained the principal places along the peninsula. In the nineteenth century Pwllheli outstripped Nefyn in importance especially after becoming a rail-head. Pwllheli is still a market town and centre of local government. And many holiday-makers come to enjoy its long sands and its fine harbour for small craft. Pwllheli is a bit short of ancient monuments. But within three miles north-east are Abererch church (medieval seats); Four Crosses (burial chamber); and Penarth Fawr (fifteenth-century hall).

Near Llanystumdwy (Lloyd George grave and museum) two

streams meet: the Dwyfach and the Dwyfor, both crossed by centuries-old bridges. Bont Fechan with its four arches is particularly fine and has the advantage of being by-passed and left as a picnic spot. Behind the council houses at Rhoslan two miles upstream from Llanystumdwy stands a fine burial chamber; and another about a mile east. From Rhoslan go three miles west by delightful lanes to Llangybi whose beautifully built curative well, reached by a path through the churchyard, has been visited by thousands down the centuries. On the top of nearby Carn Pentyrch are the collapsed walls of a small Dark Ages fort of no known history.

Cricieth, a steadily growing resort, sits in the sun on a south-facing slope with the glint of the sea in its eyes. Though more ancient as a borough than Pwllheli it never really developed until the sea-bathing age. It got its charter in 1284 when Edward I was encircling North Wales with great castles. Not that Cricieth castle is Edwardian in quite the sense of the others. A Welsh castle stood there already and Edward enlarged it. Standing apart on its hill of igneous rock (rhyolite), overlooking sea and sandy shore, the castle looks good from all angles. A minor curiosity of Cricieth is a disused sundial of 1734 on top of the churchyard wall near the gate of the old parish church above the town. It gives bearings and distances for ports and landfalls all round the world. Four miles north of Cricieth you can buy first-class weaving at Brynkir woollen mill. The Roman road from Caernarvon to Trawsfynydd evidently came this way for there were Roman sites at Brynkir (Bryncir) and Tremadoc. Many medieval stone castles had a wooden predecessor and Cricieth's may have been the motte now mixed up with farm buildings on a bend of the main road at Dolbenmaen, three miles up the Dwyfor river. Above Dolbenmaen you enter the Pennant valley, celebrated by poets and artists. It penetrates a mountain region frequented by early peoples, presumably of the Iron Age, whose groups of hut-circles are sometimes marked on maps as 'Settlement'. You can find them on the west slopes of Moel Hebog and the south slopes of Mynydd Craig-goch. And there are others not yet marked on the maps.

Moel Hebog (2,566 feet), commonly climbed from Beddgelert, is easier from the Pennant side up Cwm Llefrith. Or you can start from further up the Dwyfor and come south along the

ridge to include Moel Lefn, a delightful walk. These two summits, though so close, have their individuality. Lefn is topped by
a massive outcrop of naked rock; Hebog lacks summit rocks but
is cliffy on the south. In the col between them are wet gullies in
basic igneous rocks that bristle with mountain plants and ferns.
The south-west view from Hebog is of the diminishing hills of
Lleyn all the way to Bardsey. South you see far down Cardigan
Bay. East is a close look at Moelwyn and Cnicht. In the north-
east Snowdon and the sharp peak of Aran stand up in detail and
there is a satisfying prospect of Siabod high beyond Llyn Dinas.
You can scramble down the southern rocks of Hebog to a quiet
region of abandoned quarries above Cwmystradllyn lake. The
ruin half a mile south-west of the lake is not a medieval bishops'
palace but a slate quarry workshop. It looks worthy of preservation.

To these parts in 1798 came William Madocks, a speculator
who persuaded the government to support the building of an
embankment across the mouth of the Glaslyn estuary. This reclaimed much land and improved local communications but
destroyed a beautiful estuary. The embankment, locally called
'the cob', was only stage one in Madocks's plans. Stage two was
to get the government to replace Holyhead as the official mail-
boat port by building a new port at Porth Dinllaen. Madocks
maintained that the journey from London to Dublin via Shrewsbury, his new embankment and Porth Dinllaen would be
quicker than via Holyhead. But this time the government
turned him down and so largely hamstrung stage three of his
plan, which was to build a new town named Tremadoc, meaning 'the town of Madocks'. The town was founded but never
developed; and the name Dublin Street survives there as a
monument to his dashed hopes. So Tremadoc remains a village
with town hall and square, a hotel, some charming houses, a
spired church and an unusual classical-style chapel; in all a
pleasing fragment of the early nineteenth century. Shelley
stayed nearby and was enthusiastic about Madocks's schemes;
and here in 1888 Lawrence of Arabia was born. Great wooded
cliffs and screes of dolerite dominate Tremadoc and all the lowlands to the sea. Because hard and vertical they are frequented by
climbers; because they are the habitat of interesting animals,
birds and plants they are a National Nature Reserve.

Caernarvonshire

The other child of Madocks's brain, Portmadoc, was intended to be the port for Tremadoc. Instead it developed its own rapid momentum when in 1836 it began to export slate brought there from Blaenau Ffestiniog, nine miles away, by a narrow-gauge railway which came down the Vale of Ffestiniog and finally along the Portmadoc embankment. Most of this line, painstakingly engineered through difficult terrain, survives today as a scenic railway and claims to be the oldest narrow-gauge passenger line in the world. Portmadoc is no longer much of a port but its harbour is thronged with small pleasure craft and the town with visitors who enjoy the eye-catching but deceptive view of Cnicht looking like a sharp peak instead of the long ridge which it really is. Doubtless the Glaslyn estuary before reclamation was a considerable haunt of wading birds and wild-fowl. Even today Portmadoc inner harbour and adjacent marshes turn up some good things for the birdwatcher. One curiosity: as place names get more Celticized (Tremadoc becomes Tremadog and Portmadoc is now Porthmadog) is William Madocks in danger of being forgotten? Will the idea grow that these names are ancient, coming down from the twelfth century and commemorating one Madog who is claimed to have sailed from the Glaslyn and discovered America three hundred years before Columbus? It is a good story, once widely believed in. A pity it has no foundation.

Portmadoc has a sheltered beach at Borth y Gest. But the long Blackrock Sands, two miles west, are open to most of the winds that blow. You can rock-climb on Craig Ddu at the end of the beach or examine in Treflys church, on the hill behind the shore, an inscribed stone of the sixth century with Chi-rho monogram. Ystumllyn church a mile north-west is an isolated church of 1830 that served a scattered community of farmers. Built on an island in a marsh (now drained, alas) it has been little altered. To enter it is to step back into early Victorian times. Its box-pews are still painted with local family and house names; and it retains the only three-decker pulpit left in the county. The key is kept at the vicarage at Pentrefelin, in which village note one of the tallest, slimmest standing stones in Wales. And now we must let this stone stand for all the fine stones and many other attractions I have failed to mention in this county so blessed with good things.

3

DENBIGHSHIRE

(Dinbych or Sir Ddinbych)

Let us begin Denbighshire in a garden—the National Trust garden of Bodnant, home of Lord Aberconway, six miles south of Llandudno. Open from spring to autumn Bodnant is deservedly one of the most famous British gardens. Begun in 1875 it has constantly been added to and now covers sixty acres. The result is a superb collection of plants and trees, some in formal settings, others in wild-seeming dells and streamsides. Bodnant is probably at its most spectacular in spring when the camellias, magnolias, rhododendrons and embothriums are in flower, but the other seasons also have their glories. And at any time its views across to the Caernarvonshire mountains are a delight.

The tilted land that extends along the Conwy from Bodnant to Llanrwst is a complexity of little fields and woods threaded through by twisting one-track lanes. One of them, a mile southwest of Eglwysbach, takes you by a tree-edged pool called Syberi which has water lilies, moorhens and roach, a quiet water that merges at each end into alder swamps. Then south again the lanes go across Maenan, a narrow tongue of land belonging to Caernarvonshire because so allocated in 1284 by Edward I in order that Maenan abbey could be under the protection of the new Principality of Wales (Caernarvonshire, Anglesey and Merioneth) in compensation for having been shifted from Conway to make room for Edward's castle.

High-level lanes south of Maenan converge on Llanddoget

54

whose square church retains its old box-pews. From there you can drop quickly to Llanrwst, small market town and tourist centre, known chiefly for its bridge and its church. I suppose guide books will always repeat that this bridge was designed by the great London architect, Inigo Jones (1573–1652) but there is no absolute evidence of this. What is certain is that whoever did build it had an eye for an elegant shape. Note above the central arch on the south side the carving of the Stuart arms dated 1636.

The medieval screen in the church is an excellent piece of woodwork. Especially delicate are the long trails of vine leaves, stalks and grapes. There are also birds pecking fruit and pigs foraging for acorns. Built on to the church is the interesting Gwydir chapel. Erected in 1634 by Sir Richard Wynn as his family's chapel it is full of their memorials. Some are of marble but others include fine brasses protected behind glass. There is also an effigy of a medieval knight. But the prize exhibit is the huge tomb chest, hewn in stone, of Llywelyn the Great who founded the abbey of Aberconwy and was buried there in 1240. This tomb was moved with the abbey to Maenan in 1283, then to Llanrwst church at the Dissolution, then into the Gwydir chapel. It still bears a seventeenth-century brass plate commemorating this last move. To see Llanrwst's oldest house visit the National Trust cottage, now a café, called Tu-hwnt-i'r Bont ('beyond the bridge').

Both north and south of Llanrwst narrow, climbing, awkwardly kinking lanes climb from the Conwy valley up into higher Denbighshire. It is along such lanes that you find your way up to the megalithic chambered tomb near Capel Garmon, two miles south-east of Betws-y-coed. This well-restored Neolithic monument stands on a delicious upland shelf that looks to all the eastern heights of Caernarvonshire. It must have been an inspiring place to hold the now unknown ceremonies that were doubtless enacted at such burial places. For another bit of prehistory go six miles north-east to Gwytherin, last village up the Cledwen valley. Lined up in the churchyard are four ancient stones about a yard high near a monstrous old yew. One of the end stones has Dark Ages lettering but the stones look like a Bronze Age alignment and the spot could well have been a holy place for thousands of years.

South from Llanrwst the county boundary goes on along the

Denbighshire

Conwy to Waterloo Bridge and from there Telford's road[1] (now A5) keeps close to a lovely stretch of the tree-shaded river almost to Pentrefoelas whose church has a very early stone inscribed to one Levelinus. Here too is an old water-mill where you can buy honest whole-wheat flour ground between stones as it has been for centuries. South-west from Pentrefoelas Denbighshire sticks out one of those quirkish fingers that county boundaries are so fond of. This one extends eight miles nearly to Ffestiniog to take in most of the tract known as Migneint, one of the boggiest stretches of high moorland in Wales, a place of tussocky moor grass, cotton sedge, rushes, heather, peewits, snipe, black-headed gulls and golden plovers. A long lane goes up and over it from Ysbyty Ifan to Ffestiniog, joining another lane on top that comes up from Penmachno. Where they meet, a mile from Denbighshire, is the elaborate well called Ffynnon Eidda (rebuilt 1846) on which it is written: 'Yf a bydd ddiolchgar.' ('Drink and be thankful.') Migneint looks to higher mountains of igneous rock all round: most imposing is Manod Mawr, a high bulge close on the west; most shapely is Arennig Fach in the other direction.

Ysbyty Ifan, first village down the Conwy on its swift course from Migneint, is a place of history. The name, meaning 'hospice of St. John', goes back to the days of medieval pilgrimage when the three holiest places in Wales were St. David's, Bardsey Island and Holywell. Ysbyty Ifan presumably catered for pilgrims to Bardsey. Today there are just a few houses and a narrow, humpy, two-arched stone bridge which looks old. But probably only the church remembers the pilgrim days.

East from Migneint the land drops to where A5 climbs through a gap in the moors around Cerrigydrudion, a name that means 'the (memorial) stones of the heroes'. But what stones and what heroes no one now knows. Could their story go right back to the days when the nearby hill fort of Caer Caradog was occupied? An old guide-book described Cerrigydrudion as 'a village situated in a cold naked district'. The place has not changed. For miles the slopes are virtually without tree or hedge. But away to the north-east on Mynydd Hiraethog the Forestry Commission has done its best to clothe the earth with a vast dome of trees

---

[1] Along A5, nineteenth-century milestones speak of 'Cernioge': now a farmhouse, this was one of Telford's change-houses for coaches. It is 2½ miles east of Pentrefoelas.

called Clocaenog Forest. It is a forest crossed by several public roads which have attractive picnic spots, one of the best being on the south by a tree-fringed pool near Pont Petryal. This is all very sparsely populated country. To see one of its few hamlets go to Pentre-llyn-cymer below the dam of the Alwen reservoir. Deep in a hollow of the moor it looks up to horizons of spruce and seems far from the world. The road climbs north through ever-spreading young forests, then past a high region where so far the ancient heather moor still survives. But only just. For there the heather is being steadily ploughed in and replaced by modern grasslands.

On one of these new grasslands three miles north-east of the Alwen reservoir is the curious earthwork called Hen Ddinbych ('old Denbigh'), a misnomer, for it certainly had no connection with Denbigh. Its remains are extremely slight and will only appeal to you if you enjoy the mystery of almost obliterated antiquities and do not jib at a mile of rough walking. Hen Ddinbych consists simply of a four-sided grassy platform enclosed by low banks. Less than a hundred yards across, it is divided into two parts one of which contains the very thick wall-bottoms of what was a long and curiously narrow building. It has been called a Roman camp, a church within a churchyard, a Dark Ages homestead and a medieval cattle enclosure. A nice problem. And a good spot to work at it, with a stream flowing below, the quiet moors all round and a glimpse of far away mountains.

From the hill above Hen Ddinbych you see a gaunt ruin stark on the northern horizon. It is a deserted shooting lodge built last century when all these moors were expensively reserved for grouse. It stands close to A543 just behind the Sportsman's Arms which, at over 1,400 feet, claims to be the highest inn in Wales. Another relic is the coaching road that came up from Denbigh through Nantglyn then over the moor and down to Pentrefoelas on a line between our A543 and B4501. It soon degenerates into a track but crosses the Brenig stream on an old stone bridge; then its onward course is still acknowledged by the footbridge across the neck of Alwen reservoir. It comes to A543 at Hafod Dinbych.

North of A543 the upper waters of the Aled have been dammed to form two reservoirs. They lie in a lovely spread of grassy, rushy uplands where the skies are broad. Here are sheep, skylarks and peewits; and here if you listen in spring you may hear the gentle singing of golden plovers. South-west lies Llyn Alwen, a natural pool with a lonely house at its edge. Aled and Elwy are twin streams which rise on Hiraethog, flow north and soon unite. Straight from its lower reservoir the Aled drops into a deep cleft, soon gathers trees on its banks and remains wooded on one side or the other along most of its length. But the upper Elwy is better known: it has a main road by it for some miles and the village of Llanfair Talhaiarn upon its bank. Here is a shapely stone bridge and, safe above possible floods, a fifteenth-century church whose churchyard is known among Welsh people as the burial place of the poet John Jones (1810–69) whose pen-name was Talhaiarn. The church itself is interesting for its iron-studded seventeenth-century door with wooden lock and latch, its pewter and other vessels and its crude pitch-pipe that led the psalm-singers of the eighteenth century.

North of here Rhos is a name you will meet in various places, for the hundred, or cantref, of Rhos was one of the former divisions of Denbighshire. Half-way to the coast there is Betws-yn-Rhos, a village of good appearance through which the Irish stage-coaches used to rumble. Follow them west along B5381 for a couple of miles then turn off right for Llanelian-yn-Rhos which looks across the sea and whose church has faded medieval paintings. Then down on the coast you come to Llandrillo-yn-Rhos, popularly called Rhos-on-Sea. Llandrillo church stands on a bend of A546. It has the date 1677 carved above the lych-gate and a tower with a tall additional turret used in the early seventeenth century as a beacon tower to warn of the approach of pirates who then infested this coast. In the porch is preserved the tombstone of Ednyfed Fychan, a thirteenth-century chieftain whose residence was possibly on the site of Llys Euryn, a largely overgrown Tudor ruin behind the housing estate up the hill from the church. It is worth seeing for its surviving great fireplace and chimney. The hill above is a delightful place for strolls with far views; and there are plenty of limestone wild flowers. To St. Trillo, the sixth-century holy man who presumably founded the church, is dedicated an ancient well down on the shore which is devotedly preserved. Over it is built a chapel eleven feet by eight.

On Denbighshire's twelve miles of coast there are no wild parts remaining. Rhos-on-Sea merges into Colwyn Bay which spreads far. Beyond that, where there is no housing, there are

caravan sites or other developments one after another to Abergele and on to Kinmel Bay. Colwyn Bay, like Llandudno, has
mushroomed as a holiday town in the last hundred years. It
offers all the usual holiday attractions and amusements. Eirias
Park has fine gardens; and above the town near the Old Highway (a former main road to Conway) you can walk in the
woodlands of Pwllycrochan or visit a small zoo.

Just behind all the Denbighshire coast is a line of limestone
hills that here and there show pale scars where their sides have
broken into cliffs as in the deep gash of the Dulas valley between
Betws-yn-Rhos and Llanddulas. The hill east of this gash, Peny-
corddin-mawr, has sizeable cliffs all round it except on the north
and was irresistible to the men of the Iron Age who defended it
with a massive bank of stones which still survives. Typical
flowers of the limestone are all about Penycorddin—rockrose,
marjoram, yellow wort—and there is a wide view of the pat-
terned farms inland. The neighbouring hill east, covered with
trees and undergrowth, has also the banks of an Iron Age fort
called Castell Cawr.

Another two miles east there is yet another hill fort. This one
is Parc y Meirch, or Dinorben, which has been intensively
studied by archaeologists. Excavation has revealed five separate
phases of fortification and has shown that the place was occupied
before, during and immediately after the Roman period. It looks
north across the coastal strip from a precipice of limestone that
is being steadily quarried away. But it is on the south side that it
must have looked most impressive. For there it had five great
banks and ditches one above the other up the slope.

As you approach Abergele from the west you see Gwrych's
walls and towers looking proudly down at you from their
wooded hillside. But disillusionment awaits you. For when you
get to the castle—it is open to the public—you find it is only a
pseudo-medieval affair erected by an early nineteenth-century
tycoon who must have had delusions of grandeur. And grand it
certainly is with its long array of towers and terraces looking
down across three hundred acres of parkland. The castle is
lavishly furnished in regency style and has a sumptuous display
of antiques. Outside are various amusements and popular music.
There are also woods to walk in. Much local history is inscribed
on stone tablets at the gateway on A55 (not the main entrance).

But I would not vouch for its accuracy. Until quite recent times Abergele was a little market town a mile from the sea. But now it has bulged out in all directions with bungalows, caravans and chalets and has a coastal suburb at Pensarn. Its church, which is Tudor, contains ancient cross-slabs and remains of a medieval screen. Walk round outside and you will see traces of four very small, blocked-up doorways. They presumably date back to the days when the naves of churches were used for all sorts of local business and entertainment. So the church must have been quite a warren on a busy day.

A favourite excursion inland from Abergele is to the deep wooded valley of the lower Elwy between the two old estates of Wigfair and Plas Heaton. Being limestone country this is also cave country. Here come the archaeologists and the pot-holers. The archaeologists have found traces of man in these caves going back to the very remotest British prehistory: his chipped tools lay with the bones of rhino, hippo and mammoth. The pot-holers have found many more caves going far into the rocks. One of the best known of the Paleolithic bone caves—the bones have long since been removed to museums—is on the hillside north-east of Meriadog bridge (Bont-newydd), a delightfully placed narrow bridge built high above the rapid, wych-elm-shaded river whose banks in summer are thick with huge leaves of butterbur. Other caves are further downstream and at Plas Heaton.

On the estate of Wigfair ('Mary's retreat') are the remains of St. Mary's well and chapel near a beautiful stretch of this deeply wooded valley. The once elegant chapel stands roofless and weed-grown; but the artistically shaped well alongside is in good condition, its water, when I saw it last, clean and inviting. This interesting building is approached along the river bank past fine copper beeches, maples and an ancient hollow walnut. South of the Elwy at the head of a wooded side-stream is Henllan, an attractive village with a thatch-roofed inn and a church tower set up like a peel tower on an isolated roadside rock high above the church.

Denbigh, as you approach from Henllan, has quite a medieval look with its castle ruins dominant above the town. This castle, whose finest portion is the gate-house, is an Edwardian one begun in 1282. It saw service in the time of Owain Glyndŵr and in the Wars of the Roses. But its greatest siege was in the Civil War when it long held out against the Parliamentarians. Of the so-called town walls, which are really the outer walls of the castle, large fragments survive. Within them are modern houses and the tower of the otherwise demolished medieval church of St. Hilary. Further down the hill are the high walls of 'Leicester's cathedral'. It was begun in 1579 by Dudley, Earl of Leicester, favourite of Queen Elizabeth who had granted him the castle. He intended this cathedral, it is said, to supersede the one at St. Asaph, presumably to boost his prestige. But it was never anything like finished, being abandoned at Leicester's death in 1588.

Down in the town are the fourteenth-century remains of the only Carmelite friary that was of long duration in Wales. In the parish church, St. Marcella's, which is curiously far from the town centre, you will find memorials of past worthies such as Twm o'r Nant, a lively and popular poet of pre-Nonconformist Wales; and of the parents of Sir Hugh Myddelton who built the New River, London's water supply in the reign of James I. Though Samuel Johnson stayed with the Myddeltons at Gwaunynog for only a few days in 1774, a cottage he used to visit near the banks of the Ystrad immediately became hallowed as a literary shrine; and in a nearby field was set up a Grecian urn that still informs us that: 'This spot was often dignified by the presence of Samuel Johnson Ll.D. . . .' It makes an enjoyable walk from the town. Just outside Denbigh on the Ruthin road look out for a good-class pottery on the right. Further on, at Llanrhaeadr church, you will find craftsmanship of several hundred years earlier—a colourful, fifteenth-century Jesse window. A mile or so south east along lanes is the primitive little church of Llanynys, where restorations in 1967 brought to light a medieval mural of St. Christopher. This little church (the west door is early thirteenth century) also has a medieval memorial cross and some good carving in wood. Tree enthusiasts will like the churchyard yews and should also visit the weather-beaten chestnuts called 'The Three Sisters' which stand on the west side of A525 four miles south-east of Denbigh and are so called because planted by three daughters of a local landowner nearly three centuries ago.

Ruthin, three miles up the vale, is a small country town with personality. It has a fine old church, some admirable black and white buildings and a castle. The church is two-aisled, as are many in this vale, the north aisle being fourteenth century, four hundred years older than the southern. The highly ornamented oak roof of the northern aisle is marvellous for its bewilderment of differing designs; and the roof of the eighteenth-century aisle is also admirable. There are a couple of notable brasses. Between church and castle you pass several timbered buildings varying in date from late medieval to eighteenth century. All are still in daily use. Of the half-timbered private houses Nantclwyd in Castle Street is the finest-looking. The red-sandstone castle is much the same age (founded 1281) as Denbigh's, being part of the design to consolidate the Edwardian conquest. It was long held by the Grey family whose dispute with Owain Glyndŵr started the rebellion of 1400. Glyndŵr made straight for Ruthin which thus had the distinction of being the first Welsh town of the many which the hero sacked. The castle was not taken. Nor did it fall until two and a half centuries later to the Cromwellians. After that it lay in ruins nearly two hundred years until it was converted into the massive, castellated private residence that still survives in its beautiful park. The castle, which is a mixture of medieval and nineteenth century, is now a hotel where you can dine in medieval style.

How many churches do you know with a knocker on the door? Or with a font made of medieval wood? Or with a big stone ball that was used in games no longer played? Or with a seventeenth-century Prayer Book displayed in a glass case? All these you can see in the chapel-sized church of Efenechtyd two miles south of Ruthin. This is an attractive countryside. All around is quiet, hilly land with generous patches of broad-leaved trees along the limestone slopes, woods that are of considerable botanical interest. One such ash wood called Cilygroeslwyd between Efenechtyd and Llanfair Dyffryn Clwyd is a nature reserve of the North Wales Naturalists' Trust, and is rich in lime-loving plants.

Above Llanfair Dyffryn Clwyd the vale gradually dies into the uplands and the Clwyd becomes a narrow streamlet finding its way down from the dark forest of Clocaenog. It flows due south then due north before it settles into an easterly course below the sloping village of Derwen whose church retains its medieval screen and rood loft more or less intact and whose churchyard keeps its medieval cross. A couple of miles east of

Derwen, in a wide and leafy side-valley, is Llanelidan, a charming sequestered hamlet whose churchyard is unusually flowery and whose church has a pulpit decorated with wood carvings from a medieval screen. In a glass case is a fine copy of the Bishop's Bible.

Going on east you reach A525 and are soon at Llandegla, a village busier in former days when several drovers' roads converged here before going over the hills to Llangollen and England. Llandegla is on the bank of the Alun (or Alyn) whose valley takes you directly north through miles of attractive, limestone, bone-cave country whose villages are Llanarmon-yn-Iâl, Llanferres and Maeshafn. So you come to the Flintshire border and the well-known Loggerheads Inn on A494. Close to the Loggerheads lived the painter Richard Wilson at a house called Colomendy. The Alun here flows below pale limestone crags with pines and beeches set picturesquely above them; and there are many wild flowers. But you soon find a difference if you go on to Esclusham Mountain. In that high treeless, sandstone country of poor soils you may see some resemblance to Mynydd Hiraethog. But the comparison soon fails. For down the farther slopes of Esclusham you come to mineral-rich ground. You descend through a zone where the rocks have been mined or quarried for lead, iron, coal, stone and fireclay. The result is the industrialized region centred on Wrexham. It is all good country for industrial archaeologists who should visit places like Minera, described a century ago as 'the El Dorado of North Wales'; and nearby Bersham where John Wilkinson pioneered the British iron trade.

Wrexham (Wrecsam) itself, once purely a country market town, was so thoroughly changed into an industrial metropolis that practically all its old buildings were swept away. There remains the remarkable fifteenth-century church whose tall, much-pinnacled tower, a landmark for all-comers, is lavishly decorated on three sides with rows and rows of saints carved in their gothic niches. Architecture apart, the church is probably best known for the grave of Elihu Yale which is west of the tower. Yale would now be forgotten had he not given an endowment to the obscure American college that is now Yale university. The name Yale comes from Iâl (pronounced 'Yarl'), the Welsh name of one of the ancient divisions of Denbighshire. There is a Yale memorial chapel at Bryneglwys church fourteen miles along A5104 from Wrexham, for here was Plas yn Yale, the family home.

Away on the coalfield to the north-east is Gresford which also has one of the finest churches in Wales though it is thoroughly English in type. Its tower, like Wrexham's, is carved with stone figures but with much more restraint. And its medieval wood-work—roof, vaulted screen and richly carved stalls—are a splendid survival. The approaches to Gresford from Wrexham are not promising, dominated as they are by the tips and wheels of a coal-mine. But then a sign turns you off the main road to 'Gresford Village' and the scene is immediately rural. You pass a pond with swans and bulrushes; you see old country cottages; then the tall brown spiky church is before you and industrial Wales seems far away. If it is Sunday and the bells are ringing you may remember that Gresford's peel of twelve was once thought a thing of real wonder. But that was no doubt a reputation gained at a time when church bells were rare in Wales. The farming country east of the coalfield, the fruitful Vale of Maelor, looks very Cheshire as, geologically speaking, it is, being on the Triassic rocks. It is also English in its language and in its position on Offa's side of the Dyke. Inevitably in this district the Dyke has had to do battle with industrialization. At Brymbo, for in-stance, a mountain-like coal-tip has been dumped on top of it.

For many wriggling miles the eastern boundary of Denbigh-shire is the Dee where it flows north past Holt towards Chester. In this corner of the county, on A483, is the village of Rossett, a name that looks thoroughly Saxon but is in fact the Welsh Yr Orsedd in disguise. At Rossett the Alyn river has for centuries turned the wheels of picturesque flour-mills but not any more: the wheels are still there but the machinery turns by electricity. At Holt, which is on the Dee, stood a great Edwardian castle, shown in old prints as towering in majesty above the river. But all its highest walls are gone. An old name for this castle, 'the Castle of the Lions', could well be a wrong interpretation of some Dark Ages name such as 'Caerllion'. And this, like Caer-leon in Monmouthshire, would have evolved from the Latin 'Castra legionis', meaning 'the camp of the legion'. And in fact there was a Roman pottery at Holt: copious traces of Roman ware, tiles and pipes have been found. Close by the castle is the bridge: and on a river that has so many memorable bridges all the way down from Bala this one at Holt is perhaps the oldest and most attractive. It is multi-arched, narrow and fourteenth century.

Upstream from Holt the Dee is altogether beautiful in its lowland way and remains so past Bangor, Overton and Erbistock until you get close to Wynnstay park, Ruabon. Wynnstay was long the seat of the Wynns who owned a vast amount of the country between here and Pumlumon nearly fifty miles southwest. Along the summit ridge of Pumlumon you can still find slate stones inscribed 'W.W.W.' (Watkin WilliamsWynn) to mark the boundary of that empire. South of Ruabon is a region much loved by canal enthusiasts for through it came the canal from Ellesmere in Shropshire to be thrown across the deep valleys of the Ceiriog, then the Dee, on aqueducts that were at that time (1805) marvels of engineering and which today are still completely fascinating. This was, however, not entirely a success among canals because it never achieved its final object of getting to Ruabon and Wrexham. The trouble up there was lack of water. Telford who built these narrow, iron-troughed aqueducts, also built a canal reservoir at Ffrwd, near Wrexham, but it soon ran dry and was abandoned. Water taken from the Horseshoe Falls near Llangollen kept the lower parts of the canal going and still does. The canal, after long railway-age doldrums, has revived as a pleasure-boat waterway. You will find the Ceiriog aqueduct linking England with Wales half a mile southwest of Chirk: it is 70 feet above the river on ten sandstone arches. The Dee aqueduct, called Pont Cysylltau, is the longest in Britain (1,007 feet). It is 120 feet above the water, has nineteen sandstone arches and is three and a half miles east of Llangollen.

Chirk is a village right on the border. It stands on the Welsh bank of the Ceiriog, has a fifteenth-century church, and a war memorial carved by Eric Gill. The place is best known for its unusually intact, rather squat Edwardian castle built on high ground a mile and a half west of the village. It is one of the rare medieval castles that has remained in continuous occupation down to the present day. Though structurally a genuine Middle Ages castle its walls and towers have been so pierced by many-mullioned windows that the medieval look has largely gone. It is open to visitors on several afternoons a week from May to September. The interior is handsomely furnished and the gardens

colourful. You approach by a long drive curving through parkland from a pair of magnificent eighteenth-century wrought-
iron gates made by local craftsmen. There is a fine walk through
the northern part of this park, starting near Offa's Dyke, going
up through woodland then along curving slopes high above the
Dee to Llangollen.

A popular motorist's-eye view of the Llangollen country is
from the Horseshoe Pass four miles north-west of the town along
A542. From up there, in a world of short turf, gorse and bracken
you have a great prospect down the valley to Llangollen and to
long lines of hills further south. On a fine summer's day the
Horseshoe Pass can look more like a farmyard than a main road.
There are sheep wandering everywhere, sheep being fed by picnickers, sheep scratching themselves ecstatically against car-
bumpers and sheep being photographed as if they were game in
an African national park. The scenery is a bit marred by old
quarries on slopes to the west but if you walk up past them you
can soon get to the top of Moel y Gamelin which is a superb
viewpoint. From there the whole ridge of Llandysilio mountain
is before you all the way to Carrog on the Dee in Merioneth.
Between Moel y Gamelin and Moel Morfudd note the high-
placed Iron Age hill fort, Moel y Gaer. East of the Horseshoe
Pass the scene is different. There, in a long impressive line, miles
of outcropping Carboniferous limestone show as a beautifully
stratified escarpment of pale rocks hanging along the hills. If you
want a more intimate view of those rocks—they are called
Creigiau Eglwyseg—there is a lane up from Llangollen that
skirts along their feet to the World's End then dives into conifers.
Just before that it passes a famous old Tudor house, Plas Uchaf.
Above the plantations it climbs steeply away over high moors
and drops you down at Minera.

Close to Llangollen are the ruins of the Cistercian abbey of
Valle Crucis established in 1201 by monks from Strata Marcella
near Welshpool. The substantial ruins of the abbey church and
monastery used to sit beautifully in their valley but the picture is
now marred by a welter of caravans next door. Here in the
sheltered valley the monks found what they sought: solitude, a
fertile soil and wide slopes on which to pasture sheep for wool-
production. They lived simply and ate no meat, the protein part
of their diet coming from fish. They had fishing rights on the

Dee and a large fish pond just to the east of the abbey. The poets
Iolo Goch, Guto'r Glyn and Gutyn Owain have left vivid first-
hand descriptions of being entertained at Valle Crucis in its
latter days when austerity had given way to luxury and the
monks were living like gentry.

The name Valle Crucis ('vale of the cross') came from the
Pillar of Eliseg, a sorry relic now but once one of the most
interesting wayside crosses in Britain. It still stands, a lone stump
on a mound near the east side of A542 a few hundred yards up
the road from the abbey. This cross shaft bore a long inscription
(now practically invisible) which said that the pillar was a
memorial to Eliseg, prince of Powys, and was set up by his
great-grandson, Concenn. Eliseg is thought to have flourished in
the middle of the eighth century and the pillar to have been
erected in the early ninth century. A grave and skeleton discovered in the mound in 1779 were possibly those of Eliseg.
The monument was broken up by the Puritans during the
Civil War, what was left of it being re-erected in 1779. The
Latin inscription, carved on the opposite side from the Dark
Ages one, records this re-erection.

From many places, including Llangollen, you see the ruin-
topped hill of Dinas Brân a mile north-east of the town. Embanked as a fort in the Iron Age this sharp hill was crowned in
the Middle Ages by a thick-walled Welsh castle which though
never playing a great part in history, was, because of its 'romantic' position, much praised by the early tourists. The result is
that, at least by name, it has become one of the best-known
castles in Wales. What power it ever had faded at the Edwardian
conquest if not earlier and when Leland saw it in about 1536 it
had already long been in ruins. Dinas Brân is easily reached up a
lane from Llangollen, a lane which then goes on up the end of
the Eglwyseg rocks to some great panoramic viewpoints above
the vale. On the other side of the town Barber's Hill and also the
lanes above Vivod give other lovely views of the Dee. Another
favourite walk is along the canal to the Horseshoe Falls and from
there to other lovely meanders of the Dee further upstream.

Llangollen, popular ever since Welsh tourism began, has become famous for its July festival of folk music and dancing when
competitors gather from many countries to enjoy the annual
international eisteddfod, an occasion of much colour and gaiety

when the town is packed with people. Most of them visit the
parish church with its intricately carved medieval roof floodlit
so that you can see the full detail. Do not miss on the south wall
the amusing marble of two ladies in tall hats apparently out for a
walk. They are the Hon. Sarah Ponsonby (died 1831) and Lady
Eleanor Butler (died 1829), eccentric Irish ladies who 'eloped'
from Ireland in 1776 and lived in bliss at Llangollen ever after.
Witty and cultured, they entertained distinguished people from
all over Britain at their house, Plas Newydd, which is now open
to the public. Past Plas Newydd you can go on along a lane
which makes a delightful walk that circles you back to the town
following an ancient meander of the Dee. Or you can be more
ambitious and take the climbing lane that goes over and down
to Glyn Ceiriog, a good road to walk but severe on cars.

There remains the final tip of Denbighshire, the stubby thumb
it pushes a dozen miles south-west into the wide-skied uplands
it shares with Merioneth and Montgomeryshire. Here is the long
wide ridge of the Berwyn, rising to Cadair Fronwen, Cadair
Berwyn and Moel Sych. And here are many small rivers of delight which come from those high moors—Ceiriog, Twrch,
Tanad (or Tanat) and their sidestreams. For the lover of wild
country this could well be the best part of Denbighshire. A B-
road gets you into the heart of it up the Ceiriog valley past the
grounds of Chirk castle to Pontfadog, a good-looking village
deep under wooded slopes and thence to Glyn Ceiriog, a quarry-
village once served by a narrow-gauge railway. And so for
several more lovely miles to Llanarmon Dyffryn Ceiriog which
is both the highest and most attractive village on the river.

From Llanarmon a lane continues upstream full of promise
but at last becomes a mere track that dies into the hills. But
though it fades today it may have been a regular route for
medieval foot and hoof. For it seems a likely link between
Owain Glyndŵr's two favourite residences, the one at Glyndyfrdwy near Corwen and the other a dozen miles south at
Sycharth near Llansilin. Glyndŵr's road or not it makes a good
walk over from the Dee and though it may fox you a little in
places it comes down blithely enough at last into the head of
Cwm Ceiriog past waterfalls and brackeny slopes. We know
vividly what life was like in Glyndŵr's wooden castle at
Sycharth from a description by the contemporary bard Iolo

Goch. His 'Sycharth' is one of the most fascinating medieval Welsh poems and you can read a famous English version of it in Borrow's *Wild Wales*. In it the castle is described on its hillock within its wide moat. There was a private chapel, an orchard, a deer park, a rabbit warren, meadows, cornfields, water-mill, dovecote, fish-pond, cranes and peacocks. At Sycharth today it is hard to imagine all this high life when you see the quite ordinary motte in its quiet green valley. But you can see where the moat was; there are still a couple of hollows for fish-ponds; and excavations have shown that such a house as the poem describes certainly did crown the hillock:

> *Upon four wooden columns proud*
> *Mounteth his mansion to the cloud*

Its end was abrupt. It was burnt to the ground in 1403 by the English under the youthful Prince Henry, later Henry V, who then went up to the Dee to give Glyndŵr's other house the same treatment. Nearly two miles north of Sycharth is Llansilin whose church has a noted fifteenth-century roof; and south you come to the valley of the Tanad near Llangedwyn. It is a district of great beauty and fertility and in the past was famous for its mighty oaks. An interesting bridge crosses the Tanad just on the county boundary. It is Pont Glan Tanad-uchaf and is surely unique in having a couple of medieval cross-slabs built into its parapets.

You are now near a famous village: Llanrhaeadr-ym-Mochnant, dear to Welsh people as the place where, in the time of Elizabeth I, William Morgan, rector of this parish and later Bishop of St. Asaph, made the first translation of the whole Bible into Welsh. Printed in London in 1588 it has become known as the Bishop's Bible. It is commemorated in the lych-gate of the church. From this village you can go up the deep valley of the Rhaeadr four miles to where the stream comes down a fine waterfall, dropping 240 feet, though not in a single leap, into a wooden dingle. This lovely fall is the highest in Wales (and higher than any in England too, local patriots will tell you).

A similar valley, that of the Twrch, takes you along a winding, undulating lane high above a noisy stream past delightful oak woods. It is a road for walkers: it merely serves a few farms then becomes a pathway faltering up the brackeny slopes of Berwyn, making for a shallow gap in the skyline. In this gap there is a standing stone which at first looks tiny but when you come up to it half an hour later you find it to be taller than yourself. Probably it is prehistoric and probably people before you for several thousand years have used it to guide them over the ridge. Up there at over two thousand feet you are in the heart of Berwyn. Quiet grassy hills stretch everywhere about you. Cadair Berwyn and Moel Sych are behind you and the cairned, symmetrical dome of Cadair Fronwen rises close before you. From here the ancient road—up there called Ffordd Gam Elin —slips away left round the head of the cwm and soon begins to descend. And down you go with it into Merioneth.

This end of Berwyn is botanically unique: it is the only place in Wales for the cloudberry. To find it look for a low-growing shrub something like a bramble but lacking thorns. Quite abundant high up the slopes of Moel Sych and neighbouring summits, it is a plant well known in the district, its Welsh name being *mwyar Berwyn* ('Berwyn berries'). Its chief peculiarity is that it flowers very sparingly and so produces extremely few of the red, raspberry-like fruits. So when in the nineteenth century a local squire offered five shillings each for ripe Berwyn berries he well knew how little he stood to lose. What is probably a very ancient legend also refers to the Berwyn cloudberry. It relates that St. Dogfan, an early Celtic preacher, used to receive payment for his ministry in the form of cloudberry fruit. (Hence its other name: *mwyar Dogfan*.) You can interpret this legend in two ways. Either it means that cloudberry fruited much more abundantly back in the Dark Ages. Or it is a jocular way of saying that Dogfan went unpaid. One other plant you may discover on Berwyn. This is a tiny orchid called the lesser twayblade. But it is so small—about two inches high with tiny leaves and a minute spike of reddish flowers—and hides so deep under the heather that you really must have your eye in to spot it. Mercifully most of the delights of Denbighshire are far less elusive.

4

FLINTSHIRE
(Sir Fflint)

This, the smallest county, is unique in being in two main parts, a large and a small, separated by ten miles of Denbighshire. And curiously islanded within this intruding bulge of Denbighshire there is a third fragment of Flintshire, the little parish of Marford and Hoseley, close to Gresford. But of Marford and Hoseley I will say nothing for I have neither been there nor heard any man say anything to its credit or discredit. So I leave it to inquiring readers to explore its secrets for themselves.

Flintshire is mainly hilly and especially so in the west where sandstones of Silurian age bulge up to form a high and undulating border with Denbighshire along the Clwydian hills, a range that goes for twenty splendid miles from Diserth in the north to Llandegla in the south. In contrast the lower ridge which lies to the east of the Clwydian hills is of Carboniferous Limestone, a part of the great arc of limestone that curves round north and east Wales from Anglesey to the Shropshire border. Parts of east Flintshire have long been industrialized. So if you arrive from Merseyside or Chester you come straight into a region that has been a coalfield and, without clearing up the old mess, has turned to other activities none of which add beauty to the scene. Happily this industrial zone does not spread far. From the outskirts of Connah's Quay you need only go a mile up the Wepre Brook to find, in a woodland retreat, a most attractive castle ruin, that of Ewloe perched high above a hazel dingle and still

71

defended by stout banks. That a Welsh castle could be built so near to Chester in about 1267 shows what prestige its builder, Llywelyn ap Gruffydd, was enjoying just then. But in a very few years came Edward I; and Ewloe and everything else was soon lost.

From Ewloe castle it is two miles along the Chester road to Hawarden (pronounced 'Harden'), one of Flintshire's pleasantest little towns. The name in medieval English meant 'high enclosure', no doubt from the Iron Age fortification that preceded the early motte castle that was itself replaced in the thirteenth century by a Norman castle, part of whose walls remain, notably the large round keep that crowns the motte. The old castle overlooks a castellated house, a lovely extent of wooded parkland open to the public and, more distantly, an airport. The modern castle was W. E. Gladstone's country home for sixty years, a possession he came into through his wife, Catherine Glynne. Gladstone's statue stands near the main road; there is a Gladstone museum; the church has an effigy of him (he was buried in Westminster Abbey) and a memorial window by Burne-Jones.

Nearly five miles north-west is the village of Northop which has a large, spiky church containing old effigies in niches along the north wall, including one of a woman with costume and hair-do of the fifteenth century. A faceless, over-fed shape nearby was aptly called 'the fat knight' by Thomas Pennant. A mile or so east a fifteenth-century hall survives at Northophall Farm. From Northop down to the estuary flows the Lead Brook, a stream that has two thousand years of leaden associations. Near its mouth is Pentre Ffwrndan ('furnace village') where remains of Roman lead-smelting have been excavated. And if the Romans came here for lead it is reasonable to suppose that it was already being worked by the Deceangli, the Celtic tribe then occupying this region. Pigs of Roman lead weighing about 150 pounds and stamped with the name of this tribe have been found in the district.

From these metallic beginnings began the settlement that officially became Flint town on 8th September 1284, when Edward I granted a charter to this walled and castled borough. The town walls have gone but the bastide street plan survives and so does the castle on its rock raised slightly above the saltings. It was this rock, early recorded as 'Y Flynt', that gave the castle and hence the town and the county their names. (The word 'flint' in early English meant any hard rock.) The castle was of the conventional Edwardian type—thick curtain walls with a round tower at each corner—except that the tower on the south-east was left separate from the walls so that at high tides it was surrounded by water. Alas, the present situation of Flint castle is ignoble, dominated as it is by the chimneys of the huge rayon factory next door. This castle, vital in the early Norman domination of north-east Wales, also held out later against Owain Glyndŵr. But in 1647 it was disembowelled by the Parliamentarians. In its time it was easily reached by ships; and Flint continued to be a port until well into last century. Today the Dee is far away and only the spring tides reach the castle walls. Maybe the river will soon have wriggled in its bed and the tide ebbed for the last time. For there is a scheme to barrage the estuary and turn it into areas of land and fresh water.

Lead ore, long the source of Flint's livelihood, came from Halkyn Mountain, the high limestone ridge three miles inland. Up there are still many disused workings of interest not only to archaeologists but also to botanists who find that certain plants seem particularly flourishing on lead mine spoil-heaps, especially the vernal sandwort, an attractive cushion-plant with tiny white flowers. These Flintshire lead mines were, taken all together, probably the richest in Wales. Their tunnellings continue for miles beneath Halkyn Mountain, many of them being conduits for the vast quantities of water that lie below ground. Though lead is no longer profitable on Halkyn or anywhere else in Wales some of the mines are still worked for limestone. Halkyn Mountain today, though scarred, is still enjoyable country. There is pony-trekking and high-level walking with many far views. At the south end, above Rhosesmor there is the hill fort of Moel y Gaer which may still have been occupied by the Deceangli when Roman Chester was being built twelve miles away.

North of Halkyn Mountain is Holywell, a place of the greatest medieval fame, its curative well of St. Winifred attracting pilgrims for many centuries, a practice still kept up by modern Catholics who regard the place as 'the Lourdes of Wales'. An ornate chapel was built over the well in about 1490 at the expense of Margaret, Countess of Derby and mother of Henry VII by her marriage with Edmund Tudor of Penmynydd, Anglesey. This interesting building survives in a good state of preservation. Close to it is the parish church in which a rare curio is a hand-bell with knee-pad. The bell was so hung from the bellman's shoulders that it was rung by his padded knee as he walked through the streets announcing the services or funerals or the perambulation of the parish boundaries. Religious power here in Norman times was centred at Basingwerk Abbey, a mile north-east of Holywell. It was founded for the Savignac order in 1132 but within fifteen years had been absorbed by the more dominant Cistercians. The present fairly substantial ruins are chiefly thirteenth century. Made, like Flint castle, of Talacre sandstone they do not impress by their height but there are many good arches and pillars. And though close to industry the site is surprisingly rural. The name Basingwerk is Saxon, probably meaning the fortress of some now unknown leader called Basa.

It was from close to Basingwerk (but it is now very slight there) that Flintshire's most distinctive ancient monument—Wat's Dyke—began. It finishes thirty-eight dyke-winding miles away south of Oswestry in Shropshire, going via Caergwrle and Wrexham, and keeping always east of Offa's Dyke. Though in some places the two dykes are nearly four miles apart and in one place near Ruabon less than a mile, generally they keep fairly parallel, following each other's curves. Like Offa's Dyke, Wat's is a raised bank with a ditch on the west; and like Offa's it climbs and bends to take advantage of natural defences such as ravines and hill crests. Judged by its similar construction its date was very close to that of Offa's (late eighth century) but whether it preceded or followed the greater dyke is problematical. Probably it was the Saxons' first attempt to define their frontier and then a few decades later along comes Offa, more powerful than his predecessors and able to establish a better line further west. Who Wat was is unknown.

In trying to see the thinking behind these fascinating dykes it is essential to forget most of the landscape's present features and to imagine it as extremely difficult country choked with dense forests and marshes. It is only in this context that some of the gaps in the dykes can be explained, huge gaps that in the Dark Ages were occupied by quite intractable country needing no

defence works. One of the best places to see Wat's Dyke in
Flintshire is a mile west of Northop along the lane to Rhosesmor
where you will find a good section of it forming the eastern edge
of a pheasant-loud larchwood. Do not be misled by nearby
place names such as Bryn Offa and Clawdd Offa: they are on
Wat's not Offa's Dyke and arose in days when everyone confused the two dykes. Offa's Dyke in Flintshire is a disappoint-
ment. Starting from the south at Ffrith there is a short length
nearly to Treuddyn. But north of that is a great gap of sixteen
miles to Holywell from where it goes on fairly complete to near
Gop Hill and there ends.

North-west from Holywell you come to Whitford, an
agreeable hill village in good country. Among the many fine
histories of Welsh parishes that of Whitford and Holywell was
one of the earliest and best, its author being Thomas Pennant
(1726–98) whose estate, Downing, was at Whitford. His house,
down a wooded glen called Nant-y-bi ('magpie dingle') has
gone. Pennant was a naturalist of European repute but today he
is known for his descriptions of North Wales. The rebuilt
church at Whitford contains a memorial of him; and at the back
of the church is quite a museum of old stones going back to the
seventh century. There is also a fourteenth-century sarcophagus.
Whitford parish has many past things to show. Of this and
adjacent districts Pennant claimed: 'no place in North Wales exhibits an equal quantity of tumuli . . . the tombs of ancient
heroes'. Note that in this part of Wales a tumulus or cairn is
often called 'gorsedd' or 'yr orsedd' just as elsewhere it has other
names such as 'crug' or 'grug'. Whitford's most celebrated
monument is not, however, a tumulus. It is the fine cross of
Achwyfan which stands in a bend of the road a mile north-west
of the village. This magnificently carved wheel cross, said to be
the tallest of its kind in Britain, presumably commemorates the
early Celtic saint, Cyfan, to whom Diserth church, four and a
half miles west, is dedicated.

For a view over all this region do as Pennant suggests and go
up the hill called Garreg (809 feet) a mile west of Whitford.
From there, he says, you can see Snowdonia 'from the crooked
Moel Siabod at one end to the towering Penmaenmawr at the
other'. (In his day Penmaenmawr had not yet been beheaded.)
If you can also see, he adds, 'the Isle of Man and the Cumberland

Alps', they are 'the sure presages of bad weather'. On this hill stands what looks like the ruins of a windmill but which Pennant correctly diagnosed as a beacon tower. But dating it with wild inaccuracy he called it Roman though it is really sixteenth century. Also he thought it was a light to warn shipping whereas in fact it was a light to warn people of the approach of shipping—the vessels of pirates who then infested this coast. On the subject of beacons note between here and Holywell the place name Mwdwl-eithin. Literally it means 'a stack of gorse' and used to be a frequent word for beacon. Several Welsh hill tops still have this name.

On the estuary below Whitford is Mostyn which looks a Welsh name but is from the early English 'moss' a marsh and 'ton' a settlement. Mostyn Hall, a fifteenth-century manor house, is on the site of a house of early Welsh princes. Here in 1485 the Mostyn family conspired to get Henry VII on to the throne of England and their Flintshire army had a part in his victory at Bosworth. The Mostyn district has long been industrialized. Coal was worked here from the age of Edward I until recent times and now there is an iron works. Unlike other Dee ports Mostyn Quay is still in use, the only port left in North Wales apart from Holyhead. Four miles inland is Trelawnyd (or Newmarket) whose church has a good fourteenth-century cross. To the north rises Gop Hill crowned by a tumulus (if that's what it is) of a size almost to make you think of Silbury Hill in Wiltshire. Investigation into this mound, which is of white limestone pebbles, has revealed nothing. So perhaps it is the site of a former beacon. Below on both sides of the hill limestone caves have yielded bones of prehistoric animals. Caves on the south side had a Neolithic communal burial and many separate graves as well as artefacts both Mesolithic and Neolithic. The hill is worth climbing for the views up and down the coast and back to the Clwydian Hills. And if you fossick around up there you could be lucky enough to pick up a tiny flint arrowhead for this hill was formerly called Bryn y Saethau because of the arrowheads that used to be found on it. From up there you look down the sloping land to the wide mouth of the Dee, at full tide a splendid arm of the sea, at low tide a world of shining sands and winding, muddy creeks that harbour large numbers of wading birds at the passage seasons and in winter. Far out near the Wirral side you see the low domes of the two Hilbre islands where these waders congregate at high tide in spectacular numbers.

The Dee ends at the Point of Ayr, 'ayr' being Norse for a sandbank. The name is apt for this vast pile-up of dunes and estuary sands. Alas, these fine dunes are spoilt by a vast sprawl of bungalows, shanties and caravans. But if the dunes are no longer wild and beautiful at least the foreshore remains unspoilt and there is a lovely three-mile walk along it from Prestatyn to the disused lighthouse at the point. A mile south of the lighthouse is Flintshire's only active coal mine: its workings go far under the estuary. Overlooking all this scene from the hills inland is the village of Llanasa whose church has fifteenth century east windows said to have been brought from Basingwerk Abbey at the Dissolution.

Prestatyn, like Mostyn, is an English name that has been given a Welsh look. Basically it is the same as Preston and Presteigne, its roots being 'prest', a priest, and 'ton', a settlement. Prestatyn as a mushroom holiday town of this century may look like a place of no history. But in fact the building of it brought to light a chipping floor that produced flint tools for the people of six or more thousand years ago. There have been finds of later periods of prehistory also. And in 1934 a Roman fort was discovered half a mile south-west of the parish church when a drainage ditch was cut across a field. Prestatyn and Rhyl, four miles west, are really one vast holiday centre with miles of sands, promenades and large-scale catering and amusement facilities. Prestatyn's chief claim to distinction is its horse-trotting stadium where competitors tear round a track with all the dust-raising, flying hooves and excitement of a Roman chariot race.

The slopes climb steeply behind Prestatyn and there are lovely walks. On the highest point (783 feet) the oddly named St. Elmo's Summer House, a first-class viewpoint, is on a tumulus of the Bronze Age and there is another tumulus a hundred yards or so to the west. A mile south-west of this summit you come to Gwaunysgor, a name spelt 'Wenescol' in Domesday (1086). (Parts of Flintshire are among the few districts of Wales that are included in the Domesday survey.) The little church there is interesting for its old door frame made of two massive oak uprights meeting in a pointed arch. There is also an elaborate Norman font, a medieval tomb slab and a fine fifteenth-century roof. Gwaunysgor has high ground all about. You look to Gop Hill on the south; and on the west is Graig Fawr, site of the great Talargoch lead and zinc mine which worked intermittently from Roman, perhaps pre-Roman, times to our own. Near the mines was the high-placed medieval castle of Diserth (or Dyserth), but it has been removed by modern quarrying. (As a Flintshire historian once remarked, we cannot blame Cromwell for every act of vandalism.) Ruins immediately south of the castle site are those of Siambr Wen ('white chamber'), a medieval manor house. This hill has also yielded many traces of prehistoric settlement from Neolithic to Romano–British. And being of limestone it is also botanically inviting. Both the common and hoary rockroses, spiked speedwell, blood-red cranesbill, lesser meadow-rue, ploughman's spikenard and milk thistle are recorded.

Diserth—the name comes from Latin *desertum* and suggests it started as a hermit's retreat in the Dark Ages—climbs steeply up the side of a limestone hill just south of Prestatyn. The old part of Diserth is around the parish church, largely rebuilt in 1875 but containing old crosses, a thirteenth century south door, grave slabs of Knights Templar and two fine windows. Near the church a sixty-foot waterfall drops off the hill almost into the village—a great spectacle after a storm. The stream, which has grey wagtails and dippers, then runs attractively alongside the road to the church. For a collection of old armour go to Bodrhyddan Hall on the Rhuddlan side of Diserth; it is usually open from June to September. For a celebrated hill fort climb Moel Hiraddug before these Early Iron Age earthworks are all quarried away. A quern and other finds of the Halstatt period suggest that the occupation of this fort began perhaps three centuries B.C. 'Hiraddug' looks like the name of a person and as such may explain the similar 'Hiraethog', the name of the Denbigh moors.

Two miles west of Diserth you descend gently into the Clwyd valley and come to Rhuddlan, headquarters of Edward I at the time of the conquest. Here in 1277 he began the great castle whose thick-walled shell still stands above the river. And from here in 1284 he promulgated his famous Statute of Wales, creating shires where he was powerful enough to do so and giving them certain laws. The castle was diamond-shaped with a single round tower at the north and south corners and with double

towers for the entrances east and west. There was a moat round
three of the sides and the Clwyd on the fourth. Rhuddlan means
'red bank', a reference to the colour of the soil through which
the Clwyd flows. This was a busy stream when most of the
world's business went by ship but now it is quiet enough as it
goes on its way down to Rhyl. Near the castle it flows under
Rhuddlan bridge, a crossing of vital importance in feudal times.
A bridge recorded here in 1281 was rebuilt about 1331 and either
rebuilt or repaired in 1595, which may be the date of the
smaller of the two present arches, the bigger one being thought
to be less ancient.

Rhyl is a word about which the place-names experts argue but
probably it simply means 'the hill', being awkwardly formed
from the Welsh article 'yr' added to the English word 'hill'. And
if you inquire, as well you might, where is the said hill in all that
flat plain, the crafty etymologist then postulates the existence of
some former castle mound now clean swept away! The speed of
Rhyl's growth has been phenomenal and today its miles of
sands, promenades and popular attractions give pleasure to
countless visitors. The coast here has seen vast prehistoric
changes: formerly it extended much farther north until it was
overrun by the sea in Neolithic times, a fact that is proved by the
stumps of trees still sometimes visible at low tide, forest remains
that have yielded implements of Neolithic man including a
couple of hand-axes made on Graig Lwyd, Penmaenmawr.

Across North Wales the Romans made a main road from the
legionary fortress at Chester to their important stronghold at
Caernarvon, crossing the Conwy near Caerhun. In Flintshire its
probable course was first alongside the Dee estuary to the lead
works at Flint, then on to Basingwerk to swing inland due west
more or less along the line of our A55 to the station they called
Varae which is generally accepted to have been at or not far from
St. Asaph, though nothing on the ground has yet been found to
prove it. Built on a rise between the rivers Elwy and Clwyd, St.
Asaph (Llanelwy) has been a religious centre ever since Asaph
founded his cell here in the sixth century. The place evidently
soon grew to importance for it emerges from the Dark Ages as
the centre of a see.

No doubt successive churches of wood stood here until a stone
one was built in early Norman times. But this got destroyed

during the Edwardian conquest and to replace it the present cathedral was immediately begun, built probably from the same yellow and purple sandstone and grey limestone as Rhuddlan castle its contemporary. In 1402 Owain Glyndŵr wrecked the interior so thoroughly that it was out of action for nearly a century. After the Reformation it suffered the general neglect of cathedrals and the Cromwellians found it useful for housing troops and horses. After long dilapidation it was extensively restored in the nineteenth century. But despite many changes the essential plan of the medieval building survives—smaller than any other cathedral in Wales, or in England. Visiting St. Asaph in the fourteenth century, the poet Iolo Goch expresses his appreciation of the wine he received from the bishop: not just any old wine but a vintage from local vineyards. (We also hear of medieval vineyards at Sycharth, Denbighshire and at Manorbier, Pembrokeshire.)

For a medieval cathedral St. Asaph is poorly off for ancient memorials. But it retains good early woodwork in its pinnacled stalls and misericords. There is also an interesting cathedral museum containing early Bibles and prayer books and miscellaneous prehistoric objects. St. Asaph also has a medieval parish church with a fine roof. This old church can be contrasted with the spired nineteenth-century church at Bodelwyddan, two miles west along the Abergele road, a church that catches every traveller's eye by its 200-foot spire and the whiteness of its limestone. Inside it is even whiter, being lavishly decorated in marble. It is the sort of church that people generate feelings about, not all approving.

Two miles upstream from St. Asaph the Clwyd flows through the old deer park of Llannerch where there is a small public zoo. East from here you face the foothills of the Clwydian hills, the village before you on the slope being Tremeirchion whose church has an ancient oak porch and door. There is a memorial stone, a priestly effigy of the fourteenth century and a memorial to Mrs. Thrale (later Mrs. Piozzi) so often referred to in Boswell's life of Johnson. She lived close by in a house called Brynbella, a name that is a rare union of Welsh and Italian. From the church you look north along the hill to a high-perched, thinly-spired chapel erected by the Jesuit college of St. Beuno in the valley below, a college where the poet Gerard Manley Hopkins wrote some of his verses when a student. Ffynnon Beuno is a medieval well at the farm of that name at Graig, south of Tremeirchion. Close to it are two limestone caves where Paleolithic flint implements along with bones of innumerable prehistoric animals have been excavated. Two miles south of Tremeirchion is Bodfari (Botffari) a Clwydian village looking to the setting sun and far away mountains. Above it a pine-covered hillside is topped by the Iron Age fort, Moel y Gaer, whose multiple banks are visible from afar. Bronze Age people too were active in this area: near Maesmynan between Bodfari and Caerwys, at a spot just in Denbighshire, a fine hoard of their gold ornaments were found in the eighteenth century. At Bodfari the county boundary is the River Wheeler, a corruption of the Welsh name, Chwiler, which means 'twisting'.

Caerwys is historically unique for its eisteddfod of 1567 summoned by Elizabeth's government as a means of distinguishing genuine wandering minstrels from the hordes of vagabonds masquerading as such and causing a lot of trouble in the Welsh countryside. A permit system was adopted and all applicants for these licences had to come to Caerwys to have their performances judged by experts. Those who failed the test had to 'returne to some honest labor'. Caerwys, a natural centre for the Clwydian hills, is a little rural town with an old church containing early memorials and medieval woodwork. Note also the ancient oak beam preserved in the south-west lych gate, a beam perhaps coeval with Hen Caerwys ('old Caerwys') a nearby medieval village site where some revealing finds have been made. The district is especially rich in Bronze Age tumuli in one of which, at Ysceifiog, a gold torc was unearthed by a farmer in 1816. It lay as 'a piece of old iron' in the farmhouse for some months before a passing gypsy woman spotted what metal it was. Made of Irish gold it is one of the finest Bronze Age torcs ever found. You may not yourself find any gold at Ysceifiog. But you will find a village beautifully placed above a deep valley with a tree-surrounded lake at the bottom of it. South across the main road is Nannerch, a hamlet among trees and particularly lovely in spring and autumn; and from here an alluring road climbs west through the Clwydian hills. The remains of a Bronze Age circle, now partly stones, partly old trees, can be seen from a bend in A541 where it passes Penbedw Park. It is somewhat less than two hundred yards from the roadside. This park is also known for its magnificent beeches.

In the valley of the Alyn (or Alun) is a quiet little village aptly named Cilcain, which means 'pleasant retreat'. Its church has a finely timbered nave roof and glass of the fifteenth century as well as an early font and fragments of medieval grave slabs. Note also the seventeenth-century wrought-iron gates each topped by a fish chasing its tail. On the river below Cilcain is the name Hesp Alyn (better spelt Hesb Alun) which means 'dry Alyn'. Here the river, except after a lot of rain, disappears into its limestone bed, a trick it does more than once in its course. The valley here is usually called 'The Leete'[1] and there are woodland walks, most popular being down to the main road at the Loggerheads, a curious inn name for it is an old word that meant 'dolts' or 'blockheads'. The district is rich in limestone plants.

Cilcain is a pony-trekking centre and a favourite starting point for walking or riding up to Moel Famau (1,820 feet) highest peak of the Clwydian range and a conspicuous height from many parts of North Wales, being easily known by the squat tower on its summit. Built in 1810 to commemorate fifty years of the reign of George III (and so contemporary with the Jubilee Arch near Devil's Bridge, Cardiganshire) this tower was largely destroyed by a gale in 1862. Another way up to this popular summit is from the car park at the top of the pass called Bwlch Pen-Barras between the Loggerheads and Llanbedr Dyffryn Clwyd. This is a walk of a mile and a half, first through conifers and then, in happy contrast, the open breezy hill with its wonderful views. Moel Famau is a name whose meaning, despite ingenious efforts to explain it, remains obscure. It is pronounced 'Moil Vamma'.

Close on the south from Moel Famau you see the bold height called Foel Fenlli with banks of a hill fort well defined among its short heather. Round to the west, and even closer than Fenlli, is another sharp, fort-crowned height called Moel y Gaer, an Iron Age defence with a Bronze Age tumulus within it. Both these hill forts enjoy splendid views of the Vale of Clwyd and far beyond. Both are in Denbighshire but fall into this chapter because they are part of a chain of six Clwydian multivallate hill forts extending north to Moel Hiraddug, the only one that has

[1] A 'leat' (canal) used to flow here to supply the lead mines with water.

been excavated recently and expertly. Note that Moel Famau itself was never a fort, presumably because it was just too bleak and unlivable. North of it is Moel Arthur, easily reached from one of this range's several cross lanes. It has a small, circular steep-sided fort which has yielded a little Romano–British pottery. Another mile north you come to Penycloddiau, the most extensive single hill fort in all Wales, covering over fifty acres and with four banks and ditches on the north-west. There are two incurved entrances: at the south-east corner and half-way along the east side. The Clwydian Range lacks mineral wealth. North of Moel Famau there have been trial shafts and levels for gold where nothing was found. East from Moel Famau the wooded limestone hills which conceal Mold are scarred with the tips of old lead mines.

At Mold (Wyddgrug), the county town, we are back near the edge of the former coalfield though Mold itself has remained essentially a country market town. The English name derives from Mohault ('Mont haut'), which is what the Normans called the town. A castle motte survives well on Bailey Hill, covered with beeches and two fine old sweet chestnuts; there is also a coronation oak of 1902. Though the Normans made much use of Mold they never had a stone castle there. And the church they built has gone. The present one, dating from 1485 was built by the wealthy Stanley family, enthusiastic erectors of churches in the Cheshire style. The ornate tower is eighteenth century. There is a notable roof, elaborate stone carving over the central arches, some early glass and several interesting memorials including one from the Dark Ages. The tomb of the artist Richard Wilson (died 1782) is next to the church on the north side. In the town is a statue to Daniel Owen, pioneer novelist who held up a vivid mirror to late nineteenth-century Wales. At Mold a unique object of the Bronze Age (now in the British Museum) was found in 1833. It was a ceremonial cape of gold draped round the skeleton of a man.

A 541 from Mold to Wrexham passes Leeswood Old Hall whose splendid gates are of iron wrought by the Davies brothers of Bersham in the early eighteenth century, great craftsmen who also made the gates of Chirk Castle; Wrexham parish church; Erddig Hall, Wrexham; St. Peter's church, Ruthin; and probably also Powys Castle, Welshpool. Nerquis (Nercwys), a village two miles south of Mold, has a name that puzzles etymologists. Its church of St. Mary has a chair made from what must have been a first-class rood screen for it is as good a piece of old carving as you will find in Wales. Nearby Nerquis Hall is a fine historic building. This parish and neighbouring Treuddyn are yet another Flintshire district rich in Bronze Age cairns. And half a mile north-west of Treuddyn church is a massive standing stone called Carreg-y-llech. A mile south-east of Treuddyn you pick up Offa's Dyke on the right-hand side of B5101 as you go towards Ffrith, a village built both on the Dyke and on a Roman settlement. Many Roman objects have come to light over the centuries. The stream, Nant y Ffrith, flows from near Bwlchgwyn down a charmingly wooded limestone gorge.

Caergwrle, a village two miles north-east of Ffrith, has fragments of a thirteenth-century castle sited on an Iron Age hill fort with a good view from the Dee estuary to Wrexham. It is scarcely a vista of untrammelled beauty but a mixture of coalfield unloveliness scattered among farms and wooded hills. Across the Alyn from Caergwrle is Hope which was once a chartered town and before that was recorded in Domesday. The name in early English meant a small enclosed valley. Linking Hope with Caergwrle is a fascinating fourteenth-century packhorse bridge. It has five arches, is about four feet wide with two large refuges. Though so near houses it is in a pleasant spot among willows, alders and butterburs and there are dippers along the river. In the National Museum at Cardiff is a small, rare oak bowl inlaid with gold and carved to resemble a ship. It is Bronze Age and was found at Caergwrle last century.

The larger of the two detached portions of Flintshire, to which maps tend to give the prosaic title: 'Flints. Det.', has come down through history as Maelor Saesneg ('Maelor of the Saxons'), a name that distinguished it from the adjacent part of Denbighshire that was called Maelor Gymraeg ('Maelor of the Welsh'). Probably the distinction is due to Maelor Saesneg having been formerly in the diocese of Lichfield (and then Chester) whereas Maelor Gymraeg was always in that of St. Asaph. As for the separation of Flintshire from Flintshire Detached, this goes back to Edward I's statute of 1284 when he created certain Welsh counties. That he failed to make Flintshire into one unit reflects the fact that although he had become nominally the

conqueror of Wales he was far from being master of the marcher
lords who had helped him to victory. So though he controlled
the two portions of Flintshire he had no power over the land
that lay between which was in the lordship of Bromfield and
Yale. 250 years were to pass before this lordship became the
county of Denbigh. By then tradition had unalterably fixed the
county boundaries, forcing Henry VIII to leave Flintshire in
two parts.

Maelor Saesneg today could hardly be more Sassenach. It
speaks English, most of its place names are English, it looks a
typical bit of Cheshire and it lies both east of the Dyke and east
of the Dee. Here the river is very beautiful where it so sinuously
forms the boundary between the two Maelors from Worthen-
bury Brook up to Erbistock. Some of its bridges are historic.
The one at Bangor Is-y-coed is narrow, five arched, of red
sandstone and has rectangular cutwaters. The nearby church on
the river bank, attractively surrounded by limes, is in similar
stone. The name Bangor Is-y-coed means 'the monastery under
the wood'; here in the early Dark Ages was a religious settlement of great size and importance that was destroyed when the
Saxons broke through at the battle of Chester (*c.* A.D. 600). The
monks are supposed to have fled to Bardsey Island. As long
afterwards as the twelfth century a chronicler reported copious
ruins of churches and monastic buildings still visible. All have
now gone.

Up the Dee from Bangor is Overton whose name in Old
English meant 'a riverbank settlement'. It is rare for a place to be
best known for its churchyard trees but such is Overton's distinction. Its famous yews have so taken over this churchyard
that it is now virtually a yew wood with a church in the centre.
Most of the trees are still in prime condition and are nothing
like the ancients you find in some churchyards. The church contains some good decorative woodwork embodying fragments of
the medieval screen. In feudal times Overton was the centre of
power in Maelor Saesneg and had a fair castle until the Dee got
at it. As Leland (time of Henry VIII) put it: 'There was a praty
[pretty] pile or castel at Oureton yn auncient tyme, the which
was thrown downe by the violence of Dee ryver chaunging his
botom. For of old tyme Dee ran half a mile from the castel.'

Fans of Owain Glyndŵr may like to make a sentimental

journey to Hanmer five miles east of Overton. For here in his time and for centuries later lived the influential Hanmers, a border family of Anglo–Welsh extraction; and it was Margaret Hanmer whom Glyndŵr married, she whose praises were sung by Iolo Goch after his visit to the castle at Sycharth. Hanmer to-day is a charming village standing at the end of a Cheshire-type mere half a mile long, a beautiful pool with ducks, coots and grebes and with deciduous trees nearly all round. Beyond stretches Bettisfield Park, former demesne of the Hanmers. In another mile Flintshire ends in the great stretch of peat bogs called Whixhall or Fenn's Moss. Here several square miles of deep peat have developed on the site of a prehistoric lake. It is the habitat of unusual bog plants but is being exploited for horti-culture. And now, as the old guide books used to say, this district need not further detain us. Except to say that a bend of the Wych Brook, two miles south-west of Whitchurch, is the most easterly point in Wales.

5

MONTGOMERYSHIRE

(Trefaldwyn or Sir Drefaldwyn)

As you come to Montgomeryshire from the English Midlands you see ahead of you, once you are clear of Shrewsbury, a bold group of hills standing sharply from the plain
as if stepping forward to announce the mountains of Wales. And
if ever there was an inevitable spot for an Iron Age settlement it
was on these peaky hills collectively called the Breiddens though
only one of them is properly Breidden Hill. ('Breiddin' would
be a better spelling, for it would preserve the Welsh word
'ddin', meaning a fort.) You are not surprised when you get up
there to find not one hill fort but three, looking across at each
other from their separate summits. Of these forts easily the
finest is the one on Breidden itself, a precipice-defended hill unmistakable from afar because of the spike of Rodney's Pillar on
its top. This monument, built by the local gentry in 1782 and
since kept in repair, commemorates a victory by Admiral
Rodney (1719–92). On top of one of the hills, Moel y Golfa, is a
monument to a Romany leader, Ernest Burton, who died in
1960. The Breidden hills not only stand alone, they are apart
geologically also. For here the earth has heaved up a vast outcrop of hard igneous rock (hence the roadstone quarries north
and south), a dolerite evidently rich enough in calcium and
other minerals to suit the choice wild flowers for which this hill
has been known since Edward Lhuyd made the first British record of spiked speedwell there in the seventeenth century.

South from Moel y Golfa you look across to Long Mountain

whose softer rocks have bowed to the elements much more than Breidden has. Hence the smooth flat top along which a road runs from end to end, a road well used by the centuries. Near the east end a pair of Bronze Age tumuli, now reduced to low mounds, look across to Breidden. Probably the Roman road came this way from Wroxeter to Forden though some reckon it skirted south of Long Mountain by way of Marton. Further west along the ridge, if you cross a couple of fields on the right, you can look down on to Welshpool and the Severn from the massive Iron Age banks of the Beacon Ring. The shapely hill intimately south of Long Mountain is Corndon, an open grassy summit with patches of bare rock showing. To reach it turn down the lane to Trelystan where, standing alone in fields, is a wooden medieval church, an odd specimen because since 1856 it has been encased in brick. Fragments of the former screen survive and there is a reconstructed barrel organ. The little church, above a deep wooded valley, enjoys views of Corndon and the Shropshire hills. On this south side of Long Mountain, three miles within Shropshire, are the earthworks of the once extensive Norman castle of Caus, named from Caux in Normandy. In its protection in the thirteenth century there developed a little walled market town of which only the faintest traces remain. Other nearby medieval reminders are names like Monksfields and Priestweston: they evidently go back to the time when the Cistercian abbey of Strata Marcella on the Severn held wide lands in these parts. It is fertile land and here and there has wild flowers of distinction such as alternate-leaved golden saxifrage, narrow-leaved bittercress, herb paris and masterwort (*Astrantia major*).

The south-west end of Long Mountain drops swiftly through conifers to the Severn. Tree-lovers should turn into Leighton woods half-way down the hill to see the finest stand of redwoods (*Sequoia sempervirens*) in Britain. This wondrous grove is a few hundred yards along a ride and has a notice board to tell you about it. It was on this estate that the hybrid conifer, X *Cupressocyparis leylandii*, was raised in 1888. One of the fastest growing conifers it is very popular as a shelter-belt tree. History goes with you all the way down to Forden. The eighth century nods at you from both sides as the road cuts through Offa's Dyke. Then you see the alleged Roman road going straight on where your road bends sharp right round the houses of Kingswood. Apart from one or two gaps you can follow the further progress of this road onward to the raised platform of Forden Roman fort where the period of occupation ranged, but not continuously, from A.D. 75 to A.D. 375. Its Roman name may have been Lavobrinta. Numerous finds from here can be seen in Welshpool museum.

A short half-mile south of the Roman fort the road swings round with a bend of the Severn. This in the thirteenth century was an accepted parleying place between representatives of English kings and the princes of Wales and was known as the Ford of Montgomery or Rhydwhiman. It was commanded by Hen Domen ('the old mound') an elaborate motte and bailey which overlooks it from the south-east. All this region is dominated by the large and complex hill fort of Fridd Faldwyn, close to Montgomery, where excavation has proved four phases of Iron Age construction, all pre-Roman. Neolithic tools have also come to light there. The site and its finds are displayed in the National Museum at Cardiff.

Montgomery itself can be a surprise to newcomers. They expect, because of the name, to find a sizeable town and all they find—I trust the shock is a pleasant one—is a village-sized place with an old-style town hall and square and with Georgian houses and black-and-white cottages straggling quietly up and over an isolated hill. Not that Montgomery was ever the most important centre of life in this part of the Marches despite its military prestige and castle. For even in its heyday it was overshadowed by Ludlow; and by Shrewsbury when Ludlow declined. Dominating the town is a large church with a fine nave roof of the fifteenth century, a medieval double screen, beautifully carved stalls, some effigies and the canopied tomb of Richard Herbert (died 1596) father of George Herbert the clergyman-poet and of Edward Herbert, first baron of Chirbury, a statesman-philosopher now remembered for his autobiography which, though unblushingly boastful, is worth reading for the picture it draws of his times. This church's woodwork is reckoned to have been brought from nearby Chirbury priory dismantled at the Dissolution.

Montgomery castle is only fragmentary on its rocky hill. When built by Henry III in 1224 it became known as New

Montgomeryshire

Montgomery to distinguish it from the out-moded castle built on Hen Domen by Earl Roger de Montgomery about 1075. In its early days New Montgomery was frequently besieged by the Welsh and at times held by them. But for most of the time it was held by marcher lords such as the Mortimers. It was slighted after the Civil War. From the first a chartered borough was established under the castle's protection and was enclosed by walls and a ditch. The walls have long since gone but the ditch is still traceable almost throughout its length. A mile east of Montgomery, in Lymore Park, is one of the best stretches of Offa's Dyke which here, as in few other places, has persisted as the boundary between England and Wales.

On the road from Montgomery to Welshpool (Y Trallwng) you cross the Camlad, said to be the only English-born river flowing into Wales. It is a district where you may see flocks of white-fronted and Canada geese in winter, flying over the road or grazing in the low-lying fields. A mile or so north you have a good length of Offa's Dyke on your right, as well as the mound of a former stone castle at Nantcribau. Then you cross the Severn and the Shropshire Union canal to approach Welshpool under the slopes of Powys castle. Throughout history the Severn has been this region's main traffic lane for it was navigable all the way up from Gloucester. Inevitably Pool, as the nearest castled town to the border, grew to early importance (it was not officially called Welshpool until 1835 when it was thought desirable to distinguish it from Poole in Dorset: on old milestones and in some local speech you will find it is Pool to this day). It was in the thirteenth century that the town got its charter and the right to hold a Monday market.

Welshpool, always looking east rather than west, would have nothing to do with Owain Glyndŵr and suffered in consequence. But it was well compensated by the English after the rebellion and has never looked back. An early nineteenth-century commentator reported: 'The manners of the inhabitants are thoroughly English.' (But what that may imply I leave you to decide.) Today it is a prosperous market town, with modern housing around an essentially Georgian centre with some much older half-timbered buildings. The medieval church has been restored but retains a fine timbered roof and the Jacobean tomb of one of the Herberts. On Church Bank is the museum founded by the Powysland Club, the oldest archaeological society in Britain, with continuous published records since its foundation in 1867. Welshpool's public bowling green near the railway station is neatly enclosed in the bailey of an early castle mound. A mile south-west at Powys Castle is another good motte and bailey, the Lady's Mount, which is the twelfth-century forerunner of the present red sandstone castle built in the thirteenth century. Much modified down the ages, Powys is one of the few great Welsh castles that have gone on being lived in after their military use was over. The best medieval fragment is the fine western entrance. Succeeding earls have cared for their castle and have developed beautifully terraced gardens, woodland and parkland (still with red and fallow deer). The castle and gardens (but not the park) belong to the National Trust and their historic, artistic and horticultural treasures are open to visitors from June to September. In 1170 on the north bank a couple of miles or so down the Severn from Welshpool the Cistercians built their abbey of Strata Marcella (Ystrad Marchell), now the most demolished of all Welsh Cistercian abbeys. Not a stone stands above ground. But in Welshpool museum you can see finds from there such as fourteenth-century tiles made at Broseley in Shropshire. The font in Buttington church is believed to have been fashioned out of the capital of one of the piers of the abbey church.

Not all canal lovers will enjoy the Welshpool canal. Anglers and naturalists cherish it for its wealth of fish and other wild life. But for boating enthusiasts some stretches of it are useless because its once humpy bridges were replaced in World War II by bridges too low for any sort of craft. What man has abandoned nature has turned to the advantage of plants, birds, fish and other aquatic life. The tow-path walk also brings you to picturesque cottages, locks and bridges, especially the drawbridges north-east of Welshpool which are like those painted by Van Gogh on the canals of southern France.

A cul-de-sac branch of this canal goes off to Guilsfield which is two miles north of Welshpool and has the unusual Welsh name Cegidfa ('place of hemlock'). So look out for a tall whiteflowered umbellifer, purple-spotted on the stem and smelling of mice—but poisonous, remember. You may not find it but certainly you will not miss the parish church which has a fascinating old ceiling of beautifully decorated wood and a stairway leading to the former living quarters of the priest-in-charge. Craftsmen will admire this church's ancient door, immensely thick and heavy yet swinging with a silky smoothness. Do not be deceived by the churchyard yews: they may look fairly youthful but they were not planted yesterday. A grave close to the gate records that one of them was planted about three centuries ago, which helps us to believe in the enormous antiquity claimed for some giant yews. It must be rare for the date of planting of any yew thus to be even approximately recorded. The text on the gravestone reads:

> *Here lyeth ye body of*
> *Richard Jones, Gent.*
> *Under this yew tree*
> *Buried would he bee,*
> *For his father and he*
> *Planted this yew tree.*
> *December ye 10th 1707 aged 90.*

Up the wide valley of the Severn from Welshpool you come in five miles to Berriew, a village with a waterfall and pride in its appearance. Many of its houses are good specimens of oak-framed buildings that speak of days when great oaks were easily come by. Berriew is happily withdrawn from the main road. Not so some of the other Severn valley villages such as Garthmyl and Abermule (Abermiwl) through which the traffic roars. It is odd to think that if a plan conceived by the last of the Welsh princes had been realized Abermule might have grown into a town. On a nearby hill above the Severn, reached by narrow winding lanes, Llywelyn ap Gruffydd built the stone castle of Dolforwyn in 1273 with a view to establishing in its protection a market town that would be a rival to the one created by the English at Montgomery. But the project was short-lived. When war came in 1277 the castle fell into English hands, was little used later and is now but a slight ruin. Its views are to every direction and are perhaps finest southward to the long line of Kerry Hill across that lovely reach of the Severn valley where the Miwl stream comes down a wooded, botanically rich dingle from Kerry.

Newtown was new in 1279 and was so called, says Camden's *Britannia*, to distinguish it from the old decayed borough of

Montgomeryshire

Caersŵs a few miles upriver. It was Edward I's answer to Llywelyn's frustrated ambition to establish a castled town at Abermule six years before. Medieval Newtown, neatly enclosed within a loop of the Severn, was never castled presumably because by then the power of the English was strong enough to render more castles unnecessary. Through the centuries Newtown, like Welshpool, has looked more east than west and speaks English almost entirely. It has known importance as a town of all trades and will become important again as an overspill town. The Severn still sweeps round the centre of the town in a wide loop but occasionally rushes straight through it. The central pattern of wide streets remains Norman, and Tuesday is still market day as it was in the beginning.

Newtown has a large parish church of 1847 along the main road and the tower of a medieval one by the river bridge. The newer church contains the font and part of the screen of the old. There are two small museums, one in Commercial Street to illustrate the history of the local textile industry; the other dedicated to Robert Owen (1771–1858), educational pioneer and founder of idealist communities in Britain and America. He was born and died in Newtown. His grave is outside the medieval church; his museum is above the Midland Bank, built on the site of his birthplace. Just outside the town on the left of B4568 as you go towards Aberhafesp is Cwrt yn Dre ('town house'), a sixteenth-century hall transferred from Dolgellau in 1885 by Sir Pryce Jones. It is now a Quaker meeting house. Music lovers should time their visit to Newtown to coincide with the annual music festival in May.

At Betws Cedewain, four miles north of Newtown, the church retains its fourteenth-century roof, its even older tower, oak-belfried in the Montogmeryshire style, and a brass of 1531. Note half a mile south the interesting name, Walkmill. A walking mill was the earliest type of fulling mill, so called because in that process the cloth really was walked on. To the west are the stately house, park and gardens of Gregynog Hall, a property of the University of Wales who use it as a conference and course centre. It was formerly the home of the Misses Davies, patrons of music and the arts. Here they had a fine collection of paintings as well as the Gregynog printing press whose beautiful books are now collectors' pieces.

Montgomeryshire

The land south of Newtown rises quickly out of green fertility into the sterner country of Kerry Hill. Kerry (Ceri) has an ancient church with a hefty Norman arcade. It is fascinating that we still have an eye-witness account of this church's consecration in 1176: that ever-busy fellow Giraldus happened to be present at the ceremony and wrote a description of the proceedings. Few medieval churches are so precisely dated. Kerry Hill and the neighbouring uplands are great walking and viewpoint country and especially rewarding for tracers of ancient roads. For many miles along the watershed a high-level trackway ran roughly east-west coming up from Bishop's Castle in Shropshire to Kerry Hill and thence into the west. As usual with such very old routes its course is marked onward by the relics of prehistory: a wealth of Bronze Age tumuli; a stone circle half a mile south-west of Kerry Pole; and, a mile east of Offa's Dyke, a commanding hill fort with fine views called Caer Din. In places this road is motorable. Other parts of it are mere tracks through fields, moorland or forest.

Characteristic of Kerry Hill are the earthworks called short dykes (or ditches). Made of a simple bank and ditch, they were built across the ridge roads in the Dark Ages to protect the more settled lowlands of the east against cattle-raiding parties from the highlands of the west. Seeing them today, lying out of context on the moorland, you may wonder why the raiders could not simply have gone round such obstacles. But the dykes make sense if we picture those Dark Ages trackways as the only penetrations through very difficult country thick with scrub and swamp. Under those conditions a dyke several hundred yards long lying across the road with dense forest at both ends and guarded by armed men would be a useful defence. Of these dykes the Upper Short Ditch is most easily found, a low gorse-topped bank lying across the county boundary, its Welsh half disappearing into conifers. Along this road, and just within Shropshire, is the Cantlin Stone, an ancient boundary mark. By it someone thought to be named Cantlin (the name is now illegible) was buried in 1691. A carved cross is raised above the grave.

West of Kerry Hill the land falls away, but soon rises again to even bigger country. This is the fine rampart of uplands south of Caersŵs. Along this high land note the long-distance track coming up from the north from a point on the Severn half-way between Newtown and Caersŵs. It passes the so-called Giant's Grave (which is in fact another short dyke) and then a high-placed cairn. From there it then goes on into Radnorshire, dipping to a stream but climbing again to a standing stone nick-named Fowler's Armchair which is the centre of a former stone circle. (Fowler was a squire of Cwmhir.)

One of the several paths into these attractive hills of south Montgomeryshire goes up from the village of Llandinam on the Severn. You climb through a gap called Cobbler's Gate to where you can look back to perfect views of the green vale of Severn and all the hills beyond. Just across the river you see the multiple banks of a hill fort on Cefn Carnedd. In Llandinam the highest building is the church because it was built on the earthworks of a hill fort as the name suggests, 'llan' being a church and 'din' a fort. You can still see the line of one of the ramparts in the field next to the churchyard. Restoration has long since robbed this once important mother-church of its ancient character. It contains three carved panels and a crude fifteenth-century carving in which three heads grotesquely share four eyes (and countless worm holes). Down by the river bridge is a statue to David Davies, a local farmer's son who made good as a railway contractor. He built the difficult line to Aberystwyth in the 1860's and then made a greater fortune in South Wales mines and docks. His statue overlooks a delightful spot by the river which is here crossed by an elegant iron bridge made at Hawarden, Flintshire, in 1846.

Caersŵs, downstream from Llandinam, was a Roman centre whose seven acres of earthworks are still plain to see close to the railway. Excavation has proved a long period of occupation at this important centre of Roman communications from which roads went north to Chester, south to Llandrindod, east to Wroxeter and west to Pennal. Clear-to-see raised causeways of these roads exist close to Caersŵs, especially eastwards through the grounds of the fine Elizabethan house, Maesmawr Hall, now a hotel. Lead unearthed from the Roman fort probably came from the Dylife mines near Pumlumon. A mile south-east of Caersŵs the Moat farm stands in the earthworks of a perfect Norman motte and bailey now almost hidden in trees. A mile or so north of Caersŵs is Llanwnog church whose walls have many blocks of sandstone probably from Roman Caersŵs. Inside it preserves an ancient rood loft and screen with carvings of foliage and winged dragons. The solid oak steps which formerly led up to the rood loft survive in the thickness of the wall. In the church-yard is the grave of Ceiriog one of Wales's best-known nine-teenth-century poets. He lived nearby and was manager of the narrow-gauge railway that ran from Caersŵs up to the lead mines at Van. From Llanwnog it is four miles north-west up A489 to Carno whose church has a cross-slab of the Dark Ages that was discovered in 1960 in use as a local gatepost. Here you enter the Welsh-speaking part of the county.

Above Caersŵs the Severn, narrowing and quickening, gets more and more the character of a mountain stream, especially at Llanidloes where the slopes close in sharply. Llanidloes, last town up the river is a typical little mid-Wales market town, its most remarkable building being the timbered market hall at the central cross roads. Built in the late sixteenth century this hall is the only survivor in Wales of a feature once common to market towns everywhere. In its time it has also accommodated the assizes, Quakers, Wesleyans and Baptists. John Wesley preached there. Today it houses a museum relating to farming, lead min-ing and other local industries. In the church is thirteenth-century stone work of outstanding interest—an arcade of five bays brought here when the abbey at Cwmhir was dissolved in 1536. The church also retains on show the incomplete mechanism of its late seventeenth-century turret clock which used to strike the hours but never had a dial. There are two similar in the National Museum at Cardiff. Llanidloes used to make flannel: in 1850 it had 40 carding engines, 18 fulling mills, 35,000 spindles.

Flowing from the north to join the Severn just above Llanid-loes bridge is the beautiful tributary called Clywedog which is born in a land of deserted lead mines at the north end of Pum-lumon. Here until the 1870's was the great mining settlement of Dylife (pronounced something like 'deliver') where a vast number of men were employed, living and working under vile conditions. Today practically no one lives in that high bleak place full of unhappy memories. There are a few ruins of mine buildings, workers' barracks and deserted smallholdings; and there is an ugly grey spread of mine spoil. In contrast one of the highest of Welsh waterfalls, Ffrwd Fawr, drops directly out of this waste land into one of the loveliest of valleys, making spec-tacular scenery.

Montgomeryshire

Below Staylittle the Clywedog is lost for a few miles in the depths of a long, elbow-shaped reservoir west of the hamlet of Van (Y Fan). This was another place with vast lead mines but, unlike the ancient Dylife mines, these were not productive until 1866. They flourished exceedingly in the next few years and attracted enormous investment, for this was one of the richest veins of lead ever struck in Wales. But the bubble burst in the late 1870's, the mines merely lingering after that until finally they closed just after World War I. Extensive ruins of Van mines still survive overlooking an attractive little reservoir. But nearby is a grey sprawl of poisonous spoil tips. Y Fan hill (1,580 feet) is worth climbing for its far views—east to the border, west to the bold ridges of Pumlumon, north to the wide moorlands of Trannon and south beyond Llanidloes to Radnorshire.

West from Llanidloes a road climbs up with the Severn, here called Hafren, between woods and green hills until both road and stream are engulfed in vast conifer plantations that rise before you high up the slopes of Pumlumon. Along the way the Forestry Commission has provided several picnic places and a map showing sites of scenic interest. You will not find the shepherd's house of Blaen Hafren that is mentioned by old travellers' accounts for it has been demolished. But its site is still by the infant river at the side of a cascade—a good spot for a picnic. The forest road marked 'Severn Source' curves gently across the contours as if making for the summit of Pumlumon Arwystli. But where it crosses the tiny Severn a sign points right and you leave the forest for the open moor. Do not expect a path. You simply follow the winding streamlet up a little grassy cleft. The ground becomes wetter and you come up to a landscape pillowed over with black, heather-topped blocks of peat several feet high—the last remains of an eroded blanket of peat that obviously once covered the whole mountain. Through this spongy world many runnels of peaty water converge among cotton sedge and bog moss. You are just concluding that the source could be any one of a hundred similar springs when you see a little signpost deciding for you which of them is in fact the source. In dry weather I daresay you could believe it. In wet weather the claim is manifestly false for you can see water flowing down to this point from higher up. No matter. This whole bog is the source of the Severn and this spot where the sign is can be reckoned as good as any for you to have the drink that is proper to such sacred occasions. By drinking you have, in Borrow's phrase, 'taken possession of the Severn'. You stand up and look round and notice two large cairns on the skyline half a mile north-east. These are the cairns of Carnbiga, unusually large and apparently unopened. Not so the cairn called Carnfachbugeilyn ('the little cairn above the shepherd's lake') which is now wasted and hollowed. But its view over lakes Bugeilyn and Glaslyn to Cadair Idris and Aran Fawddwy is one of the great views of Wales. In peat bogs close to Llyn Bugeilyn many perfect little flint arrowheads have been found especially after heavy rain has washed them out of the peat. From the summit ridge other cairns become visible to the west crowning the hill tops on either side of the Hyddgen stream. Somewhere over there in 1402 Owain Glyndŵr fought and won a wild battle among the mountains, probably to nobody's profit except that of the kites and the ravens.

Now you are on the watershed at over two thousand feet. With the bogs behind you and lichens crisp and dry under your feet you are well placed to walk the five or six miles that will take in this whole splendid ridge and land you down on the main road at Eisteddfa Gurig. But it would be a waste of a good opportunity if, a mile south-west of Pumlumon Arwystli, you do not also 'take possession' of the Wye (Borrow, remember, 'possessed' the Rheidol also while he was up there). But if you want to make the source of the Wye a separate trip altogether you can come up from Llanidloes to the village of Llangurig, then after five miles proceed on foot up the Wye along the former mine road that leaves A44 at Pont Rhydgaled. That way you reach the source in four miles. Roman fort enthusiasts can visit Cae Gaer, left as a pale space amid the dark conifers a mile south-west of Pont Rhydgaled and visible from the main road. From Llangurig a minor road goes south-west over the hills to Cwmystwyth in Cardiganshire. At the end of the eighteenth century, before a road was built through Pumlumon Pass, this then rocky trail was used by the gentry travelling in carriages from the Midlands to taste the newly discovered delights of Aberystwyth.

Although only ten crow-miles separate the source of the Wye from that other famous Montgomeryshire river, the Dovey, they are ten miles that include the vast hump of Pumlumon. This has always meant that the world of the upper Wye has had little to say to that of the lower Dovey though they are in the same county. In fact Machynlleth has at least as much contact with Merioneth and Cardiganshire as it has with the rest of Montgomeryshire. It is an old town, its market being chartered in 1291 and probably the wide spaces of its Maengwyn street have accommodated the Wednesday markets of seven centuries. But it never had a castle and was possibly never a borough. Machynlleth has a high symbolic value for nationalistic Welshmen who remember that here in 1404 the rebellious Owain Glyndŵr, then at the height of his power, convened what proved to be the last independent parliament to meet in Wales. (So far.) The Owain Glyndŵr Institute probably stands where this parliament assembled. A black-and-white house on the other side of the road is dated 1628. Machynlleth's massive clock tower (1873) is an architectural monstrosity, all spikes and knobs. But I suppose lovers of Victoriana adore it. Dovey bridge (probably built 1533) stands at an ancient river crossing. This is a favourite gathering place for anglers to fish this famous salmon water but Machynlleth itself has kept well away from the often flooding river. The town is fortunate in the possession of the Plas (built 1671) and its acres of parkland (but no deer). Formerly owned by the Marquis of Londonderry it houses a permanent exhibition of Welsh crafts, especially woollens and pottery, organized by the Council for Small Industries in Rural Areas who are a mine of information on crafts throughout Wales.

A few miles west of Machynlleth, Montgomeryshire dips a finger into salt water at the head of the Dovey estuary and so we find a few seaweeds and saltmarsh plants included in the flora of what is otherwise a thoroughly inland county. Before the railway age it even had a port at Derwenlas, a village now remote from all thought of shipping. Here lime and other goods were imported, lead ore and slate exported, all passing through the port of Aberdovey. Until the 1860's when the main line superseded it there was an extension of the Corris narrow-gauge railway as far as Derwenlas, some of its banks and bridges being still intact. Narrow-gauge relics are on view at Corris.

From Machynlleth up to Mallwyd the Dovey valley is wide and fertile with pastoral farms and a few small villages such as Penegoes in whose rectory the landscape artist Richard Wilson was born about 1713. There is a memorial to him in the church; and in the churchyard flourishes the rare keeled garlic whose distinctive pink flowers begin to appear before midsummer. On the other side of the valley Llanwrin's church has an ancient screen and a churchyard full of wild garlic in spring. At Cemaes (or Cemais) the church, on a former river-terrace, retains a good fragment of its old screen—a delicately carved trail of vine leaves and grapes now behind the altar. South-east of Mallwyd rise uplands that might be described as the unknown heart of Montgomeryshire. It is a region varying from grouse moors and high lakes in the west to a mixture of upland farms and curlew bogs further east. Good quiet country, it is crossed by few roads.

Interesting villages encircle these central moors. On the south there is Llanbrynmair which is in two halves: its old part is on a hill clustered round a church interesting for its crude oak timbers; the rest of Llanbrynmair has come down to live on the main road a couple of miles north. Here where three valleys meet was the castle of Tafolwern. Its tump, attractively sited between two streams, looks poor enough now. Yet in the twelfth century it was important: from it, for instance, was granted the charter for the founding of Valle Crucis abbey thirty miles away. For a fine view of Llanbrynmair in its fair setting take the climbing lane east from Dolgadfan and then look back. The deep Twymyn valley is below you and you look across to steep, bare-topped ramparts that guard a secluded region of hills and wooded valleys, ancient farmhouses and hamlets such as Aberhosan, Darowen and Abercegir. Above this viewpoint a level-topped summit called Newydd Fynyddog has the remains of three stone circles. East you come down to the main road at Talerddig. Here the words 'Natural Arch' on the ordnance map refer to a noteworthy upfold in the rocks on the roadside just downhill from the village, an arch that is beautifully repeated in a hollow beyond the railway. Note too how the stream here flows in a tunnel under the railway for 150 yards.

From this central moorland whose highest point is Carnedd Wen (1,716 feet), streams flow in every direction, the best known being the Banwy (Banw) along whose valley A458 goes for thirteen miles. It has some beautiful tributaries, notably the Twrch and the Eira, and by the time it reaches Cann Office (Llangadfan) it is a fine fishing river. It is especially lovely at

Llanerfyl where its bend protected a motte of the twelfth century. Llanerfyl church contains a Dark Ages gravestone inscribed in Latin to 'R——, thirteen years old, daughter of Paterninus. In peace.' It is rare to find so early a memorial set up for one so young. Also in the church are a reredos (frame only) and a reliquary (in the form of a model of a church) both carved in wood in the fifteenth century. This churchyard has, I think, the most remarkable yew in Wales, an ancient monster of five great trunks blasted apart yet all still leafing prosperously.

At Llanfair Caereinion you can take a trip on a picturesque narrow-gauge railway which goes for several beautiful miles towards Welshpool. Below Llanfair the Banwy, having flowed east all the way, suddenly snakes round to the north and flows into the Vyrnwy (Fyrnwy). In the eighteenth century Thomas Pennant called the Vyrnwy *amnis piscosus* ('the river abounding in fish') because of the exceptional number of species in it. Most North Wales rivers have trout and salmon and little else. But in the Vyrnwy, he said, were also grayling, minnow, perch, ruffe, carp, tench, roach, dace, gudgeon, bleak, chub, loach, bullhead, shad, eel, lamprey and flounder—a remarkable tally if reliable. Shad and flounder may seem a bit far-fetched in a stream so remote from the sea. But in fact both do go far up rivers. It is not many years since a flounder was caught in the Severn at Llanidloes which is about two hundred miles above Gloucester. At one place Pennant admired how the Fyrnwy had been dammed 'for the sake of a mill and forms a fine reach'. What then would he have thought of the great reservoir which Liverpool Corporation created on the river a century later? Time has helped this reservoir, mellowing the stonework and producing tall forests all about. And ever since its completion in 1890 it has attracted increasing numbers of tourists who walk, motor or cycle round its eleven miles circumference. Narrow roads connect with Bwlch y Groes to the west and Bala to the north, so making the western end of the Berwyn easily accessible. The reservoir drowned the little village of Llanwddyn together with its parish church. The lectern of the old church is now in the church which replaced it in 1888. Also in the church is a stone ball weighing three-quarters of a hundredweight formerly used in village games. It looks a dangerous plaything.

In the church of Llanfihangel-yng-Ngwynfa, four miles south-east of the reservoir, are interesting medieval sepulchral slabs, one of them with a floral carving. Outside is the grave of the remarkable Ann Griffiths who died in 1805 aged twenty-nine, a mystic religious poet whose hymns are still widely cherished by Welsh people. Old-trackway enthusiasts might give their attention to Ffordd Gefn ('the ridge road') two and a half miles north of Llanwddyn; or to Llwybr Heulen (or Heilyn) that goes south over the hills from Hirnant. Near Llwybr Heulen is Clawdd Mawr ('the great dyke'), an impressive ridge-top earthwork five hundred yards long which looks like the Kerry Hill dykes. From the reservoir the Vyrnwy flows past attractive hamlets and villages such as Dolanog, Pont Robert and Meifod. Two miles below the great dam it collects the Cownwy streamlet at a charming little roadside spot by a bridge. West lie extensive, unfrequented hills, birthplace of the Cownwy and the Twrch. The Vyrnwy soon passes between large woodlands to flow under B4395 at Llwydiarth (Pont Llogel) where there is a Forestry Commission picnic place beside the river.

Another stream which Pennant found particularly rich in fish was the Tanat which rises on Berwyn just within Merioneth, soon makes fine waterfalls at the head of its cwm then goes on down one of the most celebrated valleys of mid-Wales, a valley known for its beauty and even more for the tradition that it contains a sanctuary for wild creatures (though I doubt whether its multitude of pheasants find it much of a sanctuary come the first of October). The sanctuary idea is associated with a saint called Melangell (Monacella) who in a medieval story gave shelter to a hunted hare beneath her skirts, her miraculous power stopping huntsmen and hounds in their tracks. Though this is a fiction of many centuries later there is no need to doubt that Melangell did exist, probably in the eighth century, and founded a primitive church in this remote place. The present church of Pennant Melangell contains a fifteenth-century screen, a part of which shows the saint protecting her animals. There are also two medieval effigies: one a knight with sword and shield, the other probably of Melangell. A separate room at the east end of the church called Cell y Bedd ('the cell of the grave') is Melangell's traditional burial place. It contains her reconstructed twelfth-century shrine, sculptured stones of which, long scattered and built haphazardly into the church walls, were carefully reassembled in 1959. Such a survival of a Romanesque shrine, even one so incomplete, is an extreme rarity. In the large churchyard —the bounds of the ancient sanctuary?—are ancient yews.

Two miles down the Tanat from Pennant Melangell where two valleys meet under crag-topped slopes is the village of Llangynog, a beautiful district but scarred by old quarries and lead mines. Here you are on the road that takes you over the Berwyn to Bala by way of Cwm Rhiwarth whose head looks back over a splendid view down the Tanat valley. Up this road botanists will note the parsley fern bristling in great quantity in the walls as soon as you cross the cattle grid. The heyday of Llangynog lead mines was in the first half of the eighteenth century when the ore from this rich vein was carted down to a smeltery on the Severn at Pool Quay which in those days, as the quay of (Welsh) Pool, was an important place of trade and manufacture at the head of the navigable river. A revival of Llangynog lead-mining towards the mid-nineteenth century was short-lived. Dominant above the village are the fine rocks and screes of Craig Rhiwarth beyond which, on the north-east slopes of the hill, are relics of presumed Iron Age settlement—many traces of hut circles defended by a long stretch of walling.

Tanat, Cain, Vyrnwy—these rivers flow through fertile soils that have produced many of the great oaks for which Montgomeryshire used to be famous; and inevitably the district is rich in delightful half-timbered houses. The woodlands along the Cain look especially fine as you approach Llanfyllin, yet another handsome little valley-bottom market town. Unexpectedly its church is eighteenth-century red brick and takes a bit of getting used to. The independent chapel, the oldest in the county, is also eighteenth century. On it is the following notice: 'This Protestant Chappel was rebuilt in the Year of our Lord 1717 Being the 172 year after the Reformation, the xxix Since the Revolution And the IV Year of the reign of King George.'

Meifod, on the Vyrnwy four miles south of Llanfyllin, is one of those places of remote historic importance most traces of which have long vanished. But in early medieval times this was the political centre of Powys, the castle of the princes being at nearby Mathrafal before they moved to Welshpool. So Mathrafal was to mid-Wales what Aberffraw was to North Wales and Dinefwr was to the south. If Meifod church stands today in spacious, park-like surroundings it is because these several acres of open ground were once covered by ecclesiastical buildings whose foundations presumably survive below the turf. The church has been greatly altered from its original twelfth-century form but a few good Norman arches remain along with work of subsequent centuries. It has an elaborately carved Celtic cross and there are six diamond-shaped heraldic shields made of glass in the mid-nineteenth century illustrating armorial bearings of local families. Meifod village sits contentedly under steep wooded slopes as if quite happy to be rid of its former importance. Close to Meifod is the site of a huge radio telescope operated by remote control from Jodrell Bank in Cheshire.

From Meifod the Vyrnwy goes snaking along its flood plain all the way to the English border. Near Llansanffraid in one of its former loops it enclosed the motte of a thirteenth-century castle (Plas yn Dinas) which is now a few hundred feet from the river. Two miles east an attractive aqueduct carries the Shropshire Union canal over the Vyrnwy. Then the river soon reaches Llanymynech where the border and Offa's Dyke are on the same line, cutting right through the village. In fact the Lion Hotel, built upon the course of the Dyke, is partly in England and partly in Wales. A fine hill of Carboniferous Limestone—the only site for this rock in the county—rises to the north of Llanymynech. It has been terribly gashed by former quarries, burrowed into by now disused lead mines and planted extensively with conifers. Yet despite all it stands in beauty above the plain and is notably rich in wild flowers. When Pennant went there in 1776 the quarries were at work turning out vast quantities of limestone that was burnt on the hill and carted off as fertilizer. He reports Roman coins found in the lead mines and also 'the skeleton of a man at full length; on his left arm a bracelet and by his side a battle-axe'. Pennant stayed the night at Llwyn y Groes, a charming house that still stands at the roadside a mile into Shropshire from Llanymynech. Here lived a famous mapmaker, John Evans who, Pennant says, 'is undertaking a beautiful map of North Wales'. This map, which appeared in 1795, was a great advance on previous maps of the region.

At Llandrinio, three miles south-east of Llanymynech, we are back nearly into the shadow of Breidden which on this side presents a craggy front to the world. Llandrinio church is the usual patchwork of many styles beginning at least as early as Norman. It has two fragments of a decorated Celtic cross. Just as in the far west Montgomeryshire dips a surprising finger into estuary water, so here it points another to take in, east of the Dyke, an odd shaped bit of territory along the Severn as if Wales wanted to hang on to the river as long as possible. But away it flows at last to meander across the plain to Shrewsbury. One final curiosity as perhaps you depart for England: along B4393 close to where it crosses the border stands the Prince's Oak. A brass shield informs you that here on 9th September 1808, the then Prince of Wales was introduced to his principality by an assemblage of the local gentry. Not much of an event, you may say, nor much of an oak. But gave it time. It may yet become one of the great Montgomeryshire oaks. Meanwhile it can be a reminder of the oaks that have flourished in this tree-blessed county. And will flourish again some day when the softwood craze has passed.

6

MERIONETH
(Meirionydd or Sir Feirionydd)

Merioneth is rugged, most of it, adding much to the wild beauty of the Snowdonia National Park. It begins in the north on the sharp ridge of Cnicht; its southern edge is that lovely river the Dovey (Dyfi); its west side is thirty miles of sea coast; and east its border goes far away along the high moors of Berwyn and comes wriggling back among countless smaller hills north of the Dee. Within these frontiers is enough good country to keep you happy for a lifetime if you are going to explore it all. There is only one town of any size—Blaenau Ffestiniog. Otherwise, because its soils are poor and its minerals only very locally exploitable, Merioneth is sparsely peopled and unindustrialized. In the west it continues the Cambrian and Ordovician rocks of Caernarvonshire and its uplands have true mountain qualities. In the east the hills have the softer outlines of the Silurian rocks of Denbigh and Montgomeryshire.

It is among these gentle hills that you enter Merioneth if you come up the Dee from Llangollen, an alluring entry into Wales with the road curving under steep, high slopes on your left and glimpses of the river below you on your right. Soon you reach Glyndyfrdwy and are immediately waist-deep in Welsh history. For this unpretentious village enjoys the prestige of close association with Owain Glyndŵr. Here was one of his estates; and here in 1400 he raised the standard of a Welsh revolt that was to go on for ten years. Inevitably in these nationalistic days he has become one of the greatest heroes of Wales. Just as inevitably

106

the nearest castle mound to Glyndyfrdwy is called Owain Glyndŵr's Mount. It appears tall and pine-topped between main
road and river a mile and a half upstream from Glyndyfrdwy.
But 250 yards east of the mount in a saucer of the pasture near a
little pool is a levelled place surrounded by a faint ditch. This
could well have been the site of a moated manor and perhaps is
more likely to have been Glyndŵr's Dee-side home.

A little upstream is Carrog, a village under wooded slopes.
Here a five-arched bridge, with four pointed refuges on each
side, has 1661 carved on it but that is perhaps only the date of one
of its more recent renovations, for it looks extremely old. It is a
good spot to stand and think of time that flies and water that
flows and watch the dippers that frequently pass up and down
the river. From Carrog you can follow B5437 along the north
side of the river past many lovely horse-chestnuts till you come,
in a mile, below Caer Drewyn, a treeless hill whose summit has
a sprawl of fragmented walls which have obviously been great
Iron Age fortifications. At the top corner (the whole camp slants
downhill) is a well-marked incurved entrance and some extra-
mural enclosures which may be a homestead of the Dark Ages.
Caer Drewyn gives you views of all the surrounding country
and of the ever-curving Dee. And it looks Corwen straight in
the eye across the valley.

If you want to compare Caer Drewyn with an even bigger
hill fort you should go by devious lanes four miles north-west to
Dinas Melin y Wig where a knobbly limestone hilltop of
thirteen acres is enclosed by solid turf banks. Not that they impress you as you approach along the farm lane below. But once
you are up there and have crossed over to look down the other
side you see how spectacularly this fortress's flank drops through
the trees to the Clwyd. To visit this good spot you should ask at
the farm beside it. Half a mile south-west a lane drops you into a
hollow containing a neat village with a streamlet and a large
Bethel chapel. You are at Melin y Wig, a cared-for little place
far from anywhere. Its apt name means 'the mill in the retreat'.
Over a hill and down again and you are at Betws Gwerful Goch,
a lovely name which means 'the oratory of Gwerful of the red
hair'. She who founded this oratory was, it seems, the daughter
of a twelfth-century lord of Meirionydd. Betws is a quite un-
hurried, secluded village. There are medieval carved panels in

the church and a good bridge over the Alwen. But the bridge really worth seeing—it is erroneously called Roman—spans the river in a graceful arch nearly a mile upstream at Cefn Ceirch where the wine-red Alwen flows under the shadow of trees.

This eastern corner of Merioneth is called Edeirnion, a name that goes back to the Dark Ages. Its principal place is Corwen, a long narrow Welsh-speaking market town, squeezed between flood-plain and wooded cliffs and unable to escape very far from the main road that thunders though it from Llangollen and out again over a long and ancient seven-arched bridge with a date stone of 1704 which, as at Carrog, may be only the date of a renovation. Corwen's most interesting building is the church which has inside it a fifteenth-century effigy and outside has the shaft of a possibly ninth-century Celtic cross. Note also the former standing stone built into the outside wall of the main porch (on left as you enter) and the ancient cross cut into the lintel over the south door. On that side too I like this record of an unusual performance: 'This corner stone was laid by the Hon. C. H. Wynn August 22 1871. Removed by him June 25 1898.' Across the Dee on the Wynn family's estate at Rug (pronounced 'Reeg') is a highly ornate private chapel built in 1637 and containing wood-carvings of human and animal figures. It may be seen by appointment.

Which part of the Dee is loveliest I leave you to decide: but for many it is these dozen miles from Corwen up to Bala. Along it are good stone bridges, one after another, as if bridge-building has been a popular local pastime. Cynwyd, for instance, has two. There is a four-arched one over the Dee, claimed to be the oldest in Merioneth, with beautiful riverside walks on either hand. And up the village, over the side-stream called Trystion, is probably the county's solidest, if least beautiful bridge whose massiveness looks out of proportion with the stream it spans. From Cynwyd you can follow the north side of the Trystion up a lane that for two miles keeps above a gorge loud with falls and cataracts and comes to a charming spot by a little reservoir. From there the lane takes to the hills to become the ancient trackway Ffordd Saeson.

For lovers of past things there are near Llandrillo three prehistoric burial sites conveniently visible from roadsides. Halfway between Cynwyd and Llandrillo along B4401 look out for a partly ploughed-out mound and a large capstone near the road on the north side. This is Rhyd y Glafais burial chamber which still retains some of its earth cover. The second site is the circle in front of Tyfos farmhouse, a mile north-west of Llandrillo. Though the most depleted, this in its way is the most impressive. For when you see the fourteen big boulders in a ring round the slightly raised platform your imagination easily puts a vast Bronze Age tumulus on top of them. At the third site, between lane and former railway at Branas Uchaf, a mile and a half west of Llandrillo, there remain three massive uprights and part of the covering mound of a Neolithic burial chamber. Best Iron Age representative for this part of the Dee is Caer Euni (three miles south-west of the Druid) a ridge-top hill fort with views all along Berwyn to Cadair Idris. Ancient roads also passed along that ridge, one of them probably Roman coming from the direction of Chester.

A fair land, all this country about Llandrillo and Llandderfel, with everywhere abrupt little hills rising from wooded shoulders above green farmlands. For viewpoints try the ancient road Ffordd Gam Elin which leaves B4401 a mile north-east of Llandrillo and climbs away steep and full of purpose to the south-east, at first a tarmac lane but soon a turf track through heather and getting fainter round the curves of the hills. If you have no time to follow it very far you can turn off to the first heathery hill top that greets you on the north-east side of the road. Up there you will find as perfect a Bronze Age stone circle as you could wish, high on the hill's flat top with, if you are lucky, the barking of grouse in the air. The forty-one stones are set close together in a ring twelve yards across with an entrance south-west and the hollow of an opened grave in the centre. There is another ring white with quartz eighty paces down the southern slope but this is evidently the base of a demolished cairn.

Here in this heathery land you are on the flanks of Berwyn, the high moorland that is shared with Denbigh and Montgomeryshire and stretches for twenty miles into the south-west where it merges with the Aran range. Then the high ground is taken on by Cadair Idris nearly to the coast to complete one of the great upland barriers of Wales, forty miles from near Corwen to the coast and descending below a thousand feet at one point only, the top of Talyllyn Pass (938 feet). So if you are looking for a long-distance ridge walk here it is. Not that Berwyn is quite the open moor it was for it is now invaded by forestry. But presumably its summits are high enough never to be submerged in trees, for the central spine of this broad range is mostly over 2,000 feet and bulges up to 2,713 feet on Moel Sych. In ancient times when valleys were choked with swamp and forest and men used the hills as roads, at least two trackways crossed the Berwyn from south-east to north-west, tracks that were probably part of long-distance ways across Britain. Their names have come down to us as Ffordd Saeson and Ffordd Gam Elin. Ffordd Saeson enters Merioneth from Denbighshire at Cymro Gate and goes fairly direct for Cynwyd and straight on up the Trystion and over Berwyn. Modern lanes continue it across to Shropshire: hence its name which means 'Englishmen's road'. Ffordd Gam Elin ('Helen's winding road') presumably got its name in the Middle Ages when it was habitual to ascribe old roads to that mythical Romano–British lady. It goes south-east from near Llandrillo, crosses the Berwyn by a fine standing stone on the ridge and goes down to Llanrhaeadr-ym-Mochnant. Another doubtless ancient route over the Berwyn went from Bala to Llangynog west of and roughly parallel with B4391. Near it, a mile and a half south-east of Bala, is Plas Rhiwaedog, a fine Jacobean house now a youth hostel.

At Bala you have said good-bye to Edeirnion and the middle Dee and are face to face with the bigger, craggier, wetter country of the west. The foothills of Arennig climb away to the north-west. Down the three and a half miles length of Llyn Tegid, the biggest natural lake of Wales, you have a fine view of Aran Benllyn. And all along the south the Berwyn range continues. Although medieval Bala was in a key position in the English hold on Wales it was never found necessary to defend it with a stone castle. Which is regrettable: a great castle would much enhance this historic town which can now point to nothing more impressive than the early Norman motte (Tomen y Bala) oddly surviving amid the houses and whose sole claim to distinction is that it may be the only motte in Britain with a public lavatory built into it. In 1828 this mound was described as 'covered in summer-time with knitters of both sexes and all ages', the knitting of woollen stockings being the great Bala industry of that time. A better-looking mound stands prominent on the slope about 150 yards up the lane north from Llanfor church. And branching off this lane a beech-embowered Lovers' Walk may be useful to some readers. Llanfor church has a Dark Ages stone built into an inside wall of the tower; and a disused eighteenth-century bell. A great man of Bala in the eighteenth century was Thomas Charles, founder of the British and Foreign Bible Society. His statue stands in the town. A great house close to Bala was Rhiwlas, home of the ancient Price family. It was demolished in 1951 but specimens of its Elizabethan wood carvings are preserved in the National Museum, Cardiff.

Bala lake (Llyn Tegid) is a splendid yachting water capable of causing excitement when south-westerlies come squalling up its length. It is about 140 feet deep in the middle and its numerous fish include roach, perch, trout and, surprisingly, grayling which is usually a river species. But its pride is the whitefish called gwyniad, a member of the salmon family and remarkable for being found nowhere else in Britain though it has very close relatives in the vendace of Cumberland, the pollan of Ireland and the powan of Scotland. These whitefish can be caught only in nets for they scorn all the lures of anglers. The southern slopes of Bala lake form a gentle, quiet region climbed into by lanes dead-ending at high-placed farms, lanes that are crooked, narrow, gated and best not motored up. This is a region more flowery than much of Merioneth for its soils are less lime-deficient than elsewhere and produce a richer assortment of wild plants. In such meadows and pastures as have not yet been 'improved' by being re-sown with modern grasses you may find frog orchid, moonwort, upright vetch, perhaps even small white orchid. One road takes you right away over the Berwyn. It goes from Rhos-y-gwaliau up the wooded Hirnant valley and then down to Lake Vyrnwy. For walks up wooded dingles go to Glyn Gower and the twin valleys that branch off it. In the lakeside church at Llangower is hung a bier that was carried by two horses, one at each end, a reminder of days when roads to high farms were often too rocky for wheeled traffic. Note in the churchyard that the oldest graves are grouped upon a low mound that doubtless supported a medieval cross. It could also be a Bronze Age tumulus.

'Arennig mountain rises to the north of the lake of Bala and sheweth itself very boldly. It is beautifully shaped, having two summits of nearly equal height and falling in a ridge singularly broken to the west.' So an eighteenth-century topographer described Arennig Fawr (2,800 feet) and Arennig Fach (2,264 feet). These peaks are twins not only in name: for both are of the same largely volcanic rocks and both hang east-facing crags above deep, glacier-gouged lakes. There is a third member of the group which also 'sheweth itself very boldly'—Moel Llyfnant, intermediate in size between the other two but less visited because remoter and lacking crags and lakes. The Arennig peaks are easily reached from the Celyn reservoir which lies between them; Moel Llyfnant from the Lliw valley on the south. A delightful approach to Arennig Fawr can be made from Parc, a village on the south-east side. And to return through the sunlight of a calm spring evening with all the curlews bubbling is to experience these moorlands at one of their moments of perfection.

If you follow the road across the moors north-west from Llanuwchllyn you will see, less than two miles up the Lliw, a prominent little ruin on a hill to your left. This is Castell Carndochan which, as the name suggests, is both a castle (possibly fourteenth century) and a cairn (presumably Bronze Age), an unusual combination of ancient monuments. Ruined almost to its foundations this castle is worth visiting for the high perch it enjoys. It has no real history and one guess is that it was 'the refuge of some ferocious chief who lived by plunder and rapine'. It is an ironical thought that whoever was the gold-greedy villain who set this castle on Carndochan he had no inkling that gold lay in the rocks below, for not until the nineteenth century was it discovered there. You will recognize the gold mine by the crushed white quartz of its spoil heaps. This road up the Lliw valley and down the Afon Gain is probably part of the medieval road from Bala to Harlech. And near it, almost a mile south of Llyn Gelli Gain, stands the medieval memorial called Bedd Porius ('the grave of Porius') whose roughly inscribed stone says: *Hic in tumulo iacit Porius. Homo planus fuit.* ('Here in this grave lies Porius. He was a plain man.') A curious epitaph. But maybe this Porius was not so much plain as destitute for *planus* can mean that too. On the slope 300 yards south-west stands the massive ten-foot slab called Llech Idris

9. Medieval packhorse bridge over the Alyn between Caergwrle and Hope, Flintshire

10. Sepulchral slab in Meifod church, Montgomeryshire. Meifod was an important centre in early medieval Wales

11. Grotesques on the walls of Llandderfel church, near Bala, Merioneth

12. The Mawddach estuary, Barmouth, Merioneth, with the Cadair Idris range beyond

('the stone of Idris') a legendary giant also commemorated on Cadair Idris ('Idris's chair'). Note the position of Llech Idris—to its vicinity come roads from the four points of the compass, a sure sign that it has stood there from ancient times. Near it the north-south Roman road crosses the east-west medieval road. But what is more significant than either is that probably one of those trans-Wales Bronze Age roads also passed that way coming from the north-west by way of Bryn Cader Faner (rich in prehistory) and going away far to the south-east.

Having now reached Sarn Helen, the Great West Road of the Romans, you can soon be at their local headquarters by going a few miles north up A487 and turning right along a lane two and a half miles beyond Trawsfynydd. The monstrosity you see at the north end of the reservoir, so incongruous in the heart of a national park, is a nuclear power-station. In Welsh it is Atomfa ('the place of the atom'). The name of the Roman fort, Tomen y Mur ('the mound within the wall'), does not refer to the Roman but to the medieval period, the mound being an outsize eleventh-century Norman motte which used the Roman enclosure as its bailey. Roman finds have been many: tiles, pottery, bricks and fragments of inscribed stones; but what the Romans called this fort is not known. A tankard of excellent Iron Age workmanship, found at Trawsfynydd, is in the City of Liverpool Museum. East of Trawsfynydd the Prysor stream comes hastening from the boggy slopes of Migneint. You can motor that way along a main road but if you want to explore Cwm Prysor on foot and in peace there is the disused railway which contours along the slopes high above the road. In three miles you will observe below you between railway and stream a stony-sided, tree-covered knoll of artificial appearance—the motte called Castell Prysor which retains low walling on its crown and may have been a place of strength in early Norman times. But as with so many castle mounds its known history is flimsy. Steeply above it Llyn y Garn, a shapely little tarn with clear water and stony margins, is beautifully cradled in the moorland. The old rail-track goes on towards Bala, soon crossing a viaduct of nine high stone arches which stand up in some grandeur on the moorland skyline.

Your feelings on first seeing Blaenau Ffestiniog, Merioneth's largest town, are not likely to be neutral. If the weather is gloomy you will probably be so appalled by all the dismal mountains of tipped slate that you will drive on without stopping, even if, as you depart, you may admit it is an achievement of the human spirit that a population can remain intact and even cheerful close to such desolation, at 900 feet above sea level in a rainfall of nearly 100 inches a year. (In 1954 it was nearly 150!) But arrive in Britain's wettest town on a bright and shining day and your reactions could be different. You may see splendour in the way the crags soar up directly from backgardens; and you will find beauty along the slopes behind the town, especially in late summer when they are colourful with yellow gorse and purple heather. For the best view go up Moelwyn, the mountain across the valley. From there you will see how Blaenau sits in the whole scene, a grey town with thirteen hundred feet of bare mountain intimately above it, a place of rugged strength and personality. Besides, how many other towns in the world can claim to have choughs on their doorstep (sometimes literally so in hard weather)? Look out for these beautiful red-billed cousins of the crow especially near abandoned quarries.

But whether you like Blaenau or not the country all round is good. If you feel the fascination of long-deserted quarries you can see them in plenty up Cwmorthin; and from there you can climb Moel yr Hydd or Moelwyn Mawr whose summit is a great viewpoint over the Caernarvonshire mountains as well as over Cardigan Bay and most of Merioneth. Or instead of mountaineering you can go down the Vale of Ffestiniog, long famous for its streams, its old bridges (as at Dôl-y-moch), its waterfalls and its surviving oakwoods rich in mosses and ferns. These splendid woodlands have not been preserved by a lucky chance but by the efforts of conservationists. Two villages, good centres for this district, are Ffestiniog (not to be confused with Blaenau) and Maentwrog. Ffestiniog has exquisite waterfalls one mile north-west (Afon Goedol), half a mile south (Rhaeadr Cynfal) and a particularly grand one three miles east (Rhaeadr-y-cwm): and there are several old houses of character in the vicinity, Cynfal Fawr, for instance. Maentwrog has a waterfall just over a mile south, the celebrated Rhaeadr Du in the wild ravine of Ceunant Llennyrch. The stone of Twrog (early Celtic Christian) which gave Maentwrog its name is a four-foot sandstone pillar outside the west end of the church.

Merioneth

The large house overlooking the Dwyryd half a mile west of Maentwrog is Plas Tan-y-bwlch, famous in the late eighteenth century when its owner, William Oakley (died 1811), created one of those earthly paradises so fashionable at that time. And he earns our gratitude today for having planted some of the oaks that still make the slopes 'romantically embowered with woods', to use an expression of that age. The house is now a residential study centre for the National Park. If you travel on the narrow-gauge railway from Portmadoc you pass close above Plas Tan-y-bwlch, overlook much of the woodlands and come near to the beautiful water called Llyn Mair ('Mary's Lake') which is on the roadside between Tan-y-bwlch and Llanfrothen. If you go down the lane from the lake, look out on the left for a notice indicating the start of a nature-trail through the woods.

Just as Snowdon has its Horseshoe so, in a modest way, has the Cnicht-Moelwyn range. Starting from the highest point of the lane about a mile south of Croesor, follow the path that heads east for the col between Moelwyn Mawr and Moelwyn Bach. From the col you look down on Llyn Stwlan, an unattractive reservoir that is emptied by day to generate electricity, some of which is used to pump the water back up into the reservoir by night. To get to the top of Moelwyn Mawr you now have a little scramble up turfy slopes and rocks to a summit that looks down sharp crags across a lake-studded moorland to all the heights of Caernarvonshire. For the maximum horseshoe you now descend to the east and follow the edge of the fine hollowed cliffs aptly called Ceseiliau Moelwyn ('the armpits of Moelwyn'), and thence over Moel yr Hydd and down to the head of Cwmorthin. But on a shorter circuit bear north-east off Moelwyn with a spectacular quarry-chasm on your right and Llyn Croesor on your left, noting the glacier-smoothed rocks lower down. Go through the ruins of quarry buildings above Cwmorthin and press on north along a scantily cairned track. You ascend a slope remarkable for the huge rectangular blocks of hard, grey dolerite which cover most of it. Then you look down on Llyn yr Adar ('the lake of the birds' but no birds, usually), a largish, round lake with a rocky islet in the centre. You are now on the ridge of Cnicht which you can easily follow to the summit. From there, given clarity, you will see far along Lleyn in the west; Llyn Dinas, Snowdon and much else in the north; Siabod and a far peep into Denbighshire in the east; and on the south an aeroplane view into the deep gulf of Cwm Croesor. It is then a simple scramble down slopes and rocks to Croesor village.

Near the mouth of Cwm Croesor you pass Plas Brondanw, home of architect Clough Williams Ellis who gave an encouraging lead towards creating the National Park when he donated a piece of land near the foot of Snowdon. Across the lane from his house is a public path leading up to a prospect tower which looks to all the mountains. It also gazes over the site of the former Glaslyn estuary, long since reclaimed, an estuary whose loss is mourned by a statue of the sea-god Neptune in Plas Brondanw garden. One of Clough Williams Ellis's best known works is the colourful holiday village he built at Portmeirion on the shores of Traeth Bach between Portmadoc and Penrhyndeudraeth. The houses and other buildings, arranged up a steep south slope, are mostly in Italian styles and the atmosphere of the place is gay and Mediterranean. There are trees and flowering shrubs everywhere.

If from Penrhyndeudraeth you wish to go south you can cross the estuary by a toll bridge and soon be in Harlech, chief town of Merioneth in the Middle Ages because of the castle Edward I built there in about 1280 as part of the great arc of forts he set round North Wales from the Dee to the Ystwyth. In those days Harlech had access to the sea, perhaps along a creek that went north to the Dwyryd estuary. Hence the castle's back-door—a water-gate that evidently led down to a quay. Since those days vast accumulations of sand, probably beginning soon after the building of the castle, have built up on this coast and the castle is now land-locked. But, high on its rock and looking north to Snowdon, it remains the most picturesquely sited of all the castles of North Wales.

Morfa Harlech (*morfa* means sea-edge land), probably an area of saltings and creeks in the Middle Ages, is now largely piled with dunes enclosing damp hollows and marshy pools, forming in all a most attractive region for naturalists in search of birds, insects and wild plants. Marsh helleborine and other marsh orchids are particularly abundant. The northern part of the area is a National Nature Reserve; the southern is a famous golf-course. And the best view of it all, with Caernarvonshire's mountains as a background, is from or near the main road a mile south of Harlech. As Harlech's sands piled up, a similar dune

116

system developed off Dyffryn a few miles south. Here the sand nearly buried the medieval church of Llandanwg and it moved the mouth of the Artro river from the south of Mochras to the north of it. Mochras, no doubt once an island at high tides, is still popularly known as Shell Island, a name dating from last century when shell-collecting was very popular. A section of these dunes, rich in fauna and flora, is a National Nature Reserve.

Barmouth (Abermo) until the end of the eighteenth century was a village port doing a little coastal trade, especially taking the products of local cottage weavers to Liverpool. Its chief contacts with Dolgellau were the small craft that went with the tide to Llanelltyd six miles up the estuary. Difficult to reach by road along the steep estuary-side slopes, the Barmouth of those days was largely by-passed, most road traffic crossing the hills from Bont Ddu to Dyffryn Ardudwy by way of Bwlch y Rhiwgyr ('the drovers' pass'). That road still exists as a fading grassy track over the pass and is difficult to picture as a main road of the eighteenth century but here and there the milestones of that time survive to prove it.

Like many seaside places Barmouth was put on the map by the coast-visiting fashion which began when doctors started to recommend sea bathing in preference to spa-water drinking. So in 1793 we find the Hon. John Byng while on a visit to Bala remarking: 'But since I was here ten years ago times are altered. Post-chaises are now kept and people go to Barmouth for the sea bathing.' They have continued to do so ever since and Barmouth has squeezed itself ever tighter between the shore and the dark cliffs that tower above the houses and hotels. On the slopes above the town is Dinas Oleu, the first property ever acquired by the National Trust. Being comparatively new Barmouth lacks historic buildings except for fragments of the old village that survive along the quay and on the hill. For a good building go north to Llanaber whose thirteenth-century church is perhaps the best surviving bit of medieval Merioneth. It has an ancient stone inscribed: 'Caelexti monedo rigi', which I leave you to translate how you will, for the scholars disagree. Pedestrians can cross the Mawddach estuary by ferry boat to the tip of Fairbourne dunes; or by walking across the long railway bridge and so to Arthog, a village that has fine waterfalls and colourful gardens and is a gateway to Cadair Idris. In the boggy land between Arthog and the estuary botanists will find interesting aquatic plants.

North from Barmouth to Maentwrog and east from Harlech to Ganllwyd stretches the Rhinog range, a tract of wild uplands penetrated by many deep and wooded valleys loud with streams, cascades and waterfalls. Its tops make that exciting, deeply undulating black skyline you see against the western sky as you travel down the road south from Trawsfynydd. Though its summits are higher in the south they are wilder and more intractable in the north. For in the south they dome up as high grasslands on Llethr (2,475 feet) and Diffwys (2,462 feet); but in the north they are thickly mantled with heather and block scree and the going is hard. The two central heights, Rhinog Fawr (2,362 feet) and Rhinog Fach (2,333 feet) are partly grassy sheep-walks and partly bare rock fit only for the goats which, descendants of the domestic goats of centuries ago, roam wild on those inhospitable tops.

Small lakes are a special delight of Rhinog, many of them in high rocky places. In the north, for instance, there is Llyn Tecwyn-uchaf, a fine pool with naked cliffs under deep-looking water. The track that edges along under these cliffs may not strike you as much of a road but it was, until early last century, a frequent line of communication from Maentwrog to Harlech by way of the flowery-margined pool called Tecwyn-isaf and then down the long, tree-lined valley to Eisingrug. East of Eisingrug is the heart of the north Rhinog country, a region of fissured rocks that rise to two thousand feet. From there you can walk or rather scramble, often waist-deep in heather, for two or three miles south to the twin pools Twr Glas and Pryfed and on to Llyn Morwynion deep amid the debris of long-shattered cliffs. But beware of ankle-turning rocks deeply bushed by heather.

Llyn Morwynion ('the lake of the maidens', though I do not guarantee you will find them) lies close under the pass called Bwlch Tyddiad through which an important medieval road went from Harlech to Bala and so was part of the line of communication between Harlech castle and London. No doubt it was also a pack-horse trading route. To ease the passage of traffic up its roughest stretch from Cwm Bychan to Bwlch Tyddiad, hundreds of stone steps were carefully laid presumably soon after Harlech castle was built. And these steps, kept in repair ever since, still go striding purposefully up through the rocks. In later centuries the steps came to be called 'Roman' which in that context simply means that their origin had faded beyond the memory or hearsay of the oldest inhabitant. What is believed to be a far more ancient route goes from Llanbedr (an important haven in prehistoric times?) towards the north-east, its way still marked by standing stones, circles, a hill fort (Moel Goedog), some 'Irishmen's Walls' (Muriau Gwyddelod) and various cairns and hut sites on Bryn Cader Faner. Having rounded the uplands the track drops into Cwm Moch and turns south-east towards Llech Idris. Bronze Age finds that could have been associated with it include a gold torc, a bronze shield and a collection of bronze rapiers. At Cwm Moch you are close to Trawsfynydd reservoir whose rocky slopes at Coed y Rhygen, covered with ancient, twisted, lichen-covered oaks, are a National Nature Reserve.

Llanbedr (accent on the first syllable) is most people's gateway to the Rhinog. That way you can go up the Artro to Cwm Bychan lake and the Roman Steps; or turn up the Nantcol for Drws Ardudwy ('the door of Ardudwy'). The uplands of Ardudwy are a district of wooded valley-sides rising quickly to the open hills; of streams flowing under ancient high-arched stone bridges; of remote, upland, seventeenth-century houses like Cwm Bychan and Maes y Garnedd, birthplace of Cromwell's brother-in-law, Colonel John Jones. From Cwm Nantcol you can climb the extremely rocky slopes of Rhinog Fawr. But do not neglect Rhinog Fach: its long smooth slabs of Cambrian rock dipping steeply into Llyn Hywel are beautiful to see. From any of these Rhinog tops the seascapes and landscapes are all rewarding, especially of the Lleyn Peninsula in the west; and round the east an arc of mountains: Arennig, Dduallt, Rhobell, Aran and Cadair Idris. The southern Rhinog ramparts lie for eight superb miles along the Mawddach estuary, divided by many valleys and secret glens. From all along these heights the views are among the best-loved prospects in Wales because they take in the incomparable Mawddach estuary and the Cadair range. I leave it to you to decide between Barmouth's Panorama Walk and Llanelltyd's New Precipice Walk.

Old mine roads make these southern skirts of Rhinog easier going for walkers than more northern parts. Some of the mines were for low-grade manganese which could still today be useful

to the steel industry in an emergency. You will find their trackways going up from Barmouth; and one from near Llyn Cwm
Mynach will help you climb Diffwys. Scattered all over these
hills from Bont Ddu north-east for about eight miles are innumerable trial holes, levels, tips and old roads connected with
centuries of success and failure in the effort to find copper, lead,
silver and gold. The chief gold mines[1] are on Y Vigra, the
1,076-foot hill north-west of Bont Ddu; Clogau, north of Bont
Ddu; and Gwynfynydd by the famous falls six miles up the
Mawddach from Llanelltyd. Modern gold-mining in Merioneth
began in the 1840s and it is now a tradition for the royal family
to have their wedding rings made in Welsh gold. Mining is only
sporadic but optimistic prospectors believe that much gold remains in these Welsh rocks. Or they tell you it might be got out
of deep holes in the river by frogmen armed with vacuum suckers.
So why waste your time fishing?

The Rhinog is good country for archaeologists, especially the
delectable shelf of moorland north-east of Barmouth. Here are
various burial chambers, tumuli and hill forts representing the
Stone, Bronze and Iron Ages. The two cairns known as Carneddau Hengwm are the showpieces. They form long, narrow,
parallel heaps of loose stones (one heap is 150 feet long) and have
probably contained several burial chambers in each. Before they
were despoiled to build local walls they must have been of huge
size. As for hill forts, you could hardly better Craig y Dinas
which stands on a spur of Moelfre above the Ysgethin stream
and still shows relics of good walling perhaps two thousand years
old. South of it lies Llyn Irddin ('the priest's lake') in a wild
scatter of rocks. East is Bodlyn in whose cold, dark depths are
Merioneth's only char. There are also burial chambers at
Dyffryn Ardudwy; and in Llanbedr church is a stone with a
spiral ornament commoner in Ireland than Wales. It was found
over a century ago amongst some 'Irishmen's huts' on the nearby hills. The spiral seems to have been an important symbol
for ancient peoples. Llanbedr also has an eighteenth-century
milestone saying: 'Harlech 111 M 1765.' See if you can find it.

Down the centuries the principal bridgehead on the Mawddach
has been a mile north-west of Dolgellau at Llanelltyd. Here at
the confluence of Mawddach and Wnion was the abbey of

[1] Mining still goes on but only sporadically.

Cymer ('waters meet'), Merioneth's only monastery. The Cistercians who built it were energetic sheep farmers, probably also owned mines and had property and rights over an extensive tract of country. Cymer abbey was never large and its remains are unimpressive. An eighteenth-century visitor complained that 'attached to it on the outside are pigstyes and cow-houses which entirely destroys the outward effect'. A twentieth-century visitor might complain that caravans have achieved a similar result. In its circular churchyard Llanelltyd's parish church bids you welcome on a notice at the gate and its fine old door usually stands open. The walls within are hung with notes about the church, local history and Illtud, most celebrated saint of North Wales. One curiosity is a medieval stone whose very worn lettering seems to say, when the Latin is translated: 'The footprint of Kenyric was imprinted at the head of this stone before he set out for foreign parts.' But the shape of the foot is even fainter than the lettering. The idea behind this inscription seems to have been a belief that it would guarantee a safe return to this Kenyric who was presumably off on a pilgrimage to Rome or Jerusalem. But a difficulty of such an interpretation is that no such footprinted stone is known to exist anywhere else. A photograph in the church shows the silver-gilt chalice and paten found in 1896 by a couple of gold prospectors in Cwm Mynach ('monk's valley'). These objects had pretty certainly been hidden there by the monks when the abbey was dissolved in 1536. The finders sold them for 50s. Eventually they changed hands for £3,000 and are now in the National Museum at Cardiff.

Dolgellau, the county town, has lost nearly all its ancient structures and its centre is now substantially that of a town of the eighteenth and early nineteenth centuries, the Georgian shire hall being perhaps the best building. All the same its lay-out—the square with narrow little streets coming into it—could go right back to the time of Meuric, the fourteenth-century knight whose effigy survives in the parish church. Of the several great houses that have flourished near Dolgellau the two most famous are Nannau and Hengwrt. At Hengwrt in the seventeenth century the antiquary Robert Vaughan amassed the finest collection of Welsh manuscripts ever gathered under a private roof. They passed to Peniarth near Towyn in the nineteenth century and to the National Library at Aberystwyth in the twentieth. They included some of the most precious of medieval writings such as *The Book of Aneurin*, *The Book of Taliesin*, *The Hengwrt Chaucer*, *The Black Book of Chirk*, *The Black Book of Carmarthen* and *The White Book of Rhydderch*: all literary monuments whose equivalent any nation would be proud to possess.

It was early in the nineteenth century that Sir Robert Vaughan, descendant of the famous antiquary, laid out the Nannau estate on the spacious lines then fashionable and planted something like a million trees, some of which still adorn the district. But in the main all the region north of Nannau is now swallowed up by the conifers of Coed y Brenin. Oak woodland survives along the Gamlan river at Ganllwyd, where is the famous fall called Rhaeadr Du which, with Pistyll Cain and Rhaeadr Mawddach close together two miles north-east, makes a trio of well-loved waterfalls. Just possibly in Coed y Brenin you may be lucky enough to see a deer. If so it will be a fallow or the descendant of one that has escaped from Nannau deerpark. On Nannau estate you can go along the old Precipice Walk which contours at a high level round the hill called Foel Cynwch, overlooking a tarn on the east and the Ganllwyd valley on the west. Scattered walls of a hill fort lie like a ring of scree round the south end of the hill. The views are magnificent. So are those from nearby Moel Offrwm hill fort which also looks down the Mawddach estuary and across to Cadair Idris. Old Precipice Walk (and nature trail) is signposted on the road from Dolgellau to the delightfully withdrawn village of Llanfachreth. Note all through this district the tall, ornate chimneys of many cottages and country houses: they are the hall-mark of the Nannau architectural tradition.

For an all-day mountain walk go north up the lane from Rhyd-y-main (five miles from Dolgellau on the Bala road) and find your way by forestry roads to the slopes of Rhobell Fawr (2,408 feet). Once you are clear of the plantations you have about a thousand feet of increasingly rocky slopes to the top, with its remarkably fine views in all directions. From there you could go down on the north-east side and up again to Dduallt (2,155 feet), a long north-south ridge falling craggy on the east. Water trickling down Dduallt's cliffs forms one of the sources of the Dee which rises also in the peat-bog you see below, a bog that on its other side gives rise to the Mawddach river. Lime-rich rocks which make Cadair Idris so botanically attractive extend across Brithdir to the southern flank of Rhobell Fawr—hence the ash wood and its calcicole ground flora below Craig y Benglog.

'Old Cader is a grand fellow and shows himself off superbly with ever changing light. Do come and see him.' What Charles Darwin, who often stayed near Barmouth, wrote of Cadair Idris illustrates the affection this mountain has inspired in generations of visitors. From Dolgellau nearly 3,000 feet below, Cader's north-facing scarp looks like a long wave that has come up from the south and is about to curl over. Though rocks that once overlaid it have disappeared this high ridge has so far resisted erosion because it is composed of a particularly hard, fine-grained, crystalline rock called granophyre which forms the great cliffs around Llyn y Gadair. But just east of this lake the slope has shattered into small scree up which the famous Fox's Path from Llyn Gwernan makes its arduous, ankle-testing way. There are easier ways up but to ascend by Fox's Path on the north and come down by Llyn Cau on the south, or vice-versa, is the most dramatic route. Like all North Wales mountains, Cadair Idris was intensely glaciated: the cirques of cliffs, the corrie lakes, the great scree slopes, perched boulders and scratched rocks are the abundant evidence of the passage of sheets of immensely thick ice. The crags most interesting to botanists are those above Llyn Gafr, Llyn Aran and Llyn Cau.

The top of Cadair Idris looks over a vast reach of country from Snowdon in the north to Pumlumon in the south, from the hills of Worcestershire in the east to Ireland, occasionally, in the west. (For Ireland try intensely cold weather in midwinter when there can be phenomenal clarity above the lowland haze.) Cadair Idris also looks down on the varied country south of the Mawddach between Dolgellau and Fairbourne. It is a sloping land cut into by many wooded valleys and their side-dingles. It is crossed by narrow lanes more suited to pedestrians than cars, by-ways which no doubt follow, some of them, the region's most ancient routes. Cadair Idris has always been an obstacle to north-south traffic but in prehistoric times most of this seems to have slipped round the western end along a road called Ffordd Ddu, a route possibly used also by the Romans to link Tomen y Mur with Pennal. But Roman road problems in this area are intense and the field is wide open to explorers. A later relic survives, but only just, a short mile west of the beautiful twin lakes of Crogennen above Arthog. This is Llys Bradwen ('Bradwen's court') probably a Dark Ages house now reduced to a square of banks in the turf, a ruin so faint it would not be worth visiting if it were not for the waterfalls and the widening views of the Mawddach you see as you climb up from Arthog.

Though Cadair Idris has its sheerest cliffs on the north it also hangs a magnificent line of crags high above Talyllyn Pass, crags that are continued across the pass by the rocks of Craig y Llam some of which stand up as isolated towers and stacks hundreds of feet above the road. This pass is always beautiful, its colours ever changing with the light and the seasons. And any time just after heavy rain there is a spectacular burgeoning of streams that make long white snakes down the slopes. All this water collects in Talyllyn Lake, a large natural pool in miraculously undeveloped surroundings. Here men fish for trout of fair proportions judging by the outlines of past specimens carved on the walls outside the Tyn-y-cornel hotel. And here in winter come wild swans, coots and diving ducks. By the outlet stream is a primitive church with noteworthy wood carving on the chancel ceiling—square panels with roses—which is early seventeenth century work.

Although the Dysynni which flows out of Talyllyn Lake has but a few miles to the sea it is a stream of much interest and charm. It is also a bit quirky. For when it reaches Abergynolwyn (slate village whose vast abandoned quarries are up the steep valley to the south) it no longer continues down the long straight valley ahead, as doubtless it once did. Instead it twists awkwardly to the right (an example of what geologists call an elbow of river-capture) and cuts deeply through the hills to turn again south-west. If at this point you turn north-east, you come in half a mile to the rock-perched ruins of Castell y Bere, a once sizeable Welsh castle built half a century before those of Edward I. Edward captured it after considerable resistance and for a while turned it to his own uses even granting the place borough status. But no town ever developed there, the new Edwardian castles no doubt soon making Bere superfluous and causing it to sink into rapid obscurity. At Castell y Bere you are at the start of one of the longer routes up Cadair Idris by way of the sequestered

Merioneth

hamlet of Llanfihangel y Pennant. There you can spare a moment
to respect the brave heart and strong ankles of sixteen-years-old
Mary Jones, an indefatigable, bare-footed walker of the
eighteenth century who made a famous walk from here to Bala
to acquire a Bible from Thomas Charles as is related on her
monument.

Nearly two miles down the Dysynni from Castell y Bere a
vast cliff rises up on the south. This is Craig yr Aderyn, the Bird
Rock, ancient stronghold of thirty or so pairs of cormorants
which nest on its highest ledges. Nowhere else in Britain do cormorants regularly nest so far from the sea (four miles) and it is a
reserve of the West Wales Naturalists' Trust. To see the cormorants at all closely you must labour up steep grassy slopes and
look across the face of the rock. Having climbed so high you
may as well go to the top of this 760-foot hill and inspect the
collapsed remains of walling that in the Iron Age helped to make
this summit into a well-defended fort. Look out also for wild
goats.

From Bird Rock there are two roads to the coast, one on each
side of the Dysynni. Devotees of medieval craftsmanship should
take the road on the north side and so come to Llanegryn, meeting the ancient road Ffordd Ddu on the way. In the high-placed
church of Llanegryn is one of the best-carved medieval screens
of Wales: but there is no foundation for the tradition that it
came from Cymer abbey at the Dissolution. A mile south the
main road crosses the Dysynni on a fine old bridge with a lovely
view up the wide and tranquil river to Cadair Idris and Craig yr
Aderyn. A few hundred yards below the bridge the pine-topped
hillock called Domenddreiniog ('thorn hill'), casts a lovely re-
flection on to the water. On this mound in the thirteenth century
stood a wooden, moated castle of some local importance. Seawards the river spreads itself round large reed-beds before it
enters the Broadwater, an estuary now almost land-locked but
which no doubt once opened a gaping mouth to the sea: a place
for naturalists, artists and photographers.

Up the coast north of the Dysynni is Llangelynnin where a
lonely, primitive church stands near the cliff edge. From here, to
avoid the main road, walkers can make a diversion of a mile or
two along a lane going at first inland then north past the hill fort
of Castell y Gaer to Llwyngwril, a village with walks inland and

good views seawards from the small boulder-clay cliffs. These cliffs continue north-east until in two miles they give place to the long bathing sands of Fairbourne. From Fairbourne station to the northern tip of the dunes a mini-railway of only 15-inches gauge dates back to 1916. For walkers there are steep paths up through woods and old quarries to the hills, linking with lanes to Arthog, Abergwynant and Dolgellau.

In the south-west corner of Merioneth is Towyn (Tywyn). Now a holiday resort Towyn was long a centre of pilgrimage, an alleged pilgrims' road called Llwybr Cadfan ('Cadfan's way') being still partly traceable over the hills from Machynlleth. Probably some pilgrims went on by sea to Bardsey which is linked to Towyn by long tradition, Cadfan (sixth-century Breton saint) having founded the first Christian settlement on that island as well as the church at Towyn. In the church (partly modern with twelfth-century nave) are two medieval effigies and a stone of about the seventh century that is unique because its message is in Welsh whereas all other contemporary inscribed stones in Wales are in Latin or Ogham. As it is the earliest known written specimen of the Welsh language it is regrettable that its meaning is obscure. Though called Cadfan's stone it seems to have no connection with him. The pilgrims who flock to Towyn these days come to worship strange gods with names like 'Talyllyn' and 'Dolgoch' which are engines on the local narrow-gauge railway run by enthusiastic volunteers. On this line you can travel through delightful country to Dôlgoch (waterfalls in delectable ravine) and nearly to Abergynolwyn. The line passes not far from the seventeenth-century house called Dolaugwyn which can be viewed by appointment during the summer months.

At the southernmost tip of Merioneth is the village of Aberdovey (Aberdyfi). And when you get there I hope the tide will be full, the air still, the sun shining and there are colourful yachts in the estuary. For then this little haven is not only at its best but looks, as nearly as it can today, like the Aberdovey of yesterday when it was a place of fishing and mercantile importance. From here road and railway go east hand in hand, skirting the estuary under wooded slopes and looking south across a shining world of sand or water to the rounded hills of north Cardiganshire. Soon you reach the hamlet of Cwrt where a road forks back along the

Happy Valley to Towyn. This was the main road of coaching days and there are still a few old milestones. From it you can walk up to Llyn Barfog. Barfog means 'bearded' and the name is inevitably translated as 'the Bearded Lake'. But as this makes little sense it seems more likely that the name means 'Barfog's lake', Barfog being a legendary figure associated with Arthur. East of the lake, if you enjoy echoes you can successfully shout your name at cliffs on the other side of a bog. If you like drovers' roads you can walk three miles or so from Pant-yr-on farm to Rhyd-yr-onnen, a station on the Talyllyn railway.

A little east of Cwrt is Pennal where foundations of a Roman fort—partly made of hard rock brought by boat from Tonfannau near Towyn—lie buried under a farmhouse and its fields. So look carefully at the walls of local buildings: you may spot a Roman brick or two (they are usually shallower than our bricks of to-day). And do not miss the hills: all along above Pennal is an undulation of smooth summits gradually descending from Tarren y Gesail near Corris to the sea at Towyn, their heathery tops and grassy slopes a choice ridge-walk of nearly a dozen miles.

At Dovey Bridge (Pont ar Ddyfi) close to Machynlleth, you can cross the river into Montgomeryshire. Or you can remain just within Merioneth by taking the road north to Corris with the trackway and old stations of a former narrow-gauge railway close on your right all the way. The valley winds northward through beautiful country: but there is more in the south Merioneth scene than the conventionally picturesque, as you discover when you arrive at Corris, a slate-quarry centre which most people consider ugly. Yet its great tips of shattered rock are not so very different from a natural waste of block scree. Nor is Corris in the centre of a Black Country. Ring ouzels sing and nest among its tips, ravens and buzzards soar over them, many ferns and wild flowers grow in their crevices. And if you still do not love Corris you can be out of it in a few minutes into any of the fine country all around.

From Aberllefenni, where there are more quarries, in fact a mountain quite hollowed out by quarrying, you can follow an ancient road (suggested as Roman) up the valley north-west. It brings you above Craig y Llam, the great cliff above Talyllyn Pass, and then down to A487 which it crosses to make straight for Dolgellau. Another outlet for hill walkers from Aberllefenni is up the Ratgoed valley, then by keeping above the steep faces of Craig Portas and Craig Maesglasau (splendid waterfall) you descend swiftly to Dinas Mawddwy. Alternatively you may go by foot or by car due east from Aberllefenni through miles of conifers to the Dovey at the charmingly placed village of Aberangell where, as at Aberllefenni, there is a Forestry Commission picnic site. From there it is two miles upriver to Mallwyd whose church has a seventeenth-century plank tower with large decayed Latin lettering on the outside. Preserved above the doorway are a rib and a vertebra of a prehistoric ox dug up nearby.

Dinas Mawddwy, a mile and a half upstream, had medieval importance which has not survived. In the nineteenth century it had mines and quarries but now confines itself to farming and forestry and has a woollen mill where you can watch the weavers at work. North of here the Dovey vale narrows into the mountains, the few riverside fields become steeper and hedges dwindle up high slopes. It is a valley rather apart from the world and, by a geographical peculiarity, has side-valleys most people pass by without realizing their existence. Yet there they are, large and beautiful valleys with waterfalls dropping into them off the moorland rim. There is Cwm Cywarch whose cliffs are especially grand; and the Pumryd valley which has the greater waterfall. Both these valleys give you access to Aran Fawddwy (2,970 feet), Merioneth's highest peak. Another way is to carry on north through Llanymawddwy and walk with the Dovey (lovely gorge and fall below Ogof Ddu) to its source lake, Craiglyn Dyfi, which is under Aran Fawddwy's dark, volcanic cliffs. If you continue along the road north from Llanymawddwy, leaving the Dovey where its valley turns off left towards the lake, you come after a long climb to the magnificent pass of Bwlch y Groes. Here you can choose between turning east for Lake Vyrnwy or going on, with great views of Arennig before you, down with the Twrch river to Llanuwchllyn ('the church at the head of the lake'), a church which has a knightly effigy of the fourteenth century. A mile due north of Llanuwchllyn is Caer Gai, a seventeenth-century house on the site of a Roman fort with a generous length of its walls still surviving on the south. At Caer Gai was found a votive tablet, now in Chester museum, saying it was made by 'Julius, son of Cavero, a soldier in the first cohort of the

13. Bird Rock (Craig yr Aderyn), a unique inland breeding place of cormorants near Tywyn, Merioneth

14. Eighteenth-century bridge over the Rheidol at Ponterwyd, Cardiganshire

15. Pont Einon, a bridge over the Teifi near Tregaron, Cardiganshire

16. View south-west along the cliffs of Cardigan Island with
Cemaes Head, Pembrokeshire, beyond

Nervii' who were there around A.D. 100. From here still partly traceable Roman roads went east to Chester, north-west to Trawsfynydd and south-west towards Dolgellau. Along this last road small Roman sites have been discovered in recent years near Llys (two and a half miles) and at Brithdir (about eight miles further). Some archaeologists believe that a larger fort awaits a discoverer in the vicinity of Dolgellau.

Llanuwchllyn's mountain is Aran Benllyn whose height falls short of Cadair Idris by only twenty-six feet. Though it looks a solitary, alluring peak from the north-east, Aran Benllyn is really the end of a long, high range and is one with Aran Fawddwy. It is most commonly climbed from the north beginning at Llys whence the path goes up a series of deceptive shoulders, every next shoulder fooling you that it is the summit. But you get there at last and look down high crags to a corrie lake in the east. Beyond you see how Bala lake lies along the greatest fault line in the structure of Wales, a fault that continues right to the coast at Towyn, a length of over thirty miles. You see all the heights along the fault from Cadair Idris to Arennig. And you have a great prospect of the counties of Caernarvon, Denbigh and Montgomery.

7

CARDIGANSHIRE
(Ceredigion)

Cardiganshire begins in the north in sand, pebbles and
dunes and an estuary, that of the Dovey (Dyfi) which
looks to a beautiful circle of the hills of mid-Wales.
South of the Dovey the foot-hills climb to stronger country
further back—the high shoulders of Pumlumon (which the
English have long called 'Plynlimon'). Many streams have
laboured to give these uplands a mountainy look by cutting deep
valleys in their flanks. Llyfnant, Einion, Clettwr, Leri: all have
their gorges, cataracts and falls and flow here and there under
steep oakwoods which foresters despise as 'uneconomic'. Yet
because these woods are so picturesque, so absolutely right for
their setting, they could be said to be highly 'economic' for they
are an intrinsic element in the scenery which tourists come to
Wales to see.

The Llyfnant makes a lofty cascade where it falls off the moorland rim; then it goes to the estuary deep in a valley between
woods. The Einion has two falls: the upper one is very fine but
tucked away in a secret gorge; the lower one, very much
photographed because at the side of A487 in Furnace village, is
somewhat artificial, its height having been raised to divert water
to the wheel of the eighteenth-century iron-smeltery next to it.
Not that there is iron locally. It used to be brought here by ship
from Lancashire, via Aberdovey, because this then thickly
wooded district could supply the necessary charcoal. The dingle
of the Clettwr is still densely wooded and, being cool and

shadowy, is esteemed by botanists for its rare mosses. The Leri had great lead mines at Talybont and further up; and a narrow-gauge railway ran along it from Llandre, then up its tributary, the Cyneiniog. Today it is famous for weaving mills and trout.

Many a hill in this region had its Bronze Age cairns, notably Foel Goch (1,557 feet). Between Leri and Clettwr the long-opened cairn called Bedd Taliesin ('Taliesin's grave') was certainly a burial of the Bronze Age, not of the sixth-century poet, Taliesin, who was traditionally associated with these parts. After the Bronze Age the Iron Age found the district enormously attractive judging by the remarkable concentration of their hill forts between Talybont and Aberystwyth. Then the Romans came and soon had a road heading south from Pennal round the fringe of the hills east of Llandre and Bow Street, aiming for their fort at Trawsgoed, much of its probable course being marked by present-day lanes.

South of the Dovey estuary lie wide, flat, difficult-to-drain lands which, getting wetter towards Borth, eventually reach a point where farming admits defeat in a deep, water-logged peat-bog. This quaking morass is what remains of the great bog called Cors Fochno, a name of unknown meaning that comes from far back in Celtic folklore. In the old tales a magic toad dwelt in the heart of Cors Fochno and could be consulted as an oracle. Now science reveals that there are indeed wonders in this great bog-land. Botanists have shown that the still identifiable pollen of the trees of long ago lies preserved in the depths of the peat, enabling them to say how both the climate and the species of trees in the neighbouring forests have changed in the past several thousand years. Besides being a marvellous repository of scientific and historical information, Cors Fochno is a habitat of aquatic plants, insects and birds which get scarcer year by year as more and more wetlands are drained. Parts have therefore been made into a National Nature Reserve together with the Dovey estuary, which is rich in wild life, and Ynyslas sand-dunes[1] which have a wealth of wild flowers and insects. At the head of the estuary the Royal Society for the Protection of Birds has a reserve at Ynys-hir where there are many woodland birds, ducks, waders and a heronry. And a castle mound, Domen Las, built in 1156.

Stumps of ancient trees—pines, birches, alders—still rooted

[1] Here the Nature Conservancy has an information centre and nature trail.

where they grew, are numerous on the shore at Ynyslas. They tell vividly of former land long since invaded by the sea—the land that has gone into Welsh folklore as Cantref y Gwaelod ('the lowland hundred'). The medieval storytellers put the submergence into the seventh century. But the tree stumps are in fact associated with Neolithic finds, which puts the flooding of this land back to about 3,000 B.C. All the same the saga of Cantref y Gwaelod makes a persuasive story, especially if you have seen the remarkable Sarn Gynfelin at low spring tide. Half-way between Borth and Aberystwyth this is a bank of stones going dead straight into the sea, then just under it, for a long way. It was, the old tale claims, one of the embankments that surrounded the now lost land. And it looks just like one. Scientists say it is natural, being tidally caused, though they do not seem too clear how it has happened.

Four miles of undulating, shaly, rather crumbly sea-cliffs extend south from Borth. Where they end, the town of Aberystwyth begins. As a resort Aberystwyth is much the same age as Brighton and those other seaside places that began to be popular when bathing came into fashion in the 1780's. But Aberystwyth has plenty of earlier history. It got borough status in 1277 when Edward I built the castle of which enough is left to enable us to visualize its general appearance and to recover the unusual, almost triangular shape of its ground plan. Though it was built to subdue the Welsh they were strong enough even a century later to capture and hold it for a while. Later, in 1404, it was taken by the then unstoppable Owain Glyndŵr who made it his headquarters. One of its last uses was as a royal mint during the Civil War when the mining engineer, Thomas Bushell, made coins there for Charles I out of locally mined silver. The fortifications were finally dismantled by the Cromwellians.

When first made a borough the town was officially called Llanbadarn after the important church a mile inland. Thus in 1405, when Glyndŵr confirmed a treaty with the King of France, he sealed it 'in castro nostro de Llanpadarn' ('in our castle of Llanbadarn'). But an earlier castle called Aberystwyth had long stood near Tanybwlch on the Ystwyth's south bank where its earthworks are still clear to see. And this name must have been popularly transferred to the new stone castle which Edward called Llanbadarn. Presumably the two names existed side by side until the official name was eventually ousted and the name Aberystwyth triumphed. Apart from recent housing Aberystwyth is largely Victorian but there are Georgian houses in Laura Place and elsewhere. The finest public building of this century is the National Library (1911), built here and not at Cardiff only after considerable debate. Besides a very fine stock of books the library has an incomparable collection of early Welsh manuscripts. It also has very interesting art exhibitions. Aberystwyth has no museum but there is an enterprising local one at Tre'r-ddôl, a village nine miles along the road to Machynlleth.

Llanbadarn began as a religious settlement near what in the Dark Ages was the lowest crossing point of the Rheidol river. By the Middle Ages it had become one of the mother churches of Wales and a centre of learning. Here was written at least part of *Brut y Tywysogion* ('The Chronicle of the Princes'), an invaluable source of early medieval history. A solid-looking, cruciform church still stands here, well above the river's flood-plain. Inside it are two ancient Celtic crosses, one elaborately carved; and the arch over the south door is often compared with the famous one at Strata Florida abbey.

Close to Aberystwyth on the south-east is the gorsy hill called Pen Dinas, easily identified by the tall spike on its summit commemorating Wellington. This popular viewpoint, with its triple earth ramparts, is the queen of north Cardiganshire's twenty-nine hill forts for it has yielded the most valuable information to archaeologists. It is really two forts side by side, the southern, larger one being typically 'Iron Age B'; the northern camp is more primitive.

Among former great houses near Aberystwyth two especially had vast possessions and influence: Gogerddan (of the Pryse family) and Nanteos (the Powells). Gogerddan now houses the Welsh Plant Breeding Station, a crop-research centre of world repute. If you happen upon a particularly good-looking field of grass anywhere from China to Peru its strain could well have been developed at Aberystwyth. Nanteos, a large Georgian manor-house in a delightfully wooded valley three miles south-east of Aberystwyth, is open to visitors (afternoons, June–August).

Cardiganshire has one true mountain—Pumlumon (pronounce it 'Pimlimmon') which, if you like, is a stray bit of Snowdonia for it is an outcrop of typically North Wales Ordovician rock poking through the blanket of Silurian rocks that cover much of central Wales. It is most truly mountain-like just west of the 2,468-foot summit where it breaks into scars and crags above a corrie lake. And if you want to see both North and South Wales from one peak, then Pumlumon is your mountain. There are various routes to the top. Perhaps the easiest and driest is up the slopes from Nant-y-moch reservoir. Wetter, but of more interest to lead mine enthusiasts, is the way up from Eisteddfa Gurig. The long-distance hill-walker will do the whole ridge (Pumlumon means 'five summits') from Eisteddfa to Dylife in Montgomeryshire. On his way along the bare summit he will pass several fair-sized Bronze Age cairns or their remains.

The Rheidol river, which rises from Pumlumon's lake, Llygad Rheidol, has some of Cardiganshire's most celebrated scenery along its course. If, as is supposed, the name is connected with the Welsh *rhedeg*, to run, it would mean 'the hastening stream', a good name for a river that gets to the sea in one county and six-teen miles, whereas the Severn, rising only two miles north-east of the Rheidol, does not find the salt till it is six counties and over two hundred miles away. The Rheidol is hardly out of its birth lake when it disappears into the hydro-electric reservoir at Nant-y-moch. At Ponterwyd the river flows under its first main-road bridge, an unbeautiful iron thing compared with the shapely old stone arch nearby. Below Ponterwyd the Rheidol plunges be-tween walls of rock and continues for several miles deep be-tween steep slopes, cutting for itself an incised meander famous among geographers. It curves under a jackdaw-loud crag and flows under woods of spindly oak and birch, near-virgin woods that are a National Nature Reserve. It passes close to lead mine ruins, then under Parson's Bridge where it boils among beauti-fully sculptured pot-holes at the bottom of a dramatic chasm. So it goes on in spume and thunder—see it after heavy rain—all down the gorge till it drops over the falls you see from the Devil's Bridge hotel.

At Ysbyty Cynfyn ('Cynfyn's hospice') between Ponterwyd and Devil's Bridge, prehistoric stones stand in the churchyard wall—one place among several in Wales where Christianity took over the site of a pagan church. For another prehistoric relic go down to Parson's Bridge and up the other side. Near a path across the hillside south of Bryn Bras is a small but perfect Bronze

Age stone circle. When the Rheidol gets to Devil's Bridge it does a sudden turn to the west. Geographers love this as a fine example of river capture. Long ago and at a very much higher level than today the river flowed on southwards to the Teifi; and what is now the lower Rheidol was a separate stream. Eventually this little stream gnawed its way into the course of the main river and diverted it to the west.

Devil's Bridge, where the Rheidol and its tributary the Mynach drop into a spectacular wooded basin, has been a tourists' honey-pot ever since the late eighteenth century. But to get a close look at its falls and bridges and to go round the very interesting nature trail you pay to click through a turnstile. The lowest of the three bridges spanning the Mynach one above the other is medieval and travellers must have had quite a scramble down the gorge side to reach it, then another up from it on the other side. So the eighteenth century built its bridge very much higher and the nineteenth put one higher still. The tradition that the first bridge was built by the monks of Strata Florida abbey is probably a true one. Certainly the Welsh name for it, Pont ar Fynach ('monk's bridge') is old. Who brought the Devil into it no one seems to know but his arrival may well have been a fiction of early guide book writers.

From Devil's Bridge there are twelve miles to the sea. At first the Rheidol valley remains deep and narrow but in a few miles begins to flatten and widen. It is there, three miles upriver from Capel Bangor, that you will find the lowest of the Rheidol's three hydro-electric reservoirs. All up the south side of this valley runs a well-engineered narrow-gauge railway opened in 1902 to bring lead-ore and passengers down to Aberystwyth and lime and other goods up to Devil's Bridge. Today, climbing through the beautiful valley, it flourishes as a summer tourist attraction.[1] Coaches, cars, a railway, a hotel, turnstiles, cafés, postcard stalls: Devil's Bridge has survived all and remains truly splendid. For isolationists there are days when you can muse there almost as solitary as Wordsworth. And for walkers there are the wide spaces of the hills, those skirts of Pumlumon that lie to the south of the pass. From there rise the Mynach's tributaries, Myherin and Rhuddnant, both of which come tumbling in spray and splendour off the moors.

[1] Nature trail leaflets are available both for railway and falls.

Cardiganshire

Though the age of the Devil's Bridge may be a bit unsure, there is certainty about that of the arch that spans the highest point of the turnpike road from Devil's Bridge to Cwmystwyth. It was built by Thomas Johnes of Hafod Uchdryd in 1810 to commemorate the fiftieth year of the reign of George III. The land thereabouts is now the domain of the Forestry Commission; but among the conifers just west of the arch, you will see a relict stand of beeches planted by Johnes about 1800. Go on south into the Ystwyth valley and you soon reach the site of the demolished Hafod house. Here from 1783 to 1815 Johnes lived, a typical Romantic idealist pouring wealth into grandiose schemes. Scholar, politician, farming and forestry pioneer, educationalist, improver of his fellow-men, embellisher of estates, Johnes was an extraordinary force to be let loose in a wild Welsh upland. Here he built two mansions (the first being burnt down); collected rare manuscripts (most were lost in the fire); translated French medieval romances; and printed his own works (these books are now collectors' pieces). Johnes also planted great woodlands. As an obituary notice said, he 'developed and enhanced the sublime scenery of nature by planting millions of trees upon the cheerless barrenness of the wastes and mountains'.

Johnes's house is now a pile of rubble. But close to the east on a hillock is the site of his daughter Mariamne's garden (with a monument to Johnes's friend, the Duke of Bedford, fellow-pioneer of agriculture); between mansion and river is a well-preserved ice-house; and for a really spectacular grotto with waterfall, scramble (after heavy rain) up through the forestry to the head of Nant Gau, a mile south-east. Another interesting Hafod relic is Pont Blaen-y-cwm, the bridge over the Ystwyth two and a half miles upstream from Cwmystwyth. It bears the Hafod crest and is thus described by a nineteenth-century guide book: 'There is an elegant stone bridge over the Ystwyth, built for public accommodation by Baldwin of Bath, at the expense of Mr. Johnes.' In Hafod church is a pathetic Johnes memory— the charred remains of a memorial by Chantry of the dying Mariamne. It was ruined in a fire that burnt down the church in 1932.

The Ystwyth, like most north Cardiganshire streams, flows through lead mine country. These mines, though some may be pre-historic, mainly yielded from the seventeenth to the nine-

Cardiganshire

teenth centuries, the last great fling being in the years before 1885 after which British lead was priced out of the world market. Among the largest derelict lead mines are Cwmsymlog, Cwmerfin, Goginan and Cwmystwyth but there are countless others. Fortunately, although ugly they are scattered over such a wide area that they do only very local harm to the scenery. In fact some of the reservoirs created to serve them are really beautiful; and their leats are most interesting. These were shallow furrows along which water was led from the reservoirs down to the mines which were sometimes several miles away. To provide a steady flow of water these leats were most cunningly engineered, descending so gently from contour to contour, winding circuitously around the slopes and through the hills, that they appear almost level. Though none now contain water they are still visible along many a hillside. Mine buildings are becoming scarce as more and more decay but here and there enough detail survives to show how the ore was processed. Naturalists enjoy these lead mines because the buildings may house wagtails, stock doves, kestrels, barn owls, even ring ouzels and ravens. Or there may be bats in the levels. Or certain plants which, as in North Wales, seem to like lead mines: alpine pennycress, sea campion and forked spleenwort.

The Ystwyth flows down a widening vale to Llanilar whose church is notable for its short, thickset tower and a stone carved with Celtic knots. Six miles south-east, on a tributary of the Ystwyth, are the well-hidden Caradoc falls which drop about a hundred feet into a deep wooded glen at the hamlet of Tyn-y-graig between Trawsgoed and Ystrad Meurig. The tradition is that some local chief named Caradoc was killed by falling down this crag. Inevitably a fictitious connection has been invented linking this event with the ancient memorial stone in the church of Llanwnnws west of the falls. The stone, a Celtic cross, bears ninth-century Latin lettering asking your blessing for the soul of one Carotinn.

West of Llanwnnws the land begins to climb to Mynydd Bach, the moorland that dominates this part of the county. Few people live up there but the frequent ruined cottages tell of more populous times. The land is poor, often sodden, and much of it has gone under conifers. There are peat-bogs and two attractive tarns called Eiddwen and Fanod. From such wet places spring many streams that flow either east to Tregaron Bog or west to the sea. The best known of them is the Aeron which flows down to Llangeitho, a good-looking village with its houses grouped attractively round a square. Here in the eighteenth century a fiery-tongued parson, Daniel Rowland, played a key part in the foundation of Methodism; for whenever he preached thousands flocked to hear him with wild enthusiasm. Below Llangeitho the Aeron valley continues amid verdure and plenty, its floor and sides a mosaic of little pastures and occasional cornfields all neatly squared in by hedges. It comes to the sea at Aberaeron, a former port whose chief product, judging by the gravestones, used to be master mariners.

The coast from Aberystwyth to Aberaeron is, except for a few blemishes, very fine. For the first eight miles there are wild cliffs and steep seaward banks, the breeding place of sea birds and a few grey seals. A mile south of Monk's Cave, in the full rage and spray of the ocean tempests, a stunted oakwood, complete with anemones and bluebells, grows down the slopes in a situation you would think no trees could endure. Because so unusual it has been made a reserve of the West Wales Naturalists' Trust. At Llanrhystud the cliffs fail and for a few miles there is a low-lying coastline of boulder clay and pebbles. Steep hills rise close behind on which are Iron Age forts and also Caerpenrhos, a castle mound built in 1149 and still notable for the size of its earthworks. The Middle Ages also survive on the shore at Llannon where curving banks of stones are the remains of ancient fish-traps which were kept in use until recent times. The tradition that they were first built by the monks of Strata Florida is reasonable, for the abbey's holding came down to the coast.

Visitors to Aberaeron are struck by the neat plan, the wide streets and the late Georgian houses of this New Town of the early nineteenth century grouped round its attractive, narrow-entranced harbour. Once a centre of commerce Aberaeron has become a holiday place particularly frequented by artists and yachtsmen. Four miles south-west is Llannarth, which has come down the hill to embrace life along the main road, leaving its old church behind. Large and Norman, this stands aloof on its rock and is worth visiting for its thirteenth-century tower, its ancient font and its still more ancient Ogham stone which remembers someone of about the fifth century called Gurhirt.

Cardiganshire

South-west of Aberaeron the shore becomes cliffy again for a few miles. Then there is a sandy bay and you are at New Quay, a former sea-trading and ship-building village with a harbour sheltered by an old stone pier. In summer New Quay is a haven for many small yachts but its once beautiful view along the coast is ruined by an excess of caravans. Twenty minutes up-hill walking through gorse and bracken to the cliffs by the coast-guard station brings you to Craig yr Adar (Birds' Rock), Cardiganshire's largest sea bird colony, a congregation of herring gulls, guillemots, razorbills, shags, kittiwakes and fulmars. The fulmars are especially endearing, passing and repassing along the cliff tops, sometimes eyeing you closely. But the kittiwake colony under the cliff is more easily heard than seen and in calm weather is best viewed from a boat. Note here also the intricate folding of the Silurian rocks. Inland for a mile or two the boulder clay is particularly rich in wild flowers.

High cliffs go on south-west of New Quay Head, only seldom parting to admit hamlets with tiny coves squeezed in at the bottom of winding, wooded glens. In such places, Cwmtudu and Penbryn for example, cars are a problem at the height of summer and the best time to enjoy these idyllic spots is the early spring when fewer people are about, the woods are in fresh leaf, the cliff flowers are sheets of gaiety down the slopes and birds are singing and nesting everywhere. Between Cwmtudu (pronounced 'Cumtiddy') and Penbryn is the larger village of Llangrannog with a popular sandy beach. Here are fine cliff walks, especially north to the peninsula of Ynys Lochdyn. For one of the great viewpoints of the Welsh coast climb to Pen Moel-ciliau which at 710 feet is the highest point on the Cardigan coast. From there you command most of Cardigan Bay but the gem is the lovely curve and shape of Lochdyn itself, especially at full tide when its tip becomes an island. One day at Ynys Lochdyn some local singers unknowingly sang their way into Elgar's *Introduction and Allegro for Strings*. As Elgar wrote later: 'On the cliff, between blue sea and blue sky, thinking out my theme, there came up to me the sound of singing. . . . Fitting the need of the moment I made the tune which appears in the *Introduction*.'

In a field in a triangle of lanes between Penbryn and Tresaith stands a stone of about the fifth century whose inscription means: 'The stone of Corbalengus. Here he lies, an Ordovician.' So

Cardiganshire

Corbalengus was a man from North Wales who died in Cardiganshire; and the great interest of the stone is that it shows the tribal divisions of the Iron Age Celts persisting into the early Dark Ages. The coast goes on westwards in wildness and beauty except at Tresaith which has caravans and Aberporth Head which has been developed as a rocket research station and looks decidedly squalid. Otherwise the cliffs are magnificent and the contortions of the rocks extraordinary. Mwnt, with its fine sandy beach, has so far not been spoilt. But when you admire its ancient church and the open space around it remember that it is so preserved only by virtue of an anti-caravan campaign that was fought and won here. In this austere little medieval church pilgrims used to say a final mainland prayer before sailing across to Bardsey Island over forty miles north. Mwnt means 'mount' and is so called from the 250-foot viewpoint hill that shelters the church from the westerlies. From Mwnt stretch three miles of little cliffs to Gwbert at the mouth of the Teifi. In May the cliff-edge turf is patched blue with vernal squill and all summer you may see house martins racing like storm petrels over the waves and swooping up into the cliffs where they glue their nests. Offshore is Cardigan Island, a reserve of the West Wales Naturalists' Trust who have introduced a herd of small, dark-brown Viking sheep. A few sea birds nest there and, as all along this coast, there are choughs and seals.

The Teifi estuary winds beautifully from Gwbert up to Cardigan which, now a market and holiday town, was until last century a busy port and ship-building yard. In the Middle Ages and long after, it was a centre of authority over a wide area and there was a castle at what is now Old Castle farm until in the thirteenth century it was replaced by one which stood dominant above the Teifi bridge; and near where the parish church now is there was a Benedictine priory: but both castle and priory have gone. Along the river relict wharfages tell of ships that came and went. Over the river is a massive six-arched bridge of the seventeenth century but partly rebuilt and of course widened since then. An inscription above one of the cutwaters reads: 'This arch was built in ye year 1726 W. Jones.' But you have to lean over to see it, so be careful.

Fair Tivy, how sweet are thy waves gently flowing,
Thy wild oaken woods and green eglantine bowers.

Cardiganshire

Yes, the Teifi has always brought paeans from the poets, for it is a totally beautiful river. The oaken woods still survive, a few of them, especially as tongues up the side valleys; and honeysuckle bowers still hang along the hedges. At the waterside are dippers and grey wagtails; and more kingfishers than anywhere else in the county. With extreme luck you might see an otter; or even one of the mink that have naturalized themselves here as the result of escapes from fur farms: but both are nocturnal. No good at all to look for beavers for they were already extinct by the twelfth century. But Giraldus says they survived in the Teifi when gone from everywhere else. Sea-trout and salmon are the outstanding Teifi fish and have always been netted from coracles which in prehistoric times were made from animal skins but are now of tarred fabric. Not only used for fishing they are now popular pleasure boats and there is an annual coracle regatta in August at Cilgerran. Coracle handling calls for skill so learn to swim first. Should you fancy taking one home it will cost you £15 or so. You carry it on your back as a tortoise his shell.

The Teifi is the longest river of Cardiganshire. And because for many miles it was the frontier of the old Welsh province, afterwards the Norman lordship of Ceredigion, it has seen a great sweep of history along its banks. Not all its towns and villages are in Cardiganshire; some belong to Pembroke, others to Carmarthenshire; but it will be convenient to bring them all into this chapter. At Cilgerran, on the Pembrokeshire bank, the Teifi winds deep, green and slow under the ruins of a high-placed Norman castle with two great round towers and a massive gatehouse: though not built by order of Edward I they are very much of that style and century.

Upstream the gorge is soon left behind, the valley widens and you come to Llechryd which has a picturesque nine-arched bridge that is old beyond the telling. It bears the date 1695 (that of a repair?) on the upstream side near the Pembrokeshire end. Nearby is a delightful river-bank walk, flowery with tall waterside plants such as balsam and hemp agrimony. At Manordeifi you come to an abandoned thirteenth-century church. It retains its medieval font and has box pews, two at the front fitted with fireplaces. (So the gentry sat snug and warm while the plebs suffered Arctic draughts further back.) This much-flooded church was equipped with a coracle—it is still there—to rescue the prayer books as the waters rose. A feature of the churchyard is the elaborate wrought iron round some graves, the work of a school of local craftsmen. This has also been a region of wood carvers and turners. One of their centres was the valley of the Cych, or Cuch (pronounced 'keek'), a north-flowing, wooded stream dividing Pembroke from Carmarthenshire. Welsh love-spoons, now in demand as antiques, were carved in great numbers here and a few still are, usually from sycamore wood. In former days young men used to carve them as presents for their sweet-hearts.

Cenarth, a picnickers' paradise east of Aber-cuch, is popular for its lovely cataracts, its leaping salmon, its eighteenth-century bridge and its coracles, here at what is traditionally their highest point of the river. Perhaps built about 1800 the bridge, judging by its weight-saving, circular openings, was copied from William Edward's bridges at Pontypridd, Dolauhirion and elsewhere. Upstream on the Carmarthen side is Newcastle Emlyn where the river makes a couple of sportive loops, one of which neatly en-closes the castle. When built in the thirteenth century the castle was called 'new' to distinguish it from the motte and bailey castle whose mound still survives at Adpar on the Cardigan bank. River-moated on three sides the 'new' castle has a lovely site. But the castle itself has stood pitiably ruined ever since Crom-well's soldiery blew it up with a thoroughness unusual even for them. The present remains are not from the thirteenth but the fifteenth century when the castle was rebuilt as a fortified resi-dence. Plant-seekers will be interested to see Danish scurvy-grass on the walls—a long way inland for this normally sea-coast species. Across the river in Adpar a slate tablet commemorates the setting up in 1718 of the first printing press in Wales. The first book printed in Wales was issued the following year.

Henllan, three miles upstream from Newcastle Emlyn, has one of the Teifi's loveliest reaches and a shapely, three-arched bridge. See if you can find the rather elusive inscription dating it to 1774. With this bridge compare the one which soars high over the river at Allt-y-cafn. For details of its building in 1839 consult an inscription on the parapet. At the end of the bridge is a weaving mill with shop attached. In the days when every little tributary turned the wheel of at least one mill the weaving industry used to be centred on Llandysul, the next place upriver from Allt-y-cafn. Llandysul is now a little market town where the Teifi rushes through narrow rocks and is exciting for canoeists. The Early English church has an altar stone (in the Lady Chapel) and an inscribed stone, both of the Dark Ages.

If you want a good viewpoint hill fort in this district go to Dinascerdin four miles north-west of Llandysul. It stands above a valley that comes down from heather moors through a land full of subtle and quiet beauties. Connoisseurs' country you might call it. It is crossed by delicious lanes some of which soon languish into tracks abandoned by modern traffic. Dinascerdin is named on the one-inch map. But a more striking fort, three-quarters of a mile east across the valley, is not. This is Carn Wen whose defences on the south-east still include a wall of loose stones twelve feet high. This fort too has a fine view down the Cerdin to another fort-crowned hill, Pen Coed-foel, which in turn looks across the Teifi to another good hill fort, Craig Gwrtheyrn ('Vortigern's rock'), by tradition one of the several places in Wales where that fifth-century king of all Britain lurked after his fall from power. Craig Gwrtheyrn has two special points of interest: it is a rare example of a hill fort connected by name with an historically authenticated person living when some Iron Age forts were still occupied; and its entrance is guarded by slight remains of *chevaux de frise*. Look for them on the left near the bottom of the south-west entrance.

The lack of thirteenth-century castles for many miles of the Teifi above Newcastle Emlyn suggests that by then the conquerors felt themselves secure enough not to need any. But before then the middle Teifi was in the thick of the bloody side of life, for castle mounds of about the twelfth century are many. There are for instance Castell Pistog, two miles west of Llandysul; Castell Hywel, a mile and a half north of Rhydowen; and Tomen Rhydowen, a few hundred yards south of Rhydowen, a village where the memory of a great schoolmaster is ever green. He was the Reverend David Davis (1745–1827) through whose hands passed many who later achieved distinction. He is remembered too for his elegant Welsh version of Gray's *Elegy*. Tree-lovers will like the old hedgerow oak guarded by a fence just south of Rhydowen crossroads: under it Davis received ordination.

Upstream from Llandysul the Teifi valley broadens, giving room for farms and fertility. The slopes remain high, there are scattered woodlands and, on both sides, winding lanes give you sudden glimpses of the river. At Llanllwni an embattled church tower stands like a castle above the trees. Below is a gorge and a flowery river-bank walk; and a bridge which has two curious coffin-shaped decorations, one at each end of the upstream parapet. For fine craftsmanship go to the tall-towered church of Llanwenog where a pictorial local history has been well carved on the bench ends, beginning with Giraldus's famous journey of 1188. The work, which has been disparaged as un-Welsh, is by the nineteenth-century Belgian sculptor Joseph Reubens and was sponsored by the former owners of Highmead house (now a school). The church also has a font with, presumably, the twelve apostles carved round the outside. They have faces that grimace at you from the dark side of the Middle Ages, faces with huge grotesque eyes and flat noses, looking more Aztec than Welsh. Even more ancient-looking is the little effigy showing three carved figures preserved above the altar. A stained-glass window at the west end was fired at Highmead and may be the only surviving stained glass made in Cardiganshire. There is good black lettering on the walls, three beautifully embroidered panels, a fifteenth-century bell-frame in the tower; and on the outside by the west door are worn faces and escutcheons. From the top of the tower is a great view of the vale of Teifi towards Llanybyther (Llanybydder), a quiet enough village except on the last Thursday of each month when you meet horsy people from the four corners of the world gathered for the biggest horse-fair in the British Isles. Every sort of horse-flesh is on sale from English hunters to Irish donkeys.

The name Lampeter is an ancient Anglicization of Llanbedr (both are stressed on the first syllable) and to give the place its full dignity we must call it Llanbedr Pont Steffan ('the church of St. Peter by Stephen's bridge'). Not that we know who this beneficent Stephen was or when he built his bridge; but it was known to Giraldus as Stephen's bridge when he crossed it in 1188. The present four-arched bridge is nineteenth century. Lampeter never had a stone castle. Strong Norman influence was early in these parts and no castle was needed after the wooden one decayed on its mound which is in the grounds of St. David's

College. This college, Lampeter's most important building, grants B.A. and B.D. degrees, has long specialized in theology but now leans towards the arts. It was long a male preserve, women students not being admitted till 1965. Its oldest part (1827) is neo-Gothic, in imitation of an Oxford college.

The names of former great houses near Lampeter: Peterwell, Falcondale and Derry Ormond show how until recent times the Welsh gentry strove to be as English as possible. Peterwell, just outside the town on the west, is a desolate ruin approached down a long avenue of old limes. In its heyday it was towered and palatial. Derry Ormond, three miles north, is still known for its tower conspicuous on a hill though the house no longer exists. It is a viewpoint tower with steps up inside but is now too ruinous for use. A roadside curiosity close to Llangybi is the milestone known as the sightmen's stone. ('Sightman' presumably meant a surveyor.) The inscription on the stone reads: 'To Lampeter four miles by Timothy Jacob and Samuel Davies sight men in the year 1768.' In a field on the same side of the road a little nearer Llangybi is St. Cybi's holy well, now in a neglected state, in contrast with Cybi's other well in Caernarvonshire.

Above Lampeter you can, if so minded, get stuck with some choice Roman road problems. For though there is nothing left above ground of the fort at Llanio (which the Romans may have called Bremia) there are roads going off north to Trawsgoed, south to Pumsaint and south-west to Lampeter. Whether you trace these roads very far or not you will always be in splendid country, often close to the Teifi and its green, trout-ringed pools. And there are fine bridges such as Pont Gogoyan and the one at Llanfair Clydogau. You will find a fragment of one of Llanio's Roman stones at the church at Llanddewi Brefi, a place deeply involved in Cardiganshire's early history. The name means 'the church of David on the Brefi' a stream that hastens down through the village and under a stone-arched bridge. The large medieval but much altered church contains a striking modern statue of St. David barefooted and carrying staff and bell. There are five inscribed stones in the church dating from the sixth to the ninth centuries. A sixth stone, recalling one Idnert, is built into the outside north-west wall. It is in two pieces, one of which is upside down because it made a better

corner stone that way. So you have to be rather athletic to read
it. In this church in the seventeenth century Lhuyd was shown a
relic that had long been safeguarded there—the core of a massive
ox-horn seventeen inches round the base. Now kept at St.
Fagan's Museum, Cardiff, it has been identified as the horn of
the prehistoric ox, *Bos primigenius*. No doubt someone dug it out
of a local peat-bog and, thinking it might be a holy relic, put it
in the church.

South from Llanddewi a climbing, winding road goes over
the hills and down to Ffarmers in Carmarthenshire. It has always
been a fine viewpoint road but conifers along both sides are
changing all that. North from Llanddewi you are soon in Tregaron, a name that goes back to Caron, a holy man of about the
seventh century. Tregaron is a small town whose life is farming
and rural trading. Its sheep sales are famous and on market days
(Tuesday) farmers from a wide area meet here and talk of sheep,
cattle, ponies and each other for hours on end. When some years
ago the military authorities tried to commandeer a tract of the
local mountains the whole neighbourhood rose and said no. And
the military, perhaps a bit astonished at the strength of the rebuff,
went elsewhere. They doubtless had no inkling of the influence
bequeathed by leaders such as Henry Richard, M.P. (1812–88),
'the apostle of peace', whose bottle-green statue stands in
speechful pose in Tregaron square.

East of Tregaron stretches the heart of the central Welsh
moorlands, a vast area mostly of grassy hills rising to about
1,600 feet. Traditionally a domain of sheep it is being increasingly invaded by conifers. A road through it all is the drovers'
road up Cwm Berwyn and eventually down to the Towy. Or,
when still two and a half miles west of the Towy, you can fork
south-east down the Camddwr and come to the loneliest place
of religion in all Wales, the chapel of Soar-y-mynydd, built to
serve a community now quite drained away. The Bronze Age
peoples throve on these hills and their cairns still crown many
summits. Then the Iron Age had their hill forts, notably the
high-placed camp of Castell Rhyfel, three and a quarter miles
east of Tregaron. In the Middle Ages was built Cwys yr
Ychain-banog ('the furrow of the yoked oxen'), a simple ditch
and bank climbing for a mile and a half over the cairned hill
marked Garn Gron, a little north of Castell Rhyfel. It probably

helped to divide the lands of Strata Florida abbey from those of some potentate on the south.

About a mile north-west of Tregaron the main road to Aberystwyth crosses the Teifi on yet another admirable stone bridge, Pont Einon. From it you look north across the greatest surviving Welsh peat-bog, a four-mile stretch of undrained wilderness occupying a wide saucer between the hills. In summer it is lovely when hundreds of its acres blow white with the tassels of the cotton sedge. In winter the stems and leaves of this sedge glow a deep rich red, a colour that gives the name Cors Goch to many a bog in Wales and gives to this bog of Tregaron the name Cors Goch Glanteifi ('the red bog along the Teifi'). Go in spring and the place yodels, sobs and scolds as you disturb curlews, peewits, black-headed gulls, sedge warblers, reed buntings and other marsh birds. In winter it is a place of ducks and snipe and foraging birds of prey. Botanically it is similar to Cors Fochno, Borth: a final refuge of the three sundew species, of bog rosemary and other diminishing plants. Its pollen-preserving depths, like those of Cors Fochno, tell of the natural history of thousands of years. Understandably it has become a National Nature Reserve.

Set between hills at the north end of the great bog the Norman castle of Ystrad Meurig controlled an important east-west route, so acting as a support for the castle at Aberystwyth. But it early fell ruinous and its remains are slight. And Ystrad Meurig today is better known for its tiny grammar school, St. John's College, that survives from the eighteenth century and has educated many famous Welshmen. Nearby the Teifi comes down from the moors to pass under its highest important bridge, the humpy, single arch at Pontrhydfendigaid ('the bridge by the blessed ford') a name clearly linked with the nearby abbey of Strata Florida. To this district in 1164 came some of the Cistercian monks of Alba Landa (Whitland, Carmarthenshire) to found a daughter-abbey in these solitudes between the great bog and the hills. They made a preliminary settlement in Ystrad Fflur two miles south-west of the present abbey, at a site still called Old Abbey. And following their quaint custom that was ridiculed by rival orders they Latinized Ystrad Fflur to Strata Florida ('the flowery vale'). Eventually they moved to the present site, building there a fine abbey which was completed in the thirteenth century. This they achieved under the protection of the house of Dynefwr, Carmarthenshire, the most powerful family then in South Wales.

At its height Strata Florida controlled a real commercial empire in central Wales, dealing in sheep, wool and lead. It was a centre of learning and had such repute for sanctity that the nobility were brought here from distant parts for burial. Here too, probably, was buried the fourteenth-century poet, Dafydd ap Gwilym. The abbey was built of local stone but dressed with sandstone which must have been brought from afar. If, as is claimed, it came from Somerset it may well have been shipped from there to Aberarth, a harbour known to have had Strata Florida connections. Alas, of the noble abbey very little remains, the elegant west doorway being the most noteworthy survival. The ground plan is clear to see and there are grave slabs, tiled floors and a collection of well-carved stones.

The source lake of the Teifi lies close to five others in a far-stretching moorland solitude. To reach these pools you can take the lane that goes east from the hamlet of Ffair-rhos, once a more important place whose annual fair was for centuries one of Cardiganshire's most eagerly attended events. After some climbing and twisting you come up to the watershed and see the lakes gleaming attractively on your right among rocks, ridges and heather. All this beauty quite escaped Leland in the sixteenth century: 'The ground al about Tyve and a great mile toward Stratfler is horrible with the sighte of bare stones.' But he had to admit that in the lake there are 'veri good trouttes and elys'.

If you go on along the track east from the Teifi lakes you see on your left a hill crowned by a low cairn. Near it lie interesting old lead mine reservoirs, the Fyrddon pools, from which you can trace a skilfully engineered leat that took water winding gently south-west down to the mines at Esgair-mwyn. Far away in the south-east you look across miles of grassy hills to the prominent cairn on Drygarn Fawr in Breconshire. This little road east from the Teifi pools was the link between the abbeys of Strata Florida and Cwmhir. But here and there it takes a bit of finding, especially where it forks left off the main track (which I take to be a drovers' road) about 450 paces beyond the crossing of the Claerddu. A hollow rush-covered path it climbs shyly away, loses itself in bogs, dips down to the Claerwen then up the

148

other side into Radnorshire, passing south of two small lakes then north of the Elan reservoirs. If you walk that quiet path on a day when the cloud shadows are playing across the wide pale grasslands you will have seen what is perhaps the very best of Ceredigion and will understand why Wordsworth called it 'the sweet shire'.

8

RADNORSHIRE
(Maesyfed or Sir Faesyfed)

Whenever I travel west across north Herefordshire I feel a growing delight as stronger country builds up ahead, shaping itself at last into the many highhills of Radnorshire. Herefordshire in its lowland way is altogether beautiful. But near the border you begin to feel a more exciting, wilder sort of beauty. Once you are over the Roman road at Mortimer's Cross (Mortimer is a name to remember as you go on into Radnorshire) you are faced with an increasing barrier of uplands where main roads are rare. Instead there is a bewilderment of hills with twisty lanes going round them, dipping you unexpectedly into hidden hamlets and abruptly out again, lifting you in the end to exhilarating viewpoint ridges. Along those lanes you are rarely sure whether you are in England or in Wales. Where the main roads cross the frontier the fact is made known to you by signs that say 'Croeso i Gymru, Welcome to Wales'. But the little lanes say nothing. They slip back and forth across the border without hail or farewell.

Gradually the greater roads are losing their worst bends but the lanes for long years yet will keep close to the wriggling streams, perpetuating the lines of ancient footways. And what delicious streams they are that flow east across this tilted borderland. There is the Arrow that springs from heather moor near Glascwm. Go, if you can in early spring and see the Arrow when the alder catkins are out and the whole length of the river is a

purple ribbon waving down the valley. A little to the north of
Radnor Forest springs the Lugg and its tributaries and their exploration will take you to splendid places like Beacon Hill and
Bailey Hill where there is enough scenery and natural and
human history to keep you happy for as long as you like. It was
down the Lugg valley that the forces of Owain Glyndŵr came
rampaging in June 1402, and amid terrible carnage overwhelmed an English army under Edmund Mortimer. A sad
thought to inflict on you in such an agreeable place; but should
you go there you may wonder what are the two great mounds
that stand near the river's edge at Pilleth. Some say (but others
deny it) that these huge heaps were piled over the eleven hundred
men who died that summer day. North of the Lugg flows
another good river, the Teme, which flirts with the boundary
between Radnorshire and Shropshire for a dozen miles from
Felindre down to Knighton and beyond.

Arrow, Lugg, Teme—their names may look English enough:
yet at heart they are pure Welsh. Arrow was once Arwy, Lugg
was Llugwy, Teme was Tefeidiad. Many other Radnor names
have been similarly Anglicized: Knucklas was Cnwclas,
Monaughty (a 1636 farmhouse with monastic associations) was
Mynachdy, Clyro was Cleirwy. Look around and you will find
other such changelings in this county that from an early date was
penetrated by English influences. For Radnorshire lies within a
horseshoe of high moorlands, a horseshoe that opens towards
England. Its life and its trade have gone the way of its rivers. It is
not just Lugg, Teme and Arrow that flow east. So do all the
others: for even those which go first to the west turn east with
the Wye at last. So Radnorshire has had less contact with the rest
of Wales than perhaps any other Welsh county and the old language has virtually gone. You will find that even the shepherds
on the far western moors above the Elan speak English only. Or
go round the churchyards and see how few are the Welsh
epitaphs on the stones.

North Radnorshire continues those Silurian rocks of mid-
Wales whose characteristic upland scenery is gently undulating
moorland here and there cut into by deep valleys. Radnor Forest
is typical—a great dome of shales and flagstones reaching to over
2,000 feet and given mountain qualities where the Harley
Dingle nearly cuts it in two, forming steep slopes that climb to

crags such as Great Creigiau, a name that is typical Radnor mixture. Though invaded in our day by conifers the Forest is traditional sheep country. Now largely depopulated it was never a kind place to live in. As some one put it in 1599: 'The air thereof is sharp and cold for that the snow lieth and lasteth long unmelted under those shadowing high hills and overhanging rocks. The soil is hungry, rough and churlish and hardly bettered by painful labour.'

Not that peaty, acid moorlands and deep intervening valleys are all of Radnorshire. Here and there the Silurian cover has worn away to expose hard igneous rocks that stand up as rough, distinctive prominences such as Llandegle Rocks, Gilwern Hill and the Carneddau—all not far from Llandrindod; and Hanter Hill, Worsell Wood, Old Radnor Hill and Stanner Rocks—all in the east. These igneous rocks are often known locally as 'roadstone', which indicates their commonest use. Some of them have a distinctive wild flora comparable with that of similar, semi-upland, basic igneous rocks in North Wales, Stanner Rocks being particularly well known for their show of rockrose, rock stonecrop and other gay species. Let me quote what a guide book of about a century ago said of these dark-grey Stanner Rocks: 'From their peculiarity of form, rather than from their height, they are truly grand and romantic. The hollows in their rugged sides and summits abound with a variety of rare and beautiful wild flowers, and hence they are popularly called The Devil's Garden.' But why the Devil should have been credited with the provision of beautiful wild flowers is a mystery. Botanists regard the conifers now covering most of this hill as more like the Devil's work!

Further variety in Radnor's rocks and therefore its flora comes from the presence of limestone which forms hills at Nash Rocks near Presteigne, and Dolyhir near Old Radnor. But both sites are being extensively quarried and are far from beautiful. Then just as the Ordovician rocks of north-west Wales dive beneath the Silurian in mid-Wales, so the Silurian in their turn disappear under the less ancient rocks of the Old Red Sandstone. This division is clear to see as you go south-east across Radnorshire and suddenly come to the red soils along the north side of the Wye between Boughrood and Clyro. In that fertile strip of farmland you are in Herefordshire before you get there.

Radnorshire

In Radnorshire birdwatchers should take to the uplands—which is not difficult in a county which in only 470 square miles has a hundred hills over 1,500 feet. On these grassy and heathy tops there are plenty of grouse, skylarks, meadow pipits, cuckoos and wheatears. And where streams have cut back into the heather zone to form little craggy places you may hear the four or five piped notes of the ring ouzel or get a glimpse of a merlin. Here and there on the moors are what the map calls Mawn Pools. They are little peaty tarns (*mawn* is Welsh for peat and rhymes with brown) and though usually rather bird-less they occasionally harbour colonies of black-headed gulls. And at such pools there is always a chance of some unexpected rarity, even a nesting pair of dunlin. This corner of Radnorshire was formerly a stronghold of the now rare red kite. Just over a century ago a man near Rhayader used to sell young kites as pets to passengers on the stage-coaches that ran from London and Cheltenham to Aberystwyth by way of Rhayader and Cwmystwyth. Today one is lucky to see a kite anywhere in Radnorshire so nearly exterminated were they by ruthless nineteenth-century gamekeepers.

Most botanists will be happiest in those central and southern parts of Radnorshire where the soils are varied by the presence of igneous rocks and limestones. There are not only Stanner Rocks. There is also the fertile Wye valley below Builth and delightful Wye tributaries such as Edw and Bach Howey (Bachawy) which go dropping down ravines and dingles in cool shade and the spray of waterfalls. (Plant-seeker or not you will enjoy the falls of the Bach Howey under the rocks of Craig Pwll-du.) Jacob's ladder, impatient bittercress, wild chives, Solomon's seal, spiked speedwell, perennial knawel, red catchfly and both the hellebores: these are among the choicer plants recorded for south Radnorshire. For bog plants go to Rhosgoch common; for water plants there are lakes such as Heilyn, Llanbwchllyn and Gwyn. For a fertility symbol see the massive yew in the churchyard at Llanfaredd, two miles east of Builth.

If you enjoy following ancient trackways, especially those that need a bit of ferreting out, you will find plenty of sport in Radnorshire: towards the Montgomeryshire border, for example, or on Radnor Forest or between there and Llandrindod. Or follow the monks' road from Abbey Cwmhir to the west

over Moel Hywel, crossing the Wye near the Marteg confluence and up past the head of the highest Elan reservoir, soon
to cross the Elan and climb away over the hills on a delicious
line for Strata Florida abbey in Cardiganshire. Note near the
head of the reservoir the significant name Aberhenllan ('the
stream-mouth by the old church'), significant because doubtless
there stood here a chapel in medieval times, a half-way port of
call for the brethren as they journeyed between these two Cistercian abbeys. The chapel's exact site is now lost but why not try
to discover it? For old routes in general read a quaint book called
The Old Straight Track by Alfred Watkins (1925). Though you
believe not one word of his theories about the origins of trackways his enthusiasm for them will probably get you out in the
field looking for them. If so, though the north may offer the
best long-distance tracks, you will find good shorter routes in
the centre and south: using Gladestry, for instance, as a centre
you can walk over Caety Traylow to Llyn Heilyn, or over
Colva Hill to Glascwm or, quitting Radnorshire, there is a walk
with fine views over Hergest Hill to Kington in Herefordshire.
Hergest, by the way, though English for the past many centuries,
is a name inseparable from the annals of Wales: one of the most
treasured of ancient Welsh manuscripts, *The Red Book of Hergest*,
which contains some of the *Mabinogion* tales, was once possessed
by the Vaughans of Hergest Court.

Radnorshire is not famous for traces of early man. In fact it is
possibly the only Welsh county that never had a Stone Age
burial chamber. But in recent years hundreds of chipped flints,
including many tools, have been found in ploughed fields between New Radnor and Evenjobb, finds that prove the existence
of a considerable Mesolithic culture previously unsuspected in
central Wales. In the Bronze Age the signs of man become
plentiful in the form of the tumuli and cairns that are still scattered about the hills. Bronze Age man seems to have had a particular liking for the district around Rhayader, both to the north
towards St. Harmon and to the south where there are several
cairns on Gwastedyn Hill. It was in a crack in the rocks on this
hill in 1899 that a local youth found a Bronze Age gold necklet,
two armlets and a ring. They are now in the British Museum.
On the other side of the county in 1955 three gold torcs were
found buried in a ploughed field on the north slope of Bailey

Hill near Knighton. The gold of those times is reckoned to have come from the Wicklow Mountains of Ireland.

Of Iron Age hill forts, so liberally scattered throughout Wales, there are notable examples in Radnorshire, none being finer than Burfa Camp which is almost on Offa's Dyke near Evenjobb. Occupying twenty acres on top of its 1,000-foot hill this camp's splendid ramparts lie in an oval 2,000 feet long and 600 feet across. If from this great camp you follow Offa's Dyke two miles north-east you reach another good, though less elaborate Iron Age fort called the Castle Ring. Unfortunately it has now been planted over with trees. Another worthwhile hill fort which, from the west side of Radnorshire spies upon miles of Breconshire, is Caer Einon on the Carneddau hills near Builth, hills that are rich in traces of prehistory and history. From nearly 1,300 feet Caer Einon looks upon one of the classic views of Wales—the Wye valley below Builth with the Brecon Beacons high beyond.

Iron Age hill forts bring us to the Roman time for within them the Celtic peoples had their homesteads while the Roman legions dominated the lowlands. In Radnorshire the chief Roman fort was at Castell Collen, a good defensive position by the Eithon a mile north of Llandrindod. From here a Roman road ran northwards over the hills and down to the Severn at Caersŵs in Montgomeryshire. Another went south to Brecon. But, especially on the north road, their exact courses offer many problems. Another Roman road edged along the south from Clyro to Brecon but to follow that one also calls for patience and determination. Offa's Dyke, at its best in Shropshire north-west of Knighton, continues south into Radnorshire where you can easily pick it up in the sections marked on the one-inch map between Knighton and Burfa Camp. And as well as Offa's there are several short dykes which could belong to the Dark or the Middle Ages. One easily visited example is Ditch Bank, a well-preserved short dyke breached by the main road a good mile south-west of New Radnor. It is reckoned to be the remains of a manorial boundary. Other short dykes are high up on Radnor Forest.

If you are a castle enthusiast you may find Radnorshire rather unspeakable. It has had castles, lots of them, but stone by stone they have collapsed and been carted off for other purposes. So much so that the sites of even the biggest look little different from the earth banks of Iron Age forts. For this there are doubtless good reasons. When Edward I conquered Wales he had no need to build great Harlech-style castles in Radnorshire for the district had long been subdued by the de Braoses and the Mortimers. Besides it may well be doubted whether really enduring castles could have been built even by Edward out of the rocks of most of Radnorshire. For instead of splitting into the square blocks needed for great castles these rocks mostly break into small irregular shapes unsuited to high walling. So what castle walls were built presumably soon fell down or were easily destroyed.

So the castle-seeker has to be content mainly with sites only, some of them in forlorn and lonely spots with little or no history and which would have been forgotten long ago if their mounds were not so enduring. For an easily reached motte and bailey I recommend Castell Crugerydd four miles from Penybont on A44. Even castle-despisers will enjoy this one for its far views south and west down the Edw valley and over the Wye to Breconshire. At nearly 1,300 feet this was a high-placed castle: hence its probable original name of Crug Eryr ('the eagle's mount'). An even higher castle site is at Castelltinboeth (1,332 feet), a Mortimer castle built on an Iron Age fort. It stands high above A483 nearly two miles up the road from Llanbister. Leland in the sixteenth century refers to it as a castle 'cawllid Tynbot, set on a stepe crage'. In the Middle Ages the establishing of a castle was often followed by that of a town that sheltered in its protection and has endured into the modern world. In Radnorshire this has happened only at Rhayader, Presteigne and Knighton, leaving once-important castled places such as Knucklas, Norton, Painscastle and Cefn-llys to decline into small settlements.

For a castle mound of lavish extent visit the dwindled village of Painscastle. Not a stone of this once considerable castle remains above ground but the motte and encircling banks and ditches are quite remarkable. Similarly extensive, the massively formed, lofty castle earthworks above the church at New Radnor are delightful for their view across the vale. In that view is the site of the much earlier Old Radnor castle quaintly called Castle Nimble which is perhaps a pre-Norman relic whose mound has almost gone, leaving only the encircling banks. But on the way down to it from Old Radnor church, the remains of an avenue of great ash trees make the walk worth while. Some of them are very thick in the trunk and swollen by great burs. They march up the hill presumably to form a vista to take the eye from Harpton Court up to a noble view of the tall tower of the church. (Near this church ignore the castle-site marked on some maps: a moated house, not a castle, probably stood there.) Among other castle sites are those at Rhayader (perched above the Wye), Aberedw, Boughrood and Knucklas (where some Mortimer walls remain). A prominent moated house-site, Court Llechryd, can be seen from A483, a mile and a half north-west of Builth.

Time, the weather and, most of all, destructive man have reduced several Cistercian monasteries in Wales to pitiful fragments. But few have suffered more than the abbey that stood in Cwmhir, the name given to part of the Clywedog valley six miles north of Llandrindod. A path from the road down a grassy bank overhung by large sycamores leads you to flat fields along the stream. There you find only the stumps of walls picturesquely overgrown by wych elms, hawthorns, birdsfoot trefoil and crosswort. Out of such fragmentary signs it requires all your imagination to build up the monastic church with nave eighty yards long—the greatest church in Wales—that once stood here with its attendant buildings and its fishponds. In fact the fishponds are easier to visualize than anything else, for the stream still flattens out into the marshy shallows that mark their sites, and traces of the dams are still there.

Some beautiful fragments of stone masonry have been found on the site of the church but as an account of 1822 reported: 'The fine freestone of this abbey has tempted the predatory hands of modern architects who have plundered its ruins to repair the church at Llanidloes and other public edifices.' But even when Leland went there (in the 1530's) the devastation was already formidable: 'Comehere an abbay of White Monkes stondith betwixt ii great hilles in Melennith in a botom wher rennith a litle brooke. No chirch in Wales is seene of such lenght as the fundation of walles there begon doth show; but the third part of this worke was never finisched. Al the howse was spoilid and defacid be Owen Glindour.'

If medieval Radnorshire has little to say to us through its castles or its abbeys, at least a few of its churches are eloquent.

Radnorshire

Not eloquent of past glories but of the simple life of people living far up the remotest valleys, many of which are reached even today only by narrow, crooked lanes. Among them are primitive little churches that are practically deserted because of the depopulation of the uplands and which, despite efforts to preserve them, smell inside of dankness and decay. Still, they have stood squat and solid on their thick walls for many centuries and will stand a while yet. I think of Rhulen, a church that will appeal to lovers of homespun churches that have not a scrap of pretence or pageantry. This thirteenth-century churchlet is white-washed on the outside, its west wall is leaning outwards while its east wall has long done battle with the roots of an ancient yew. It stands alone up a little hill at the side of a narrow lane with high hedges. The population of its parish in 1847 was 129; in 1901 it was 59; now it is down to 30.

Not far away is the sister church of Cregrina, also thirteenth century and very simple with its crude, ancient screen. It seems fitting, in so primitive a building, that the chancel should be out of line with the nave. Cregrina hamlet stands quietly by a musical stretch of the Edw river. Like other Radnor villages it has known far more life in the past when cattle drovers used to pass that way. One of its claims to historical distinction is that in nearby Penarth wood the last wolf in Radnorshire was killed in early Tudor times. Both Rhulen and Cregrina are daughter churches to Glascwm, a delightful little village high up the narrow valley to the east. Glascwm was important in medieval church affairs, which is why its church is outsize for so small a place.

For elegance and historical interest perhaps no church in the county competes with Old Radnor. English in style it contains a finely executed medieval screen reckoned to be the work of Gloucestershire craftsmen. There is a splendid panelled roof and a rare and beautifully carved organ case of the early sixteenth century. The large font, hollowed out of a block of rock, was presumably a glacial erratic like the Four Stones a mile north. It is certainly a very early Christian relic and may well have been a standing stone before that. Old Radnor church has long since lost its rood loft. So in fact has every Radnorshire church that ever had one except Llananno. But Llananno church, delightfully alone on the banks of the Eithon eleven miles north of

Llandrindod, is most famous for its screen, the finest surviving in Wales. That it should still be in existence is almost a miracle for the church was entirely rebuilt in the restoration craze of last century when nearly all remaining screens, despised as nuisances and obstructions, were chopped up for firewood. But Llananno's screen was carefully set aside and rebuilt into the new church, thus preserving a magnificent specimen of the native Welsh woodcarver's art of the fifteenth century. It was bought, probably at considerable expense, from a school of Montgomeryshire craftsmen, the money being raised by a series of ale-evenings, the medieval equivalent of our coffee-mornings. Its motifs include many from nature: leaves, stalks, flowers, tendrils, grapes and pomegranates. A three-petalled flower in the design may have been inspired by water plantain which the craftsmen could have seen in Montgomeryshire streams and pools.

For another rare survival go a mile down the road to Llanbister whose church has an early eighteenth century singing loft, a reminder of the days when psalms were led by the village band whose instruments were often provided at parish expense. Pipes, flutes, clarinets, bassoons—some of these are still preserved in the churches at Aberedw, Presteigne and Llanbister. For a really atmosphered church go further down the Eithon to Disserth. You could believe that nothing in this church has been disturbed for three hundred years. Its box pews, looking like cattle stalls, are there just as they were in Stuart times (one of them is dated 1666) and they still have the names of old families painted on them. The three-decker pulpit dates from 1687. An outsize box tree in the churchyard is also worth seeing. Here at Disserth are records of those games, including football, which were regularly played in churchyards. In fact churchyard dancing may have survived in Radnorshire after it had died out everywhere else in Britain. For another old interior go to the Dissenters' chapel built in 1697 at Maesyronnen, Glasbury, which is still furnished much as it was in the beginning, and externally is so acceptable compared with the unlovely nineteenth-century chapels which dominate so many Welsh villages. For Quaker simplicity visit the Pales, a thatch-roofed house on the hill nearly a mile north of Llandegle. It is the oldest Friends' meeting house in Wales (1745) and enjoys wide views of the Eithon valley.

Radnorshire

Depopulation in Radnorshire has not only meant deserted houses in the uplands. It has also inhibited the growth of towns. For people have not drained off Radnor hills into Radnor towns. They have gone off to America or South Wales, Birmingham or Slough. So in the whole of the county there are still only four little towns—Llandrindod, Knighton, Presteigne and Rhayader. Presteigne may seem no more than a village yet for many centuries it was a power along this border, having achieved borough status about 1225. In more recent times it was a centre of gaiety and fashion along the coach road from London to Aberystwyth; and it is still the county town of Radnorshire though also the smallest. The well-proportioned church has architectural features of many centuries from the eleventh onwards. Its prize possession is a beautifully worked Flemish tapestry of the early sixteenth century.

Coming up Broad Street from the church you see attractive Georgian houses and round the corner the resplendent black and white Radnorshire Arms hotel. Built in 1616 as a private house, it became a coaching inn in 1792. But eventually the road through Presteigne was superseded by a new road by way of Kington, leaving Presteigne rather isolated from the mainstream of progress: for which it ought to be thankful but probably is not. No town could be more of a border town than Presteigne. For at the bottom of Broad Street flows the Lugg and half-way across the ancient bridge you are in England. Inevitably there is little that is Welsh in this town. Its church looks English, its name is English and it stands on the English side of Offa's Dyke. And being so English it suffered at least twice at the hands of the wild Welsh soldiery. Llywelyn the Great brought fire and sword in 1262. Glyndŵr did the same thing later.

If you like Presteigne because it sits so well on the banks of the Lugg, you will also take to Knighton sitting likewise on the banks of Teme. But not so quietly. For Knighton is a busier place, a good shopping centre, a mecca for marketing farmers, a rendezvous where shepherds from miles around discuss Clun and Kerry sheep for hours on market days. Knighton, unlike Presteigne, stands squarely on the Dyke and is the only town to do so. The origin of its English name is in dispute. But its Welsh name is a statement of fact: Tref y Clawdd means 'the town on the Dyke'; and its early Norman motte and bailey, still conspicuous

17. Detail from one of the finest medieval Welsh screens, Llananno church, north of Llandrindod Wells, Radnorshire

18. Cairn on the top of Drygarn Fawr, north Breconshire

19. The Irfon valley, part of which is a National Nature Reserve, above Abergwesyn, Breconshire

20. Three prehistoric monoliths called 'Harold's Stones' at Trelleck, Monmouthshire

as a wooded knoll in the town, was built almost exactly on the Dyke.

Then there is New Radnor which, to the hurrying traveller, is just a village where the main road jerks round an awkward right-angle. But New Radnor too is a place of history as the words 'Town Wall' on the one-inch map suggest. But New Radnor's right to townhood has lapsed long since. The town wall is visible as a bank on either side of the road as you come in from Hundred House. Note also the curious carved stone with Maltese cross built into the farm wall on the left as you enter the village. This was evidently once the top of a cross shattered perhaps by some Reformation image-breaker. The church, well above the houses, is more attractive inside than out and has two ancient effigies in the porch. From the castle mound above you look down upon the village and see how well it sits in its steep-sided flat-bottomed valley. Opposite you on the south is The Smatcher, a broad-bosomed hill on which the Forestry Commission has made whimsical patterns with conifers of various greens.

Ever since the late seventeenth century people have been going to Llandrindod Wells to take the waters. The English wealthy flocked there in the eighteenth century and turned the place into a gambling and whoring hell. And although the spa fashion there has largely died out, if you think it will do your gout or your scrofula good you can still take your pick of waters rich in sulphur, salt or iron. More likely you will go there to play golf with far views from every hole, or play bowls on the famous greens on the banks of the Eithon; or picnic under the white poplars round the lake (in which you may fish provided you put the fish back afterwards); or see the work of Welsh artists at the Temple Gallery. Or you may attend a congress, for congresses are a Llandrindod speciality. But you could well go to Llandrindod for its own sake, just to see a town that has not its like in all Wales. After Knighton and Presteigne which look like what they are, old towns that have been put together a bit at a time by the centuries, Llandrindod is a surprise. For this was a new town of a hundred years ago, a successful attempt to revive the place as a resort after years of being out of fashion and forgotten.

To get the full impact of Llandrindod leave it till last. See Radnorshire first, get soaked in old stone-built towns and villages, castle mounds and medieval churches, slow-to-change farms and green valleys leading up to dark Celtic moorlands. Then for the contrast go to Llandrindod. It is very red-brick and green-domed, very spa, very Malvern, totally un-Radnorshire. It looks spacious, swept and welcoming: one of the better specimens of nineteenth-century towns. But if the age of Victoria is not to your taste you can escape into the very good little museum and go back nearly 2,000 years with the many fragments of Roman life found at the nearby fort of Castell Collen; and the perhaps even more ancient boat dug out of the silt of the Eithon; and further back with the tools and ornaments of the Bronze Age, including replicas of the Bailey Hill gold torcs. Or you can be quickly out of Llandrindod altogether, out among deep wooded valleys and sharp little hills. For Llandrindod, having a river on both sides of it, is blessed with agreeable walks of which the best is the eastward one to Shaky Bridge (made unshaky long since), then across a meadow past a lonely church and up to the bold hill of Cefn-llys that is looped around by the Eithon and has fallen Norman walls on its summit. Or you can walk from there to the Alpine Bridge a mile or so upriver, a delightful streamside amble. The mound there, close to a farm on the east side of the river, was presumably the site of the first castle of Cefn-llys.

Does the town council of Llandrindod sometimes look a little enviously at Rhayader when it thinks of the thousands of visitors who annually go to Elan or stream down the Wye valley missing Llandrindod by only a few miles? For Rhayader (in Welsh Rhaeadr Gwy—'the falls on the Wye') is emphatically a touristy spot and has been ever since the 1770's when Welsh tourism seriously began. Eventually the Wye's side-streams were discovered, notably the Elan which soon had an honoured place in the guide books, much lavish description being bestowed on the woods and waterfalls and on the beautiful estate created in the valley just before 1810 by Shelley's relative Thomas Groves, formerly of Wiltshire, who planted many trees there. This Arcadia was drowned in 1902 by Birmingham Corporation, since when it has become the famous reservoir round beloved of coach parties. In 1952 the round was increased by the opening of the Claerwen reservoir whose four miles reach nearly to the Cardiganshire border. With all these hills, crags and lakes on its doorstep Rhayader is the obvious tourist centre for this part of the county.

If I were asked to recommend where else to stay in Radnorshire my thoughts would go first to Knighton, Presteigne or New Radnor for the exploration of the border and of Radnor Forest. New Radnor is a particularly good starting point for the county's best mountain walk: up round the head of Harley Dingle by way of a shapely dome called Whimble, then to the highest points of all at Black Mixen and Great Rhos, and back by way of Radnorshire's best natural waterfall at Water-break-its-neck where, to quote an enthusiastic nineteenth-century guide book: 'a small stream drops seventy feet into a rugged and gloomy dell amidst the wildest alpine scenery'. But be warned: in dry weather it shrinks to nothing. For the Eithon valley which goes through many miles of good country from the Montgomeryshire border to the Wye, Llandrindod is the obvious choice. For the fertile, gentler south I would go to one of the several well-placed villages along that lovely southern sweep of the Wye; Boughrood, Glasbury, Llowes or Clyro. (Pronounced 'Bock-rood', 'Glazebury', 'Llow-is' and 'Cligh-ro'.) Above all these villages are hills of much delight, notably the curiously named Begwms which is crossed by many old tracks and visited for its views of the mountains all round the south. On the Begwms in the Dark Ages there stood the tall Celtic cross of St. Meulig. It was brought off the hill down to Llowes and stood a further 800 years in the churchyard there. Despite all its experience of the elements it remains a fine specimen of its kind and is now inside the church.

If from Llowes you make your way to Clyro note the ancient arch in the wall of the farm on your right just before the village. This arch and the range of early farm buildings in the yard beyond date back to the fourteenth century when they were part of a monastic grange belonging to Abbey Cwmhir. Clyro, formerly cursed by traffic, now has a by-pass and, quietly insular, is once again more like the village Kilvert knew, the Reverend Francis Kilvert, a lover of this countryside, who was curate at Clyro a century ago. He would no longer be remembered had he not written in his journals a charming account of his daily life. Today these lyrical journals are widely known and loved and if you like you can use them as a guide to that part of

Radnorshire and from there up Wye and Marteg to St. Harmon where Kilvert was also vicar for a while. Exploring with this vividly descriptive man you will learn more about Radnorshire country folk than you could from any other source. For only by learning about a people's past can their present be understood. So with thoughts of this gentle man let us say good-bye to Radnorshire.

9

BRECONSHIRE
(historically BRECKNOCKSHIRE)
(Brycheiniog or Sir Frycheiniog)

Those who love Radnorshire for the quiet remoteness of
its inland hills, woods and streams, must love Breconshire also, for such qualities continue across Wye, Elan
and Claerwen, the hastening rivers that separate these the only
two counties of Wales that nowhere get a lick of salt water. Go
on to a hill like Corngafallt (Carn Gafallt) that forms the
northern apex of Breconshire and look around. You will see
that the characteristic pattern of Radnorshire—the plateau-like
moorlands divided into high, isolated blocks by deeply carved
valleys—is faithfully repeated further south in Breconshire. The
wooded streams, the rock-scabbed slopes, the peaty, rushy uplands are no different either side Elan or Claerwen. It is inevitably
so, for the grey shales and mudstones of Radnorshire and Cardiganshire continue into this northern tip of Breconshire.

Corngafallt is also worth climbing for its fine view up the Wye
to Rhayader or down the Wye to where it winds out of sight
towards Newbridge. And on the west you look down on the
lowest of the Elan reservoirs and beyond to wild, empty hills.
But if you feel daunted by this hill's steep slopes there is a lane
that circles its feet completely, much of its course below a
fascinating wood of old oaks, many of them thick-trunked and
hollow—an unusual type of woodland to find in upland Wales.
This district was particularly favoured by Bronze Age man—
there are cairns, tumuli, single stones and alignments. And on

Corngafallt, as on Gwastedyn across the Wye, Bronze Age gold torcs have been found. Four of them found on Corngafallt are in the National Museum of Wales and facsimiles in Brecon museum. The church at Llanwrthwl, a hamlet at the foot of Corngafallt, has a twelfth-century font whose sides bear four crude human faces. But the best object there is the huge squat stone in the churchyard, a stone that no doubt made this spot sacred thousands of years before Christ.

South-west of Corngafallt (1,530 feet) the ground swells to greater heights. A long, broad, wet ridge that throws off innumerable streams begins on Gamriw and continues several miles across Gorllwyn (2,009 feet) to culminate in the west at Drygarn (2,115 feet). To this high dome of Drygarn ('three cairns') there are various routes. The easiest, both about an hour's walking, are from the Claerwen valley in the north and from the Irfon in the south. Either walk leads you up pathless streamsides through the grassy hills to the topmost cone, crowned by perhaps the most elaborate cairn in Wales. Drygarn is a viewpoint for those who like landscapes with little sign of human life: for this is one of the most unpeopled regions of South Wales. There have been houses here and there, shepherds' houses lonely at the heads of cwms but they are all abandoned long since. Now the only ones occupied are far down the valleys. It is a land in which to look out for surviving specimens of the old cruck-built long houses where the animals lived at one end and the people at the other. Such a building still endures at the old farm of Llannerch-y-cawr near the southern end of Caban-coch reservoir.

On the moors between Drygarn and the Towy rises the stream called Irfon. Born in the peat this short though famous tributary of the Wye soon cuts itself a deep valley which, below the farm called Llannerch-yrfa, is beautifully clothed with oakwoods one of which is a National Nature Reserve, the nesting place of buzzards, pied flycatchers, redstarts and other oakwood birds. Here too is the mountain road that goes over to the Towy and away up again to find its way at last to Tregaron. The Irfon's first place of any note is the hamlet of Abergwesyn, centre of a formerly more peopled region. For here was an inn (the Grouse) and a church. The inn has long closed its doors and the church has quite gone, leaving only venerable yews to remember the site. Opposite across the river stood an even older church in a burial ground that seems to have been circular. If you visit it try to go there in mid-June when it is coloured by sheets of bluebells.

Downstream through beautiful country you come to Llan-wrtyd once thronged because of its allegedly healing spa waters that are now right out of favour in a world that has more faith in antibiotics than sulphur springs. Here were busy pump-houses now forlornly decrepit. Llanwrtyd, though still calling itself 'Wells' has become a centre for tourists, anglers and pony trekkers. This is the only region of Breconshire where you will find any rocks other than sedimentary: north-east from Llan-wrtyd an igneous outcrop extends for several miles (here and there you may come upon what geologists call 'pillow lavas') and it is these volcanic rocks that account for the mineral springs. The road through Llanwrtyd Wells is A483 which goes south-west out of Breconshire through the Sugar Loaf pass, a popular roadside viewpoint and picnic spot. This Sugar Loaf is not to be confused with the famous one near Abergavenny.

If at Llanwrtyd you want Welsh tweed made on local hand-looms you can get it at the Cambrian Factory (formerly a corn-grinding watermill) a mile along A483 towards Beulah. If you fork left at Beulah and go up the valley of the Cnyffiad you pass through one of the best oak regions left in Wales: it ought to be preserved as such, as a contrast with the all-invading conifers. Antiquaries should go a little south of Beulah to see Caerau, a farmhouse sitting on the banks of a Roman fort with a nice straight length of Roman road going due south down to Llanga-march which was, like Llanwrtyd, a spa. But valetudinarians no longer seek health there. Like all these Irfon villages Llangamarch looks south at the sandstone escarpment of Mynydd Epynt under whose slopes, at a farm called Cefn-brith, about two miles south-west of Llangamarch, was born one of the most impassioned champions of the Reformation. He was John Penry, martyred as a Puritan in the reign of Elizabeth I. An interesting church of this district is Llanlleonfel which stands on a small hill overlooking A483 a mile west of Garth. There is no road to it, only a path up a field to where the little church stands amid trees. In it is pre-served a large crude stone carved in ninth-century Latin which translates: 'Iorwerth and Ruallaun in their graves await the dread coming of the Lord in peace.' This is one of the churches Francis Kilvert describes so vividly in his diary.

Two roads go south across Mynydd Epynt, converging at Upper Chapel, one from Garth, the other from Builth. The Garth road, B4519, climbs steeply out of Cwm Craig-ddu with great views back to the Irfon, then down and up to the now ruined Drovers' Arms where cattle and even geese used to be shod before being driven across country to markets such as Hereford. From Garth the Irfon winds on towards Builth with A483 on the north side and a much preferable minor road on the south. But the main road has the advantage of taking you to Cilmery which in recent years has become a focus of Welsh national feeling. For near here Llywelyn, the last native prince of Wales, was killed in 1282, a year as familiar to Welsh school-children as 1066 is to the English. Llywelyn's body was carried thirteen miles north-east for burial in the great abbey-church of Cwmhir. First to commemorate Llywelyn at Cilmery was, strangely enough, a local English squire. He put up a small obe-lisk in 1902. But now this has been replaced by a huge granite standing stone hewn in a Caernarvonshire quarry, bits of the old obelisk being used to edge the steps up to the newer memorial. Thirteen oaks, one for each Welsh county, are planted round the stone. A sign commemorates 'ein llyw olaf' ('our last leader') as Llywelyn is always called.

Builth (pronounced 'Bilth') is well sited on the right bank of the Wye and has a fair amount of history behind it, beginning with the castle whose large multiple earthworks still stand above the east end of the town. They were probably raised by the Normans in the eleventh century but a great stone castle subse-quently built on them has gone—the most completely destroyed of all Edwardian castles. Builth was given a charter by Edward I (who spelt the name as 'Buelt') in 1278. The parish church, which has an effigy in armour of the sixteenth century, is also interest-ing for having been turned round. The medieval tower, formerly western, is now at the east end but on its outside east wall you can still see the V-shape where the former nave roof was fixed to it.

Builth's finest building is the bridge of six high arches span-ning the Wye, constructed, says a stone in the centre of the up-stream parapet, by James Parry of Hay in 1779. From the bridge a quiet, tree-shaded promenade—the most attractive part of Builth—takes you nearly to where the Irfon flows gently in. From here the river is particularly lovely and you can cross the Irfon on a suspension bridge if you want to continue your walk up Wye-side. Botanists know this part of the Wye because it is one of the few districts in Britain where chives are genuinely wild and native. This mauve-flowered onion-like plant grows on the river banks and on rocky islands in the river. Despite the nearness of Llywelyn's memorial modern Builth is almost entirely English-speaking except on market days (Monday) when farmers from further west have a day in the town. A great Welsh occasion is when the annual Royal Welsh Show comes in July to Llanelwedd on the Radnorshire side of the river. The town's full name is Builth Wells but the spa is obsolete. The Welsh name is Llanfair-yn-Muallt ('the church of St. Mary in (the hundred of) Buallt').

If you take the Upper Chapel road (B4520) out of Builth you climb steeply out of the town as if going straight to the top of Epynt. Instead you are immediately plunged into a beautifully wooded valley by a stream amid rocks; and from here you can diverge on foot to explore the delights of the Duhonw dingle. All this region between Epynt and the Wye goes slanting down good quiet country with tucked-away farms and lovely valleys, such as Nant Offeiriad. A network of lanes, many quite unsuited to motoring, threads through it all, mostly converging on Erwood. Upstream from Erwood a lane climbs up to the Twmpath which gives you a vast view of that part of the Wye. Below Erwood the main road is squeezed against the river for a mile till the valley broadens. Then steep woods rise high above the road, and between road and river you see Llangoed Castle, one of Breconshire's many historic houses. At Llyswen the Wye turns back to flow north for half a mile before curving away southeast round the southernmost tip of Radnorshire. You reach Aberllynfi, a roadside village more widely known as Three Cocks, the name of the old inn there. Nearby, standing in its park, is Gwernyfed, a house of the seventeenth century and earlier, a twelfth-century doorway being a notable feature.

At Hay we are truly on the border: immediately beyond the town's medieval walls—of which a fragment survives on the east side—lies Herefordshire. The name Hay is connected not with grass but with trees. The Norman French 'haier' meant 'to enclose' and The Hay, as it always used to be called, was simply 'the enclosed settlement'. (The Hague in Holland has the same derivation.) Hay castle was Norman-built and often faced the gory side of life, falling to besiegers at least five times in the thirteenth and fourteenth centuries. Then, at the start of the fifteenth, Owain Glyndŵr wrecked it for the last time and burnt the town as well. It was long recovering; over a century later Leland could report: 'The town within the waulles is wonderfully decaied.' Not long after Leland an Elizabethan house was built against the castle ruins. It has been partly destroyed by fire in recent years but a section is still in use as a book store, for book-selling in Hay has become a major industry.

For miles along this part of the Wye the view south is always of the great billowing escarpment of the Black Mountains. It is not motorists' country up there, with the exception of the narrow road with passing places that goes from Hay up the Dulas valley and down the Honddu to Capel-y-ffin. But for walkers there is an infinity of southward lanes all the way from Hay to Talgarth, lanes which head for the hills full of promise but all of which falter to an end at varying heights up the slopes. From there you go on your way more and more rejoicing in the freedom of the grassy, wind-blown hills for there are fine heights to conquer in all the exhilarating miles from Pen y Beacon (2,219 feet) in the north round to the highest points, Waun Fach (2,660 feet) and Pen y Gader Fawr (2,624 feet) in the south.

Talgarth is a historic little county town but its only surviving medieval secular building is the peel tower now a private house by the bridge in the town centre. The church, up a steep hill, is partly thirteenth century and has a memorial to that strange character Howell Harris (1714–73), founder of Welsh Methodism. With fiery eloquence he preached the religious revival up and down the country with fantastic success until in 1750, having quarrelled with fellow leaders, he retired to Trefeca, a village a mile south-west of Talgarth, and there founded a community of Methodist families who lived with almost monastic severity toiling at over sixty different country crafts as well as printing and farming. Trefeca remains a religious centre; there is a memorial chapel to Harris; and in the museum next door you can learn much about his life and times.

Breconshire

If from Talgarth you go up the lane past the Mid Wales Hospital you come in two miles to Llaneleu church, perched high in a large, almost empty graveyard. This little church has an old wooden door-frame; and usually a swallow's nest in the porch as all churches should have. There are two ancient Celtic crosses, a sundial of 1686 and a medieval rood-loft topped by a tympanum that reaches to the roof. Below the church is a house dated 1676. On the other side of Talgarth along the road to Bronllys village you pass a tall single tower set jauntily on a high mound above a winding, alder-shaded stream. This is the keep of a thirteenth-century Norman castle (otherwise practically disappeared) built upon a no doubt earlier motte. High on its grassy hillock this tower has a fine view south-east over Talgarth to the shapely peak of Mynydd Troed. The church at Bronllys is unique in Breconshire for having a detached tower, Herefordshire style. Two miles south-west, at Llanfilo church, you can see a carefully restored medieval screen and rood-loft as well as old box pews.

Mynydd Troed is one of the finest viewpoints in the county: spread before you is all the fertile basin around Llangorse Lake and Brecon with the Beacons magnificent beyond. Or, instead of Mynydd Troed, try Castell Dinas on the opposite side of the valley—a most interesting Iron Age fort because its massive ramparts were turned to use by the Normans who built on them a sizeable stone castle. At 1,471 feet this site was remarkably high for either a hill fort or a castle. Is there in fact a higher castle in all Wales? Extremely little is left of it now. And even Leland reported: 'It is now ruinous, almost to the hard ground.' He adds that there were 'sumtime 3 parks and a forest, the parks be down but yet good plenty is ther of redd deere'. Happy days.

Cwm-du, a village deep among the hills half-way down the Rhiangoll valley, long had a water-mill grinding corn but this is now a sad ruin. The church has a Dark Ages stone built into an outside buttress of the south wall. Its well-carved lettering reads: 'Catacus hic jacit filius Tegernacus' which a brass-plate renders: 'Here lies Catawe son of Teyrnawe.' This church is curious in having two south porches: in the disused one is a medieval cross slab. The name of this place which means 'the dark valley' no doubt reflects the lateness of the morning sun to reach it round the shoulders of the Black Mountains. And the blackness of the mountains was presumably given them by those who live along the Wye and see the deep, day-long shadows of the steep north-facing scarp.

Below Cwm-du the valley widens and if you are following A479 you are very soon at Tretower where two medieval secular buildings have survived within two hundred yards of each other. First there was a twelfth-century motte. Then, as at Bronllys, the thirteenth century contributes this great round stone keep with nine-foot-thick walls, one of over a score of similar free-standing towers in South Wales. By the next century more settled times have arrived, the need for these towers to command the valley-routes has gone, the building of premises more domestic than military becomes possible and we get Tretower Court. This very interesting house, lived in and gradually altered until the eighteenth century, gives us as good a picture of changes in taste over four centuries as any house in Wales. Both castle and court are in the care of the Ministry of Works.

The Usk has many good-looking bridges but none finer than the one at Crickhowell with its thirteen arches extending over the river and its flood-plain, a distance of 140 yards. Its founda-tions probably date from the seventeenth century; but it was broken by a flood in 1808 and extensively rebuilt the following year. At the other side of the town are the ruins of the thirteenth-century Norman castle. Ruined ever since Glyndŵr's rebellion in 1403, all that is now left of it is a mound and a pair of tottery-looking towers. On a bend where the two main roads meet in the town, in a long castellated wall, there is a good medieval gate-house called Porth Mawr which led to a house long since gone. Conspicuous north of the town, standing up like a frontier post of the Black Mountains, is a flat-topped hill locally called Table Mountain (for this is an English-speaking region). Its Welsh name is Crug Hywel ('Howell's mount') and Crucywel is still Crickhowell's Welsh name. Who this Hywel was is lost in Dark Ages darkness. His 'mound' is in fact a multivallate Iron Age fort with an incurved entrance half-way along the east side and is a great viewpoint.

Crickhowell is a gateway to the southern Black Mountains which on this side are penetrated by the long narrow valleys of the Grwyne Fechan and Grwyne Fawr, two streams which unite amid delightful oakwoods east of Crickhowell. Of the two the

Grwyne Fawr forms the more magnificent valley-head but its lower parts are sadly conifer-strangled. Above both of them the hills keep to a level height before dropping abruptly to the Usk: for the Black Mountains are the remains of a former plateau now deeply sliced into by the streams. The lane that goes all the way up the Grwyne Fechan eventually becomes a mere hill path, leaving you free to branch out where you will over this vast spread of upland sandstone grassland, the largest area of continuous high ground in Wales outside Snowdonia. Note the height called Pen Cerrig-calch ('limestone hill'), an outlier of the limestone south of the Usk.

If you do not venture far up the Grwyne Fawr, at least go to Partrishow if you have even the slightest feeling for history of the quiet rural sort. Partrishow is a simple little church that stands above a side-dingle of the Grwyne Fawr four and a half miles north-east of Crickhowell. In this unlikely-looking building you will find preserved one of the most perfect medieval screens and rood-lofts left in Wales and fit to compare for craftsmanship with the one at Llananno in Radnorshire. On the floor beneath is another rarity—a pair of medieval altar slabs, one with five, one with six little incised crosses. On the wall at the back is painted a most convincing black skeleton symbolizing Time with his scythe, spade and hour-glass. The font is very old and is inscribed in Latin words meaning: 'Menhir made me in the time of Genillin', which dates it, Genillin being an eleventh-century prince. The oldest walls of the church are probably thirteenth century. The oldest name of the church is Merthyr Issui, meaning the shrine of St. Issui. Partrishow, also spelt Patrishow, seems to come from 'parth', a share, and 'Ishow', a corruption of Issui. So Partrishow could have originally been the plot given to Issui by some local prince. Returning down the Grwyne Fawr you come in a mile or so to Pont-Yspig (or Pont yr esgob) which means 'bishop's bridge'; so called, according to tradition, because it was used by Bishop Morgan on his famous tour through Wales in 1188 to preach the Third Crusade. In recent centuries all the way down the lower Grwyne around Llangenny there has been a string of paper mills, flour mills and fulling mills, all now out of use. Llangenny itself remains a charming little place with its old church, bridge and tree-shaded stream.

Below here the Grwyne is soon into the Usk which in a mile

or two goes off into Monmouthshire. The Usk (the word is from its Welsh name, Wysg) is a river which in South Wales enjoys as much devotion as does the Dee in North Wales. And not surprisingly for it is a lovely river ever winding between high hills and under countless fine trees, its banks not yet mauled and maltreated like those of many English rivers. Its fish are plentiful; there is a richness of birds, animals and wild flowers along its banks; and it is spanned by a galaxy of fine stone bridges. Alongside the Usk, and sometimes crossing it or its side-streams on cunningly engineered aqueducts, runs the Monmouthshire and Brecon canal. Completed in 1800 but long since discarded by industry, this canal has settled down to a peaceful rural life, winding through the countryside with all the beauty of a slow-moving river. It is still in popular use for pleasure craft. At Gilwern the Clydach falls into the Usk down a deep, wooded ravine across which the canal has been led on a remarkable aqueduct. Instead of some elegant bridge such as Telford employed to throw his canal across the Dee in Denbighshire, at Gilwern the whole ravine was blocked by a massive embankment. The canal runs along the top of it and the Clydach passes through a tunnel underneath. The embankment has long since clothed itself with deciduous trees and now looks quite natural.

Gilwern is by-passed by the Heads of the Valleys road which goes roaring up the Clydach gorge to Brynmawr and Beaufort. Great beech forests clothed much of this limestone country until the sixteenth century when, attracted by all this potential fuel and the water-power of the streams, the early iron industry moved in. For two centuries forges worked in the valley and the forests were turned into charcoal. In the eighteenth century the iron industry moved away to the coalfield but by then only fragments of the beechwoods were left—in steep places difficult of access. And because this is one of the very few districts of Wales where beeches are native and natural, fifty acres of them are protected from further depletion by the creation of a National Nature Reserve in the Clydach gorge east of Brynmawr.

On the hill between Usk and Clydach is the hamlet of Llanelli. It has an ancient church in a churchyard crammed with gravestones and hemmed closely round by a guardian ring of ancient yews. Nowhere have I felt more strongly that this was the purpose of churchyard yews—as a magic circle sheltering the dead from the forces of evil. Above Llanelli you can find a lane up to the rim of the moorland called Mynydd Llangattock (Llangatwg). Up there the name Disgwylfa ('lookout') tells you what to expect: a viewpoint that sees for miles up and down the Usk and across to the Black Mountains. All along this escarpment the Clydach limestone continues: there are caves, swallowholes, lime-kilns and old quarries; and, convenient for walking, an old tramway that once linked the quarries with Nantyglo. And there are beechwoods. But here the fascinating trees are not beeches but the several species of whitebeams, small berried trees related to the mountain ash, which grow in this district and nowhere else in the world. Hence the Craig y Cilau nature reserve that occupies one of these rocky slopes. In it also grow the large-leaved and small-leaved limes and a ground flora that includes rare hawkweeds, alpine enchanter's nightshade, angular Solomon's seal, hutchinsia and green spleenwort. Underground the heart of Mynydd Llangatwg is mined by the famous natural caverns and passages called Agen Allwedd ('the keyhole'). Until recently known only to bats they have now been deeply explored by cavers who regard them as the most extensive system of caves in Britain. The entrance is in Craig y Cilau nature reserve. At the village of Llangatwg we are only a few fields away from Crickhowell opposite across the Usk. Its church has a huge fort-like tower that dwarfs the rest of the building. Inside are the village stocks and whipping post to tell us how times have changed. And from the excellent parish scrapbook (published in the journal *Brycheiniog*) we get another reminder: 'Older inhabitants relate how Mrs. Crawshay of Dan-y-parc had tea served in her pew during service, while she also regularly brought three dogs to church with her. Other such pew-holders brought newspapers and magazines.'

Tree-lovers should take B4558 from Crickhowell. The riverside poplars here are beautiful in spring, their red catkins gleaming in the sun. Then, nine hundred paces upstream from the bridge, you find a magnificent oak beside the road, its vast trunk buttressed around with massive burs. Less than a mile further you pass under the arching boughs of a lovely evergreen oak, a hybrid between a Turkey oak and a holm oak and most striking in winter when all other oaks are leafless. From Llangynidr B4560 climbs away south to zigzag you in splendid style

up over the mountain, with superb views back north, before it
drops you into Monmouthshire and industrialized Beaufort, so
named from an early Norman family once powerful hereabouts.
Much of the surface of Llangatwg and Llangynidr Mountains is
pitted with swallow-holes of various sizes, the result of caves
collapsing as the rainwater of long ages has dissolved the limestone. On this limestone too is the largest concentration of
Bronze Age cairns in Breconshire. A fine gold torc now in the
British Museum was from this area.

Llangynidr bridge, four miles up the Usk from Crickhowell,
is a real gem: old, narrow, massively cutwatered and rising high
on its six arches over one of the loveliest parts of the river. From
it are delightful riverside walks along the south bank. North of
Llangynidr bridge you are soon at Bwlch, a village in a high gap
used by the modern main road as it was once used by a Roman
road. The ancient road can still be followed due east for over a
mile to Pen-y-gaer where a high farmhouse looks across at the
Black Mountains from the ramparts of a Roman fort. If you go
from Bwlch to Llangorse you pass close to the remains of the
once-important castle of Blaen-llynfi which was stone-built,
moated and well embanked around. It guarded the eastern
approaches of the Norman lordship of Brecon. Today its mound
is a thicket of sycamores and only a fragment of its purple walls
remain. So much for faded glory. As late as the sixteenth century
this was 'the shape of a veri fair castel now dekeiyng, and by was
a borow town', says Leland. How hard it is today to imagine a
chartered borough in that quiet spot! Further north is a hamlet
called Cathedin that looks to the lake and has in its churchyard
three stalwart yews that appear at least a thousand years older
than the un-Welsh-looking church.

Between Cathedin and the lake you skirt the grounds of an
elegant house on an historic site called Treberfedd, built and still
occupied by the Raikes family related by descent to Robert
Raikes of Gloucester the founder of Sunday schools in the late
eighteenth century. The church and former school down by the
lake at Llangasty were built in 1848 by the first Raikes of Treberfedd. From the churchyard you hear the sharp cries of coots for
the water laps very close. This is the quiet side of the lake and
long may it remain so. Here grow choice water plants such as
flowering rush, greater spearwort and fringed water-lily. And

21. Tintern Abbey: Cistercian remains by the lower Wye, Monmouthshire

22. The medieval keep inside the walls of Cardiff Castle, Glamorgan

here many small birds breed in the waterside vegetation, among them the reed warbler, a curiously rare bird in Wales.

Llangorse, the biggest natural lake in Wales after Llyn Tegid at Bala, is in Welsh Llyn Syfaddan, a name of lost meaning. Past ages have reckoned it bottomless and that it has a drowned city beneath it. I wonder could this legend be a genuine folk-memory of the prehistoric lake dwelling found built on wooden piles near the outlet stream? This crannog and a dug-out canoe now in Brecon museum may be Iron Age but could be earlier. It is the only lake-dwelling so far found in Wales though they are common in Ireland. The lake has long been famous for its pike, perch, roach and eels and in the medieval time was an important fishery. Thronged with yachts in summer, it is a gathering ground for many wildfowl in winter. Though only a mile or so from the Usk the lake actually empties into the Wye at Glasbury. About the beginning of this century the London County Council had a plan for raising the level of this lake by a hundred feet and piping water from local rivers into it. Happily the scheme died.

If you follow A40 from Bwlch to Brecon you come in two miles to Llansanffraid, at the top of whose sloping churchyard the religious poet, Henry Vaughan, was buried in 1695. Then upriver, or rather up-canal, from Llansanffraid there is a little place called Pencelli which had a large stone castle in Norman times. Now all that remains is a wilderness of brambly hummocks and hollows sloping steeply to the canal behind a farmhouse. Much more interesting is the church at Llanhamlach on the other side of the Usk. Concealed among yews this church contains a curious early stone carved all over with odd patterns, a cross and two crude human figures. Latin words on the stone mean: 'Johannis Moridic set up this stone.' Roman-road seekers will find one well indicated on the map from here to Bwlch.

Brecon is on the Usk where a stream called Honddu comes flowing down off Epynt. Hence the town's Welsh name, Aberhonddu. As a borough the place goes back to a charter of 1270. So Brecon early became an important castled and walled town dominating a powerful lordship. The castle, now mixed up with a hotel, had its ups and downs but was not finally wrecked until the Civil War. A substantial portion still stands but the old layout is confused by a road that now runs between it and the earlier castle mound. For a while the town walls survived better: they and their four gates were described as still in good repair at the start of the eighteenth century. Then the town burst its seams and now the only good length of wall is alongside the Captains' Walk between the shire hall and the river. (The 'captains' who took exercise along this walk were French officers brought here as prisoners in the Napoleonic War.) Brecon has so far escaped industrialization, its centre has not yet been modernized and you need no great imagination to visualize the present-day shops and offices as the fashionable town-houses they were in the days when Brecon was a resort of the well-to-do.

The town has several ancient buildings, besides the castle. There is the Early English chapel of Christ's College, a public school beyond the river. This chapel was originally part of a friary of Dominicans and as such is a unique survival in Wales. Nearby is the Usk bridge built on seven arches in 1563 and of course widened since. On 15th November 1535, its predecessor, says Leland, 'was thrown down by the Rage of Uske Water. . . . It was not by Rain but by snow meltid that cam out of the Mountaines.' The parish church of St. Mary in the centre of the town is of little interest because of over-restoration: it retains a tall sixteenth-century tower and inside is a fine fourteenth-century cross slab with leaf and arrow decoration. The town's principal building is the church of St. John, formerly belonging to a Benedictine priory. It became a cathedral at the creation of the diocese of Swansea and Brecon in 1923. Despite restoration this medieval church has many fine architectural features especially the thirteenth-century choir. The chancel arch is the finest in the county. Perhaps the oldest thing in the church is the ornate Norman font. In old times the building was lit by the largest cresset stove now surviving in Britain: it has holes for thirty tallow lights. Outside the church the old priory remains include fortress-like walls and a tithe barn. Brecon has an excellent museum covering a wide sweep of history. Its collection of ancient inscribed stones is especially good, particularly the Turpillius stone and a Roman one called Maen y Morwynion. There is also a military museum for Brecon has long been a garrison town.

If you want a view of all the good country round Brecon climb Pen-y-crug, an isolated hill a mile north-west of the town with a fine multi-banked Iron Age fort on top. It looks to all horizons—Epynt, Black Mountains, the Beacons, Fforest Fawr—a really splendid circle of mountains, with Brecon at the centre of it all. Also just north of Brecon is Llanddew, now a quiet hamlet but medievally important as the site of one of the palaces of the bishops of St. David's. But of this building little survives except a little pointed arch across the road from the church and some larger fragments of heavily ivied walls further back. The church is a rarity for Breconshire, for it is cruciform. A little way up the Honddu you come to Llandyfaelog church in a circle of ancient yews. From the churchyard you can often watch dippers on the river; and in the church you will see an eight-foot early memorial stone with a figure of a warrior carved below a cross.

Further up B5420 you get into the heart of Epynt. There are many lovely valleys and side-valleys to explore for countless streams have cut grooves through these red soils. You can go on to Upper Chapel and over the top to Builth or Garth. But beware of red flags betokening military activity. This, like so many in Wales, is an upland region far less populous than a century ago when little upland villages like Merthyr Cynog were centres of life for miles around. The prehistoric antiquities of Epynt are not as thick on the ground as they are in other parts of the county. But the Iron Age made a few hill forts and before that the Bronze Age had left some cairns behind. Near one of them, at Ynys-hir at the head of Nant Brân there was a small stone circle which has been excavated and thought to be Bronze Age of about 1,300 B.C. The best Roman site is their large fort at the Gaer, west of Brecon. This fort, which they seem to have called Cicutio and occupied over several centuries, was first of wood but later of stone. Roads ran from it to all directions: Llandrindod, Abergavenny, Neath and Llandovery. It has been well excavated and parts of it are left exposed. In fields close to the fort look out for a wild plant called Danewort or dwarf elder (*Sambucus ebulus*). It reaches several feet in height, has umbels of white flowers and is something of a rarity.

The Usk and its side-streams have as many old bridges above Brecon as below. One of the best is Aberbrân bridge which has three semi-circular arches, two refuges on each side with seats, and a notice saying that one James Parry built it in 1791. Would that we could all leave such good works behind us! Near here is the curious place-name, Battle. It came straight from Sussex with the Normans who included this parish in the lands held by Brecon priory which was a daughter-house of the Benedectine abbey at Battle in Sussex. So Battle, Breconshire commemorates Battle, Sussex which commemorated the battle of Hastings. A beautifully lettered Roman stone ploughed up in this parish can be seen in Brecon museum. A fine stone of the fifth or sixth century inscribed in good clear Latin and Ogham is in the church at Trallong. At Sennybridge a meagre castle ruin stands above the south side of A40. It seems to have been a keep rather than a castle, part of the Norman defences against the Welsh in a wild forest area.

A40 goes on towards Llandovery, but before it leaves Breconshire at a good boundary stone there are still one or two interesting things to note. Down a side lane just over a mile west of Sennybridge is the bridge at Pantysgallog, a fine, lofty, single arch above the Usk. Then on your right as you enter Trecastle you can scarcely miss the castle mound covered by tall slender beeches for it is one of the tallest mottes in the county. The church of this parish is a mile further on at Llywel. It stands at the roadside fronted by two yews one of which is a real veteran. The church has a cast of a famous Ogham stone now in the British Museum; on it are rare primitive drawings of human figures. The Romans' version of A40 went, as you might expect, straight over the hills from Trecastle, calling at their high, bleak moorland fort of Y Pigwn: it then went undulating on to Llandovery probably much as the modern lane does. A few hundred yards east of Y Pigwn camp there are two small Bronze Age circles. Four miles north-east Clawdd British is an obscure earthwork. Two miles south-west of it at Pantycelyn, Carmarthenshire lived Williams the great hymn-writer (1717–91).

South of A40 stretch the mountains. To all of them your best introduction is a visit to the Mountain Centre, a welcoming and attractive building on Mynydd Illtyd five miles south-west of Brecon. There you will obtain much valuable information. You can see photographs, maps, models of the whole National Park which will help you to decide what you want to see and do there. Walking, caving, climbing, nature and other interests are all very well covered. Or you can spend your time in an arm-chair drinking tea and looking at the marvellous views through the windows. Nearest objects of interest to the Mountain Centre are the church of the famous Celtic saint, Illtud, and his alleged grave, both within a few hundred yards. The church is nineteenth century and abandoned but note the big circular churchyard suggesting a church has stood here since the Dark Ages who carried on the prehistoric faith that circles had magical protective properties. Bedd Illtud ('Illtud's grave') is a more doubtful proposition. If Illtud really was buried hereabouts his grave is more likely to have been at the church; so Bedd Illtud could mark a Bronze Age burial. A mile along the road south-west you reach a rushy, moorhen pool where people picnic. And opposite it across the road, is the mound of Maes-car castle which has the stump of a round tower of thirteenth century Norman type. Its history is elusive but presumably it was set up there to guard the road from Brecon over the hills to Ystradfellte, north of which quiet hamlet there was probably a similar keep at Castell Coch, now a mere overgrown mound.

The upland through which this road passes up the Senni and down the Llia is Fforest Fawr, a great tract of open country once attached to the Norman lordship of Brecon, and called 'forest' in the word's original sense of a hunting ground. Fforest Fawr, with the Beacons to the east and the Carmarthenshire Black Mountain to the west, is an unbroken stretch of grassy, treeless, sandstone hills extending across thirty splendid miles. The heights of Fforest Fawr stand in a row from west to east: Fan Gyhirych, Fan Nedd, Fan Llia and, tallest, Fan Fawr (2,409 feet). (Don't forget that Fan is pronounced 'van'.) There are several reservoirs for the thirsty south but only one sizeable lake, Llyn y Fan Fawr, a corrie lake which is the source of the Tawe river that flows to Swansea. A landmark in the heart of Fforest Fawr is Maen Llia ('Llia's stone'), an eight-foot prehistoric monolith that perhaps began as a memorial but has always been used as a guide-post for upland roads, for example Sarn Helen.

As you come south off Fforest Fawr you cross a region of limestone outcrop; and so do four mountain streams which have cut deep gorges in this yielding rock. Pyrddin, Nedd, Mellte and Hepste, carving their rapid way through the limestone, have created exciting scenery and several notable falls (the Welsh for waterfall hereabouts is 'sgwd'). A quarter-mile up the Pyrddin is Sgwd Gwladys; above that is Sgwd Einion-Gam; half a mile below Pont Melin-fach on the Nedd is Sgwd Ddwli; up the Mellte just above its meeting with the Hepste are the three lovely Clun-gwyn falls; and on the Hepste, a few hundred yards from the Mellte, is Sgwd yr Eira. There are other wonders: streams that sink into their beds as the Mellte does at Ystradfellte; or vanish into enormous caves such as Porth yr Ogof, a mile downstream from Ystradfellte. It is a district where any weekend you meet young men in tin hats with lamps attached to them; for there are cave systems everywhere. And the limestone hills above are rough with countless swallow-holes. Adjacent areas of millstone grit are similarly pocked because of the collapse of limestone underneath. Glaciated rocks are also very common as for instance on Gwaun Cefn-y-garreg, a mile east of Ystradfellte.

Parallel to the Mellte a mile or so west flows the upper Nedd, also amid caverned and porous rocks into which it disappears for several hundred yards. Lower downriver, as in neighbouring valleys, you scramble steeply down through oaks, ashes, wych elms and wet-floored alder woods towards the thunder of waterfalls. Though it may be a really hot day it is cool down there deep in the fern and moss zone. Brittle bladder-fern is especially abundant; so are hard shieldfern and hartstongue. On the south slopes of Fan Fraith, three miles north-west of Ystradfellte, is a unique feature, Pant Mawr pot-hole—the only real South Wales pot-hole of the type familiar in Yorkshire. It goes down for fifty feet into a large cavern with a stream flowing through. And this is a good moment to mention to novices that it is totally ill-advised to go caving or pot-holing without first joining a club.

A few miles lower down these same slopes the Roman road from Brecon picks its careful way across. It is well marked on the one-inch map and you can easily find it about 400 yards west of the Nedd where it slants away south-west as a green road alongside an old wall at the edge of a conifer plantation. It continues well defined and is particularly good and straight where, after two miles, it leaves the forestry and heads for the clearly outlined Roman fort near Coelbren. Immediately north of Coelbren are the Henryd falls and Craigllech woods, a charming river-gorge property of the National Trust. Below the falls the stream hastens down its dingle into the Tawe.

In the Tawe river we have yet another fine stream from

Fforest Fawr that has cut down into the limestone. It is best known to tourists where it flows below Craig y Nos, a nineteenth-century Gothic castle once the home of the Italian soprano Adelina Patti (1843–1919). Later it became a hospital. The valley here is wide and has fine woods of deciduous trees, bold crags of pale limestone and rich bracken slopes. Half a mile upstream is the most visited cave in Wales—Dan yr Ogof, which is illuminated and open to the public for a certain distance. Beyond that there are endless passages, stalactite caves and underground lakes but all are in decidedly cavers' country. On the slope above this show-cave is Ogof yr Esgyrn ('the bone cave') which archaeologists have shown was occupied by man in pre-Roman and Roman times. Further downstream on the opposite side of the Tawe is a real cavers' cave, Ogof Ffynnon Ddu, where several miles of passages are known. It is curious that in all these Breconshire caverns that might have attracted human life no trace of Paleolithic man has ever been found.

A few miles below Craig y Nos you come to the county boundary and the edge of the coalfield, an unattractive region depressed by pit closures. Yet in only a few minutes in a car you can leave behind the coal-tips of Onllwyn and enjoy wide and lovely prospects from high-climbing A4109 before you come down to Glyn Neath. From there the main road east is much industrialized but is fast and you are soon in Merthyr Tydfil, the main gateway from industrial South Wales to the Brecon Beacons National Park.

There are two roads out of Merthyr to the Beacons. A470 to Brecon goes past a string of conifer-edged reservoirs to top the rise at 1,440 feet. Here was a lonely wayside inn, the Storey Arms, which has been replaced by a café and youth hostel. And from here is one of the shortest routes (just over an hour's walk) to Pen y Fan, highest of the Beacons. The alternative road up from Merthyr is the way the railway chose and before then all the centuries back to at least the Romans. This goes via Pontsticill and Torpantau alongside great reservoirs; for the Beacons' sandstone is great holding ground for reservoirs, being neither fissured nor porous. From the head of Pontsticill reservoir the ancient pack-horse road still goes on up the Taf Fechan, crosses the ridge a thousand feet below the summit and goes straight for Brecon down Cwm Cynwyn. As a north-south walkers' route it cannot be bettered. For the ridge-walk at right-angles to this track you can come up from Brecon to Cwm-llwch farm then to the little corrie lake, Llyn Cwm-llwch, to skirt west up round the rocks, climbing past a sad monument to a little lost boy and so to Corn Du (2,863 feet) and Pen y Fan (2,906 feet) and either down the descending ridge to Torpantau or straight on east to Craig Pwllfa (2,502 feet), thence down to Talybont. But of course there are countless variations on these routes, all the more exciting for being discovered for yourself. And if, at Merthyr, you want a good photographer's viewpoint for the Beacons, try a shot with the earthworks of Morlais castle in the foreground. The slight ruins of this Norman castle stand on Morlais Hill just north of the town.

On the Beacons the Old Red Sandstone reaches its highest point in Britain outside Scotland, forming, as seen from Brecon, three noble rounded heads above an abrupt scarp face. Few landscapes could more perfectly illustrate the effects of glaciation than this quartet of magnificent northward-facing cirques that look down their smooth U-shaped valleys from rims that are hardly yet eroded by gullying, as if it were only yesterday the glaciers melted. Behind them in the south the ground goes more gently down the dip-slope of the rocks, covered at first with eroding peat then lower down by grassy slopes. As a viewpoint the Beacons are superb: given that rare right day you see to Cadair Idris in the north and away to Exmoor in the south.

Botanists have a special affection for the Beacons for on them grow several species of plants that properly belong to the Arctic but which extend down into Britain getting scarcer the further south they venture. Here on the Beacons is their full-stop. Not further south than this will you find purple saxifrage, roseroot, northern bedstraw, least willow nor green spleenwort. These and other choice mountain plants such as lesser meadow rue, mossy saxifrage and globe flower inhabit the north-facing rocks where the sun cannot dry them up and where there is a sufficiency of the lime that seems so essential to their way of life. They are best seen in the National Nature Reserve at Craig Cerrig-gleisiad, a corrie that continues the summit ridge to the west of A470. Tree-lovers should visit the Forest Nature Reserve at Penmoelallt, three miles north-west of Merthyr. It consists of seventeen acres of woodland on limestone scree on the west bank of the Taf Fawr. Ash is the dominant tree but there are also those Breconshire specialities, the rare whitebeams. But many others of these valleys round the Beacons are rich in wild flowers and trees. And in May along some of the roads, especially roun Brecon, the white flowers of the bird cherry are altogeth . beautiful.

10

MONMOUTHSHIRE
(Mynwy or Sir Fynwy)

The modern way from southern England into Monmouthshire, over the Severn bridge, follows a prehistoric route, the line of the Aust to Beachley ferry. The car-ferry which the bridge replaced in 1966 had excruciating disadvantages but it had one virtue: as it slowly pulled across the estuary it gave you a long first look at Monmouthshire which you do not get now as you flit across the bridge and in a few minutes are far along the motorway towards Newport. So for the tourist there is a lot to be said for A48 which comes down the north side of the Severn from Gloucester. That way the traffic pushes you along with less than motorway frenzy and as you cross the Wye at Chepstow your first glimpse of Monmouthshire—a great white castle sitting high above the river—is truly encouraging.

What sort of a county is this Monmouthshire which begins at Chepstow in a ravine cut in Carboniferous Limestone and ends in the north-west in a massif of gritstone uplands? Between these extremes lies a land that is really two lands. The treeless mountains of the west that sprawl across about a third of the county and continue on into Glamorgan are deeply sliced by long, close-set, parallel valleys that were once thickly oak-clad and beautiful. Alas, under those mountains lie the Coal Measures and valley after valley has been industrialized. Only in the north, around Llanthony and the Vale of Ewyas, have the uplands retained their beauty, for they are free from coal. The rest of the county is lowland and semi-upland, a softly undulating region

centred on the Usk valley whose soils are mostly a fertile red
marl which man has always farmed intensively. Here are ancient
castles, interesting villages and fine river and woodland scenery.
The twenty-two miles of coast are flat and estuarine and the tide
recedes across miles of shining mud. Out there skies are wide, the
light often brilliant and there are many ducks and wading birds.

Very little Welsh is spoken in Monmouthshire. But Welsh
place-names are everywhere though naturally thinning out towards the east. Names like Redwick, Caldicot and Shirenewton
are English enough. Other names may look English but in fact
are Welsh in disguise. Trelleck was the Welsh Tryleg; Tintern
was originally Tyndyrn; Coldbrook was Colbrwg; and the
'Mon' in Monmouth is from the river name, Mynwy, today
called Monnow. Monmouthshire was part of the territory of the
Celtic people whom the Romans called the Silures and with
whom they seem eventually to have fused pretty closely,
especially in the town of Venta, a name which has come down to
us as Caerwent, a village south-west of Chepstow. If you have
seen how meagre are the Roman remains of North and central Wales, Caerwent can be exciting. The Roman town walls
stand high and solid for much of their length and there is nothing
like them anywhere else in Wales. Where possible Venta has
been excavated but covered up again except for one small area
left exposed. So for the most vivid picture of Roman days you
should visit the museums at Newport and Cardiff where you can
see what the town was like with its streets, shops, baths, houses,
amphitheatre, temples, basilica, forum and its four gates opening
to each point of the compass.

Do not miss Caerwent church. It is on the Roman town and
whenever a grave is dug in the churchyard the spade is soon in
conflict with ancient masonry. The church seems largely made
of Roman stones and is in part a Roman museum. There is a
Roman burial urn, a square yard of good mosaic flooring, a fine
memorial to a brass-hat, Claudius Paulinus, and another stone
commemorating the Roman god of war. An interesting find at
Caerwent and now in the National Museum, Cardiff, was a dish
marked with the ancient Christian symbol, Chi-rho. One of the
earliest relics of Christianity in Wales, it suggests that a small,
perhaps secret, Christian community existed in the Roman city.
Overlooking Caerwent from the north is the large hill fort of

Llanmelin: possibly from among its people the British citizens of
Caerwent were recruited.

From Caerwent it is a natural step to Caerleon-on-Usk
(Caerlleon ar Wysg)—hence 'Isca', which is what the Romans
called this place. For Caerleon (from Castra legionis, 'the camp
of the legion') was the military counterpart of Caerwent. But
Caerleon was not wholly military, for adjoining the legionary
fortress there was a civil settlement, the only known example of
such pairing of civil and military sites in Roman Britain. Much
of the original Caerleon, like Roman Caerwent, lies under
modern housing. But you can still see the foundations of barracks excavated in the 1920's and also Caerleon's showpiece, its
famous amphitheatre, the most perfect bit of Roman life surviving in Wales. Caerleon has a good Roman museum. Its church
lacks Roman objects but has beautiful altar cloths. Caerleon, like
Caerwent, is overlooked by an Iron Age hill fort.

With its genial earth and kindly climate lowland Monmouthshire has always been a land desired by the rapacious and was invaded by the Normans with particular violence, the excesses
they perpetrated against the Welsh being met by vengeful
retaliations whenever possible. So the castles that stand in quiet
beauty in the twentieth century are monuments to a dreadful
period and the contrast between their present tranquillity and decay and their past violence and splendour is an essential part of
their fascination. No castles express this more vividly than the
remote castles of the north, the closely linked castles called the
Trilateral: Skenfrith, Grosmont and White Castle. In that order
I think it best to visit them, from the least to the most impressive.
Begin at Skenfrith (which is an Anglicization of Ynysgyn-
wraidd), the most primitive: just four bleak walls enclosing nothing but a round stone tower perched on an early Norman
motte. Close by is an attractive church whose squat tower is
unmistakably war-like with its immensely thick walls. It is
topped less militarily—by a wooden dovecote. Possessions within the church include an ancient altar and piscina, a piece of
fifteenth-century English embroidery, and a pew and an elaborate tomb of the sixteenth century. Beside church and castle
flows the lovely Monnow which here slides over a weir that
diverts water along an alder-shaded leat to turn the wheels of a
mill that still grinds corn.

Monmouthshire

The triangle formed by the Trilateral castles is almost filled by
Craig Serrerthin, a partly wooded height reaching nearly 1,400
feet. North of it you will find the village of Grosmont about
four miles upstream from Skenfrith. Here, to quote an early
traveller, 'the lively and transparent Monnow serpentises through
woods and hollows'. It is all a world of small green hills that
look to each other across the fertile vale. Grosmont's few houses
climb up a hill between two remarkable buildings, the church
and the castle. Of these the twelfth-century church will tell you
most about the Grosmont of past time. Its purple-stoned,
cathedral-like bulk speaks plainly of the large civil and military
population it once had to serve. But the medieval town of Grosmont never recovered after 1405 when it was burnt down by
Owain Glyndŵr's forces who here, immediately afterwards,
suffered their first heavy defeat. In the seventeenth century Camden's *Britannia* reported that Grosmont's old streets and causeways could still be traced under the turf of surrounding fields.

Grosmont castle looks rather a gem, sitting cosily on its motte
surrounded by a deep ditch and almost circled by old oaks and
ashes. In many places you see such mottes but have to imagine
the castle that once stood there. But here at Grosmont you have
the reality, the high walls and shapely towers continuing the
banks of the mound and all fairly entire. Inside you look up to
fragmentary stone stairways climbing among the masonry, fossi-
lized bits of the past transfixed in space and unconnected with
steps above or below. But the masterpiece of this castle is surely
the sophisticated fourteenth-century chimney, miraculously
standing alone and inconsequential when all about it has fallen.
Yes, Grosmont is a fine little castle; but you will probably leave
it wishing that water could be restored to the moat. If so you will
approve of White Castle, the third of the trio. Prominent on a
hill some five miles south-west of Grosmont it was more spacious
both in size and atmosphere than its sister castles. And more of it
has survived. Besides, it has a deep moat with water in it and
flowery banks all round. On the south the moat widens to enclose a crescent-shaped island (the hornwork) on which extra
defences once stood. From one of the towers you look across
most of north-west Monmouthshire to distant mountain ranges.
Almost due west is one of the great views of Skirrid, the county's
most shapely hill.

Two other good things near White Castle: the old church of Llantilio Crossenny which is built on ancient earthworks and contains interesting memorial stones; and Hengwrt ('old court'), which stood in the angle between the main road and the lane leading to White Castle. Hengwrt was a moated manor whose grassy square survives, surrounded by its deep, wide moat. A strange place, where it is left to your imagination to rebuild the medieval house once standing there. The moat is decidedly for naturalists. It is full of bulrushes, bur-reeds and water figworts where hidden moorhens make sharp exclamations. One day there I heard short sucking sounds I think were made by carp. What more appropriate fish in such a medieval place?

Skenfrith, Grosmont and White: these three castles are small and austere. But you may not realize how small and austere until you get to Raglan which stands at the side of A40 six miles south-east of White Castle. For Raglan has size, splendour and ornateness that were never dreamed of at the others. There is a finer finish about its stones and more decoration. Carved heads look down from parapets. Coats-of-arms are still visible on the walls. There is all the appearance of elaborate military purpose having been outlived and replaced by a long period of comfortable domestic living. You do not need much persuading that in its heyday this must have been the most sumptuous residence in all Wales. It has a splendid portcullised gateway between great towers. Within are the still impressive remains of other towers, courts and the great hall. But most spectacular is the six-sided keep that stands apart, moat-surrounded and called the Yellow Tower of Gwent. Skenfrith, Grosmont and White are castles of the twelfth and thirteenth centuries and look it. Raglan belongs to the fourteenth and fifteenth and even later and was occupied until Cromwell dismantled it.

In the north, Monmouthshire sends out an unexpected hand to grasp at a long valley up in the Black Mountains. This is the celebrated Vale of Ewyas down which the Honddu river flows on its way to join the Monnow west of Grosmont. The Honddu rises in the north-east corner of Breconshire on the high saddle between Hay Bluff (Pen y Beacon) and Lord Hereford's Knob (The Tumpa). Soon it is deep between high level ridges, treeless on top but scattered with thorns down their slopes and here and there the red gashes of gully erosion. Soon the river is lost among trees and hedges. From the west comes a quiet side-valley called Nant y Bwch—'the valley of the stag'. (Many Welsh place-names thus remember the deer which, once common in the land, had been exterminated by about 1700.) The purple rocks of Tarren yr Esgob ('bishop's ridge'), rise in broken, tree-scattered terraces, the habitat of kestrels, ravens and ring ouzels. Near the waters-meet are the remains of the nineteenth century, brick-built monastery where the sculptor Eric Gill lived a few years; and in the burial ground of the tiny church of Capel-y-ffin, shadowed by seven ancient yews, you will find simple gravestones with lettering carved by Gill.

Capel-y-ffin means 'boundary chapel'. It marks where road and river enter Monmouthshire from Breconshire. Here, where the mountain glen ends and the broader Vale of Ewyas begins, the Augustinian priory of Llanthony was founded about 1103, a perfect place, remote and peaceful even today, to have sited a monastic retreat. As Giraldus, who visited the place about eighty years later, reported: 'Here the monks, sitting in the cloisters, enjoying the fresh air, when they happen to look up towards the horizon behold the tops of the mountains touching the heavens and herds of wild deer feeding on their summits.' Here was built a splendid cruciform church with pointed arches (there is little Norman work) with considerable secular buildings adjacent. Today there are still sizeable fragments of arches, towers and high walls; and some of the ruins have now been converted for use as a hotel. Enough is left for us to realize the fine proportions and craftsmanship of this building of the late twelfth and early thirteenth centuries. For three years around 1811 Llanthony was owned by that eccentric man of letters, Walter Savage Landor. He bought the ruins and estate for £20,000, proposed to rebuild the priory and found an ideal community. He spent £50,000, planted many trees, quarrelled with every one in sight then departed.

Downstream the sides of the vale remain lofty for this is the highest land in Monmouthshire, Chwarel y Fan, on the west between Capel-y-ffin and Llanthony reaching 2,228 feet. On the east you come to Hatteral Hill, high, green-topped and knobbly, fronting the valley with reddish sandstone crags. Spare a moment here to look across the valley at one of the curiosities of Wales, the ancient tower of Cwmyoy church that leans wildly away from the rest of the building. A final touch of history in this vale: where you reach the Monmouth–Abergavenny road stands Llanvihangel Court, a late-Tudor, H-shaped manor-house open to visitors in summer. Trees here are huge, especially the ancient Spanish chestnuts. Ysgyryd Fawr stands close and mountain-like on the south. At Llanvihangel the Honddu can get no further south: checked by thick glacial deposits it turns sharply east then north, soon to join the Monnow.

From Llanvihangel you descend to the Usk valley at Abergavenny, a very old centre of life and communications. Here the Romans had a fortress called Gobannium (nothing left now) and major roads going in several directions: north to Kenchester, south to Caerleon, west to Brecon and probably south-west to Neath (the road called Sarn Hir). Of the medieval town-walls and castle little is left. But next-door to the castle is a museum, and a walk outside the castle walls looks delightfully across the Usk. Even if there were no visible history elsewhere in the town there is enough in the parish church. For here the high-born and powerful of past times are commemorated by an impressive array of tombs and effigies which reflect the former prestige of this church when it was part of a Benedictine priory evidently well patronized by the aristocracy. But even if you dislike pomp and alabaster this church is still worth a visit for the fifteenth and sixteenth-century carvings on the stall ends and other woodwork, and for the massive carved wooden figure of Jesse. If it is Sunday you will hear the very fine bells.

Abergavenny looks at friendly hills all round. Most famous—and a favourite walk for the energetic—is the Sugar Loaf (National Trust) which rises in isolation in the north-west to nearly 2,000 feet. The same distance north-east is the Great Skirrid (Ysgyryd Fawr), less high but more rugged than Sugar Loaf because of its rocks and bristling woods. Skirrid (also National Trust) formerly enjoyed repute as a holy mountain: it was one of the many St. Michael's mounts up which pilgrimage was made in medieval times. Today virtually nothing is left of Michael's chapel which stood above the north-facing cliffs. But his memory lives on in the district for churches dedicated to him (they are called Llanfihangel) are frequent hereabouts. The path up Ysgyryd Fawr starts from the Skenfrith road a mile or so from Abergavenny and follows the ridge to the summit at the north end. To keep to tradition take home a crumb of holy Skirrid earth for good luck. It will be earth from the Old Red Sandstone; for Skirrid, like Sugar Loaf, is an outlier of the Black Mountains.

Across the Usk south-west of Abergavenny rises a fair height whose lower slopes are heavily wooded and whose shoulders and head are open heathy moorland. This is the Blorenge (Y Blorens) which can be climbed by a path from Llanfoist. Motorists take B4246 (the Blaenavon road) cross the Brecon–Newport canal and climb up the western flank of the Blorenge to the highest point of the road. From there you look far up the Usk in Breconshire; and north you see that the Sugar Loaf, far from being the pointed Japanese volcano it looks from below, is in fact flat-topped, which shows it for what it is—a fragment surviving from some long-disappeared plateau. To the south the road falls towards Blaenavon and the beginnings of an industrially damaged landscape. You stand in the heather on the lark-loud moor and there not half a mile away is the black, rain-grooved flank of a massive coal tip. The view goes on down the length of Monmouthshire's most easterly mining valley, past the smoke of Pontypool then that of Newport, with a gleam of the Severn Sea beyond the murk. For an eastward view across the whole vale of Usk take the road towards Llanelen. On the way down you will find a thoughtfully provided viewpoint showing Abergavenny in the centre of its fertile basin with Skirrid and Sugar Loaf rising in splendour beyond.

Below Abergavenny the Usk says good-bye to the mountains and settles into a meandering course through the county's richest lands. Inevitably this has been a district rich in gentlemen's seats. Llanover House for instance. Here lived Lady Llanover (died 1896 aged 94), remarkable in that century for her championship of the Welsh language and traditions. She was author of several books and a founder of the Welsh Manuscript Society. A staunch teetotaller, she bought inns all over the district and converted them into coffee taverns. A reminder of the old Llanover folksiness is a local folk-dance, the Llanover reel, which is still widely known.

The pleasant town of Usk, where the river has been crossed since ancient times, has long history. Here was the big Roman station called Burrium and there is still a medieval castle (very ruined) and a medieval church—formerly a priory of Benedictine nuns. Connoisseurs of church woodwork will find Usk an admirable centre for some of Monmouthshire's best remaining screens. These can be seen in Usk church itself where the screen is of English design; at Betws Newydd (three miles north-west) which has one of the most nearly complete screens and roodlofts in Wales; Gwernesney (two miles east); Llangeview (a mile east); and Llangwm Uchaf (three miles east) where the ornateness of the screen is exceeded in Wales perhaps only by Llananno's in Radnorshire. South of Llangwm the Chepstow road climbs round a wooded cwm to high ground where a lane to the north leads you to Caer Fawr, a twenty acre, multivallate hill fort that looks across a vast landscape of Glamorgan hills, Black Mountains and farther western heights.

The church at Tredunnock, four miles downstream from Usk, is visited for the beautifully inscribed Roman stone of the second century which reads: 'D.M. JUL. JULIANUS MIL. LEG. II AUG. STIP. XVIII ANNO R. XL HIC SITUS EST CURA AGENTE AMANDA CONIUGE.' ('To the shades of the gods. Julius Julianus, a soldier of the second legion, the Augustan, of eighteen years service and forty years of age, has been buried here by the solicitude of his beloved wife.') This memorial was found three feet down in the churchyard: so presumably here is another instance of Christians having taken over a pagan burial ground. In the days of river commerce Tredunnock bridge (Newbridge) was the highest point reachable by barges. From Usk a minor road follows the river's east bank south through pleasant hamlets such as Llanllywel and Llantrisant. The river winds between willows and red-earthed banks where sand martins twitter in their nesting colonies and tall Himalayan balsams, pink or white, crowd the water's edge. A mile south of Newbridge a sharp little castle mound stands over a loop of the stream. In another mile, also above a curve in the river, you come to the forlorn site of the dismantled Kemeys Inferior church in its quiet burial ground.

For an obscure Norman stone castle go two miles south of Usk to Llangibby (Llangybi) whose old name was Tregrug. In its lay-out it may be grouped with the Edwardian castles of North Wales for it is of their age and extent. But unlike them Llangibby was never finished and has no part in history. It was given walls, towers, keep and gate-houses but there are no signs of internal buildings. Its walls, which enclose the whole of a large hill top that has extensive views are a riot of ivy, clematis and wild roses. Oak, ash, chestnut and beech crowd all round and the wide space inside is planted with conifers. A deep, dry moat and a ravine defend the western side. Altogether a surprising place.

The ten miles of country that domes up between lower Usk and lower Wye is largely agrarian but it is easy to picture it in the Dark Ages as thick woodland from end to end, an extension of Dean, the forest across the Wye. Still today there is a fair spread of woodland (alas, mainly coniferous) on the high parts of the dome, especially above the Wye and reaching south-west nearly to Caerlon. This south-western arm is what is left of the ancient forest of Wentwood. The road from Usk to Caerwent climbs to Pen-y-cae-mawr (good viewpoint) and passes near the extremely slight ruins of Troggy castle (Cas Troggy) from which perhaps Wentwood Forest was controlled in medieval times. From there the road goes south-east in the shade of many conifers to Newport's reservoir, a quiet anglers' retreat, then to Llanvair Discoed whose church has memories of eighteenth-century churchyard games. An inscription in the porch says:

> *Who ever hear on Sonday*
> *Will practis Playing at ball*
> *It may be before Monday*
> *The Devil will have you all.*

If, after the sylvan quiet of Wentwood, you can face the din and traffic of Newport you will find extremely little left of the pre-industrial era. It was in the twelfth century that Newport was first called new, to distinguish it from the nearby old town of Caerleon. From the Middle Ages there survive only some poor ruins of a castle which guarded the chief river crossing, now the principal bridge; and the high cathedral of St. Woolos (up Stow Hill) which has an admirable Norman doorway. One Tudor building, Murenger House, remains in High Street. The civic centre, where murals depict the town's history, is modern. There is an art gallery (early water colours a speciality) and a museum particularly good on Roman Monmouthshire, local geology and natural history. Music flourishes and there is a living theatre.

For a view of the Newport region go to Twm Barlwm, north

of Risca. At nearly 1,400 feet Twm Barlwm is one of the highest Iron Age forts in Wales but you can motor right to it—a popular spot for an afternoon out. It stands up conspicuous from many miles away, its eastern end crowned by a medieval castle mound. From up there you can see every facet of this part of South Wales: sheep, conifers, farmlands; long narrow towns squeezed into valley bottoms; coal-tips like mountain ranges along the sky; pylons and cooling towers; Newport and the docks; Cardiff smoke away in the distance; and out in the sea a few ships and the islands of Flatholm and Steepholm. But if you want a close look at a thriving industrial centre go to Pontypool on the other side of Mynydd Maen. Here there have been iron works, forges and furnaces since at least the sixteenth century: it is claimed that the first forge in America was built in 1652 by emigrants from Pontypool. Eighteenth-century lacquer ware known as Pontypool Japan is prized by collectors. For the first Welsh new town of modern times visit Cwm Brân, south of Pontypool, born 1949 and still developing.

Monmouth's eastern border is the winding lower Wye whose praises were sung in 1798 by Wordsworth in his 'Lines composed a few miles above Tintern Abbey'. By then the Wye tour was already becoming popular and Monmouth was in fact one of the first Welsh towns to feel the impact of tourism. Sited in a fertile basin circled by a score of hills, it has remained a favourite centre ever since. The medieval town was so placed between Wye and Monnow that water guarded it on three sides. It had a castle (birthplace of Henry V) which has now almost gone. But it retains the thirteenth-century bridge across the Monnow, a bridge that has not its like in all Britain because of the tall, massive, fortified gatehouse it supports. Another splendid bridge, over the Wye, is also an ancient monument. A medieval preaching cross stands beyond the Monnow bridge. In Roman times Monmouth was Blestium.

Monmouth is a town of surprises. For instance you find its heroes are Nelson (Monmouth was a favourite haunt) and C. S. Rolls (of Rolls-Royce) who was born there. Rolls, third son of Baron Llangattock, was a pioneer of cycling, ballooning, motoring, aviation and aerial photography. Killed in 1910 he was the first British victim of a flying accident. There is a museum full of memories of both these celebrities. It also includes local archaeology and history from the Stone Age onwards and there is an excellent geological map. Next door to the castle ruins is Great Castle House (1673). Occupied by soldiery it is open to visitors in summer. A famous citizen was Geoffrey of Monmouth who in the twelfth century produced the most fictitious history of Britain ever written. But because it was stuffed with good stories it was a best-seller and though discredited by historians it influenced literature for many centuries. To Geoffrey more than anyone we owe the great vogue of the Arthurian legends. The fanciful notion that Arthur held court at Caerleon brought Tennyson there in search of local colour for his *Idylls of the King*. Geoffrey, a churchman, lived at Monmouth priory in whose ruins a window is still known as 'Geoffrey's window'. For a promenade along the Wye there is a park called Chippenham Mead. And for a panorama of Monmouth and its vale climb the Kymin, a National Trust hill east of the town across the Wye. Another great viewpoint is the hill called Craig-y-dorth south of Mitchell Troy (where the village stocks survive in the church).

The country from Monmouth to Chepstow, though now to quite a large extent agricultural, is by its traditions all a forest land and place names such as Penallt and Argoed are full of woodland memories (*allt* and *goed* being Welsh for wooded places). Fascinating air photos of this district show many dark circles in the pale fields, circles that were the sites of charcoal-burners' fires in the forest. The parish of Penallt, standing high on a ridge that slopes steeply to the Wye, is served by an intricacy of zigzagging lanes that eventually get you down to the church in its quiet spot among trees above the river. It is only a modest little church yet it has a high square tower. There is an an aged sundial over the porch. Tall limes stand near a yew that looks immortal.

South of Penallt much of the forest still endures or has been revived by the Forestry Commission who call it Tintern Forest —a National Forest Park. For this region a good centre is the village of Trelleck, a name evidently derived from the Welsh *tri* (three) and *llech* (stone). Three fine pillars of the local conglomerate rock about eight, ten and twelve feet tall and presumably set up in the Bronze Age, stand in a line near the side of the road a little south-west of the village and are locally called Harold's Stones. (Giraldus tells us that in his day (twelfth century) there were still many stones in existence commemorating King Harold's victories over the Welsh.) The underside of the largest Trelleck stone is a useful geological specimen showing how conglomerate rocks have formed on the bed of a prehistoric ocean as layers of gravel and sand alternating with layers of pebbles. In Trelleck itself is a red-earthed castle mound rather hidden behind the houses. A preaching cross in the churchyard looks ancient but the most visited feature of this old church is a sundial made in 1637 and now preserved inside. Crudely incised on it is a representation of the three standing stones and other local attractions such as the Virtuous Well which you pass on the southward road out of the village. This holy well of St. Anne was a place of pilgrimage from the Middle Ages to the seventeenth century. It is still cared for, its walls beautiful with liverworts, its surrounds gay with cresses and water speedwell.

From there the road winds alongside coniferous forest, passing a marshy common brightly edged with wild flowers and where nightjars reel in the summer dusk. In June the wood spotted orchid is particularly splendid along these roadsides all down the steep twisting road to the Wye at Llandogo, a village which has memories of days when all commerce was by water and barges were constantly passing on the river, some going with difficulty all the way up to Hereford. The bell of the last boat to sail up the Wye to Llandogo, the *William and Sarah* of Chepstow, is preserved inside the church. Near Llandogo there were small paper mills until the 1870's, their raw material being esparto grass imported through Bristol. This industry came here because of the exceptionally clear water of the streams (hence the name Whitebrook) which enabled the whitest paper to be produced. There were other paper mills in the charming little valley at Mounton just west of Chepstow and at nearby Shirenewton.

The best way to see the lower Wye is from a boat, which is how most of the pioneer tour-writers saw it. Though some of them had purple-passaged their way all down the Wye from its source they still found new words of wonder when round a bend of the river the ruins of Tintern abbey fell upon their easily astonished gaze. 'On approaching this venerable relic', wrote one of them, 'the steep hills and hanging woods, the rolling stream, the nodding ruin, the surviving monuments of falling grandeur and beauty in decay, the opening vacancy, stillness and retirement all aid the enthusiasm of the spectator, who forgets for a moment that he is connected with the busy world.' But better go by moonlight, says another visitor: 'Under the silvery beams of the pale orb of night, the lights and shadows are indescribably fine and solemnly grand.' Things are different now. The traffic on the main road has killed the quietness and the Ministry of Works shuts the gate long before any moonlight effects can begin to work their magic. Even so a lot of the magnificence of this Cistercian abbey survives from the thirteenth and fourteenth centuries which saw it built. Its finest fragment is the sixty-foot east window of the choir.

Today Tintern rather lives on its abbey but it was not always so. At the time when iron to be smelted was taken to wherever there were forests, there was an iron foundry next-door to the abbey. Hence all the local charcoal burning. Centuries before that other metals had been worked here. A plaque on the wall outside the abbey says: 'Near this place in the year 1568 brass was first made by alloying copper with zinc.' A brass foundry and ethereal abbey ruins: strange to think of them side by side in that fair place. Much of the nearby Anchor Hotel is obviously very old and presumably built from abbey stones. Large parts of a corn mill make an unusual sight in the lounge bar.

Below Tintern the river gets more remote. As it burrows deeper into its gorge its banks get steeper, more solid with trees, forcing the road to climb away towards the celebrated viewpoint of the Wyndcliff which you can reach either up a steep path through woods of beech and yew, or by going round the road and walking to the viewpoint along a much easier path from the west. The Wyndcliff looks down over its trees on to one of the Wye's most perfect loops enclosing, on the Gloucestershire side, the tiny parish of Lancaut that in the Middle Ages was a world apart with its own minute church now in ruins. Iron Age Lancaut was even more isolated for then there were defensive earthworks across the neck of land. All about Lancaut and down the Wye to Chepstow great cliffs and quarries rise along the river; some are wooded, others show faces of pale limestone. Beyond, the view reaches far: the rest of south Monmouthshire, the Severn estuary, the suspension bridge and deep into Somerset beyond. The Wyndcliff view is most glorious when the reds and yellows of autumn are on the beeches.

These steep woods curve north to unite with those of Black-cliff, the whole 200 acres forming a Forest Reserve of the Nature Conservancy and the Forestry Commission. If all you know of yews is the stolid specimens of churchyards you will be surprised by the wild yews of Wyndcliff, for they have long arching branches as graceful as any other trees of the greenwood. For a cross-section of the different types of local woodland take the steep lane from Tintern past an attractive chain of little pools up to Devauden (a name which may come from *ffawydden*, the Welsh word for beech). Here are woods of oak, beech and spruce mature enough to give a feeling of high forest that is rare in Wales. The Wye limestone is known for its wild flowers as well as its trees. The list is long and includes choice species such as pale St. John's wort, spreading bellflower, woolly thistle, winter-green (*Pyrola minor*) and one extreme rarity, the upright spurge, native nowhere else in the British Isles.

The Wye's final big curve is occupied by Chepstow. The name is English and means 'market town'; but to the early Normans the place was 'Striguil' which may represent their attempt at some old Welsh word such as *Ystraigyl*, meaning 'a bend'. But if this was the original Welsh name the Welsh have forgotten it for they know the town as Cas-gwent, the castle of Gwent, as this part of Wales has been called since the Middle Ages. Chepstow's Norman town walls (along the Port Walk), now incomplete but still traceable throughout, are best known at their only gate. This straddles the steep main street and was not intended for twentieth century traffic. These thirteenth-century walls ran north-south from river bank to river bank, defending the town from the west. At their north end the castle stands dominant above the river, its pale walls seeming to grow naturally from the limestone cliffs. On its long narrow platform edged by a seventy-foot sheer drop it looks extremely strong. The first and greatest foot-hold of the Normans in Gwent, it threatened the whole district so convincingly that its defences were never tested until centuries later when during the Civil War it changed hands more than once. The Cromwellians, usually so unkind to castles, actually repaired Chepstow castle and it continued well into Stuart times to house a garrison and a state prison. It eventually fell into neglect and its roofs and rooms collapsed. But the ramparts, the keep, Marten's tower and the great gate-house with its very thick doors survive. A more recent splendour is a venerable walnut tree within the castle walls. Chepstow's parish church, formerly that of a Benedictine priory, contains good early Norman work, notably the nave and the fine west door. In the seventeenth and eighteenth centuries Chepstow made bells which still ring in many churches of England and Wales. To find the last few miles of Offa's Dyke you must cross the Wye into Gloucestershire and the easiest bit to see is the very end of it where B4228 cuts through it on a hill top a mile north of Beachley.

By tradition a local hero-king of the Dark Ages was Theoderick (Tewdric) who died resisting the Saxons. You will find a church dedicated to him at Mathern nearly two miles southwest of Chepstow and on the way there, a hundred yards south of the bridge under the motorway, you will see on the right a notice indicating the well where tradition says his wounds were washed. Note the superb Wellingtonia flourishing in Mathern churchyard and the beautiful Tudor house next door which is on the site of a medieval palace of the bishops of Llandaff. Across the fields you can see the towers and tall chimneys of Moynes Court, a Jacobean house on another historic site. Beyond this is St. Pierre, a Tudor house in a 200-acre park scattered with ancient trees. There is a lake and a small medieval church with two ancient sepulchral slabs.

Chepstow's rural district council and previous owners deserve credit for their painstaking care of Caldicot Castle five miles south-west of Chepstow. It is a sizeable Norman stronghold of the twelfth century, added to in the fourteenth to make it more liveable. The oldest portion is the fine round keep standing on a motte and moated. The most imposing item is the double-towered main entrance gate of the fourteenth century. The walls are almost intact but internal buildings have gone. Flower gardens and a goldfish pond introduce an unusual note; and quite incongruous is the figurehead of Nelson's flagship! There is also a small museum and art gallery.

For a whiff of the open estuary and a further step back into history go to nearby Sudbrook. It is worth while finding your way between the houses and the huge pulp-mill where the conifers of Wales are turned into paper. For on the shore beyond, only a few feet above the tide, are the two remaining sides of an extensive Iron Age fort, coast erosion having carried the rest away. This fort, clearly built to command an ancient ferry, is large, in fact it encloses a football ground, its massive banks providing terraces for the spectators. Excavation has revealed copious traces of Iron Age occupation which continued till A.D. 100 when perhaps the Celtic occupants were removed to Roman Caerwent. There was a brief re-occupation in medieval times when a little church, now a fragment, was built close to the ramparts. A mile to the north is the ruined Neolithic chambered long barrow of Heston Brake.

Heavily wooded throughout and fringed on the south by a wide belt of swamps and mudflats, Monmouthshire must have been a daunting prospect for Neolithic man, but as his few chambered tombs show he managed to get at least a footing in the county. Iron Age times with the use of improved axes no doubt bit deeply into the forests. The Romans may have begun the reclamation of the coastal lands that for many miles east and west of Newport lie below the level of spring tides and which have long been protected by high banks. The walls have often been breached and the polders flooded but never worse than in the great inundation of 20th January 1606, which is commemorated on tablets in several coastal churches such as Redwick, St. Bride's Wentlooge and Peterstone Wentlooge. At Goldcliff a small brass plate in the chancel reads: '1606 on the xx day of January even as it came to pass it pleased God the Flud did flow to the edge of this same bras and in this parish theare was lost 5000 and od pownds besides xxii people was in the parish drownd.' Much of this coastal land is still pretty marshy and wild and there are miles of flat, rushy fields with willow-edged ditches. The Monmouthshire Naturalists' Trust preserves a fragment of the former wilderness near Magor.

11

GLAMORGAN

(Morgannwg or Sir Forgannwg)

The word has got round that Glamorgan is nothing but vast coal mines, steelworks and docks. But the image is a false one. Of course there has been scenic devastation especially in those coal valleys which, like the Rhondda, were once praised for their wild beauty. Yet despite industrialization there probably remains in Glamorgan a greater variety, though not a greater area, of unspoilt country than in any other Welsh county. If you doubt this I will refer you to one statistic: that there are more species of wild plants in Glamorgan than elsewhere in Wales—as good a yardstick as any for measuring a region's natural variety. Even the infamous valleys have their champions who will tell you that any place where vigorous communities live and work is rich in human interest. So if you have never seen a Welsh coal valley go up say, the Rhondda, the Taff or the Rhymney. You will see immediately why they so easily shock the eye. It is their narrowness. They are so closed in, so deep, so steep-sided that the mines, factories and terraced houses have been forced to develop in long, thin, winding lines. No room down there for the tips. So, laboriously and expensively, millions of tons of waste have gone up the steep slopes on aerial ropeways and been dumped on the hills. Often there have been landslides, bringing the wet muck across the roads. And in 1967 at Aberfan, three miles south of Merthyr Tydfil, there was the school that was buried and a generation of children lost.

Not that every inch of the coal valleys is dark and Satanic. As you follow the winding main roads up the banks of polluted rivers you come to occasional open hillsides colourful with bracken and heather and where sheep still graze; or to steep oak-woods that have redstarts and pied flycatchers in the spring. Between the valleys, as between the Rhondda Fach and the Cynon for instance, you will find farms that, despite the industrial revolution all round and below them, have remained in the same family for many generations. And there are vast areas of modern forest. Near the heads of the valleys, especially those of Rhondda, the roads take you up into really fine mountain country. Here there are trout in the rivers, dippers and grey wagtails on the streams, ravens and buzzards nesting in cliffs that look on towns far below. This is the highest ground in Glamorgan, rising to 1,969 feet. Here the cliffs of Craig y Llyn look spectacularly down upon conifer plantations and the pool called Llyn Fawr, famous among archaeologists for the hoard of Bronze Age vessels and weapons once found in it. They are presumed to have been cast into the water as an offering to some lake god. Mesolithic flints have also been found on these moors.

You may or may not venture up the valleys. But at least you should go to Caerphilly (Caerffili) upon which many of the valleys converge. For there amid collieries, quarries, factories and houses you will find a medieval castle that spreads hugely amid thirty acres of beautiful lakes and moats—the biggest castle in Britain except for Windsor itself. Though not built till the fourteenth century Caerphilly is a perfect Edwardian-type castle with concentric inner and outer wards. By early Tudor times it was decaying and after the Civil War was slighted by the Cromwellians who failed to dislodge the leaning tower. They blew enormous holes in it but were defeated by its medieval mortar. So it stands to this day, still deliciously tilted. The castle continued to crumble until in our century its owner the Marquis of Bute, a captain of South Wales industry, extensively restored it.

Merthyr Tydfil (or Tudful) thirteen miles north-west of Caerphilly, was a mushroom town of the industrial revolution and as the centre of what was the world's greatest iron-producing region, was for a time the largest town in Wales. But after the 1850's high-grade ores from abroad put Welsh iron out of favour and most of the steel industry migrated down to meet the foreign ore at the ports. And there it remains. Merthyr once pioneered everything made of iron: cannons, railway engines, cables and a thousand other things. Typical of its iron tycoons were men such as Guest and Crawshay. Guest lived at Dowlais where his wife, Lady Charlotte, made with some help a heroic first translation into English of the whole of the *Mabinogion* (1849).

As for Crawshay, if you want an introduction to the industrial valleys you should visit the museum now housed at his former home, Cyfarthfa castle, which stands in fine grounds at Merthyr. The name Merthyr Tydfil, often translated as 'the martyrdom of St. Tudful', probably meant nothing more than 'the church of Tudful'. The church is restored fourteenth century but contains ancient inscribed stones. With changing times Merthyr has had to turn its hand to a variety of manufactures and now there is even a factory that turns out cross-bows. (Nor is the long bow forgotten in the valleys: archery is an enthusiastic local sport perhaps nowhere more popular in Britain than in the Rhondda.[1]) One fragment of the past worth seeing near Merthyr is ten miles down the valley at Pontypridd where the Taff was bridged in 1755 by William Edwards. It is a long, slim and elegant single span of masonry. In his first attempt the key stones were pushed out by the weight of the material which he then reduced by piercing it with six large holes and it has stood ever since. When built, the bridge was in a rural spot: it is now in the town centre.

For another place that has old memories but is adapting itself to great changes go a few miles further south to Llantrisant ('church of three saints'), a small hill-top town that looks south from the edge of the uplands. A well-known landmark is its Norman church, dedicated to the Celtic saints Illtud, Tyfodwg and Gwynno. It also has a Norman castle of which one tower survives. And there are defences of far earlier date—the gorse-yellow banks of Caerau, the Iron Age fort that crowns the neighbouring hill. Llantrisant looks south across wide farming lands but its foreground is changing. In 1967 it became the home of the Royal Mint. And now a New Town is spreading below this old town that every seven years still beats its bounds.

The visitor who wants to see and understand all the faces of this fascinating county should go first to the National Museum of Wales. This superb museum which stands in the centre of

[1] The Archery Centre is at Llwynypia.

Glamorgan

Cardiff along with the municipal buildings and the university, gives you an unrivalled introduction to local prehistory, history, geology, botany, zoology, industry and art (as well as covering the rest of Wales). If I had to pick out one set of exhibits more striking than the rest it would be the magnificent collection of early Welsh decorated crosses and inscribed stones. And one of the art department's most interesting features is the show of paintings by Richard Wilson and other artists famous for their Welsh landscapes.

From the National Museum it is a natural step to St. Fagan's, a hundred-acre estate with garden, fish ponds and specimen trees four miles west of the centre of Cardiff. For here is the Welsh Folk Museum where the past life and culture of Wales, its arts, crafts and implements are exhibited. Particularly interesting are the old houses, craft workshops and other buildings that have been saved from ruin elsewhere in Wales and rebuilt at St. Fagan's. You will find a sixteenth-century cruck-built barn from Flintshire; an eighteenth-century woollen factory from Breconshire; a tannery from Radnorshire; old farmhouses from several parts of Wales; an early Unitarian chapel from Carmarthenshire; a Welsh gipsy caravan; and an English-looking toll-gate from Aberystwyth. It is good to find that where possible the buildings are kept in use. So the woollen factory still works and sells its products and there are also wood turners and basket makers. St. Fagan's house itself is Tudor, built on the site of a Norman castle.

Close to Cardiff's civic centre is the castle whose architectural history is complex. Here the Romans made a strong stone fort within which the early Normans put a motte and bailey castle whose huge mound still exists crowned by an attractive thirteenth-century keep. Later builders repaired the Roman walls and added living quarters. These now form the main block of the present castle. It continued to be lived in and its nineteenth century owners, the marquesses of Bute, Gothicized parts of the exterior. The Roman wall has been rebuilt, including an impressive gate-house which is a pretty faithful reproduction even if purists do cavil about some of the details. The castle is still a residence but is usually open to the public. Its main features are the banqueting hall (frescoes and stained glass); the Chaucer room (stained glass illustrating the *Canterbury Tales*); a richly ornate chapel; an Arab room; and a viewpoint clock tower.

Glamorgan

Allow plenty of time for visiting the cathedral at Llandaff, two miles north-west of the centre of Cardiff, for though small it is full of fine things. Here from the very earliest Christian times stood a religious house of which nothing survives except a Celtic cross discovered in 1870 in a nearby well. The present building was commenced in 1120. To boost its religious status the bones of a then much revered saint called Dyfrig were transferred from Bardsey Island and reburied in the new cathedral (an incident that is carved on the twentieth-century font). The building was long in completing: its first arches were Norman, its last were Gothic. It flourished until near the mid-sixteenth century but after the Reformation it fell into ever deepening neglect. At times in the seventeenth century it was a beer house and then a cattle shed. Early in the eighteenth century two towers collapsed and the roof of the nave fell in. Later that century and in the nineteenth the cathedral was restored only to be wrecked by a German landmine in 1941, so joining Coventry's as Britain's worst cathedral casualties of World War II. After that war the cathedral was quickly rebuilt and once again it reposes in its quiet hollow. It contains fine medieval and modern work, including an imposing aluminium Christus by Epstein. For those who prefer nineteenth-century art there is an attractive triptych by Rossetti in St. Illtud's chapel. Botanists will be interested to identify the twelve species of wild flowers depicted on the bronze panels of the reredos in the Lady Chapel: all have Welsh names linking them with the Virgin Mary just as some of them, such as lady's mantle, have in English. For a curiosity just outside Cardiff go to Castell Coch ('the red castle'). Originally built in red sandstone by twelfth-century Normans it was for long centuries a ruin. Then in 1875 the Marquis of Bute rebuilt it in the style of a Rhine castle. It is open to visitors and inside you find its walls and ceilings remarkably and lavishly decorated with paintings of many subjects including lots of plants, animals, birds and butterflies, some illustrating scenes from Aesop's fables.

Cardiff extends south across dockland to Penarth which is largely residential and also a popular holiday resort with esplanade, gardens and pier. From here steamboats go across to Weston in Somerset. Opposite the railway station is the Turner House art gallery, a branch of the National Museum. South from Penarth small cliffs extend to Lavernock Point which has views across shingle and rocks to Flatholm, a low-lying island with a tall lighthouse: three miles from the mainland, Flatholm is the most southerly part of Wales. Between Lavernock Point and the island the first radio message ever transmitted across water was sent by Marconi on 11th May 1897. Lavernock Point is useful to birdwatchers who observe coastwise migration there. To the west a wide sandy shore extends to Sully Island which becomes a peninsula at low tide. You can then walk out over the rocks to picnic on the island, examine the grassy banks of its Iron Age promontory fort and see how, at the south-east corner, the horizontal Triassic rocks lie directly on the steeply dipping strata of the Carboniferous Limestone. But keep an eye on the tide.

West from Sully Island you look a couple of miles along the shore to Barry which advertises itself as 'the playground of South Wales'. Barry also has docks which when built in 1889 were the world's largest. The name appears to come from St. Baruc, the site of whose chapel is still preserved on a cliff edge of Barry Island near the fun fair. Along the shore immediately west of Barry you come to Porthkerry from whose isolated church a path goes down to a pebbly beach through steep woodland that is hummocky with the multiple banks and ditches of The Bulwarks, a large Iron Age fort. The pale cliffs all along this coast consist of numerous horizontal strata of Lower Lias formation— thin slabs of limestone alternating with soft shales which are easily eroded by wave action. Fossil hunters love them, especially for their ammonites.

West from Cardiff and Barry to Bridgend and on to Port Talbot lies the so-called Vale of Glamorgan which is in fact a coastal plateau. A fertile farming region, it was eagerly competed for by the invaders of all history. The Romans built their villas on it. The Normans loaded it with castles. Today it contrasts with industrial Glamorgan and many of its hamlets and villages have kept their rural character. That early man flourished in the Vale is attested by the long barrow at Tinkinswood half a mile south of A48 at St. Nicholas. This is one of the most striking Neolithic burial chambers in Wales mainly because of the huge size of the capstone which measures seven yards by five and weighs about forty tons. Of a type well known in the Severn-Cotswold region it is evidently the work of colonists who reached the area by the western sea-route perhaps about 3,000

23. Britain's second largest castle, at Caerphilly, Glamorgan

24. Threecliff Bay, a place of beauty and historical interest in the Gower, Glamorgan

25. The upper Towy, in the heart of south-central Wales,
north Carmarthenshire

26. Talley Abbey, north of Llandeilo, Carmarthenshire: surviving
fragments of the medieval church tower

Glamorgan

B.C. Less than a mile down the road is another fine chambered tomb. Between these two burial chambers you pass Dyffryn House which has attractive grounds, gardens and greenhouses open to the public.

Three miles south-west of Dyffryn House you go down into a peaceful valley among trees. You reach Llancarfan, a very fair village with a streamside church and a cawing of rooks. The church, which has the only wooden reredos in Wales, a fine piece of Welsh medieval carving, is on the site of a Dark Ages monastery. Many centuries earlier the Iron Age had a large settlement on a hill half a mile to the east—the Castle Ditches. This is all a charming region. The hedges in summer are hung with roses and wild clematis; the banks are gay with scabious and greater knapweed; the lanes go up and down and twist round with every whim of the streams. So you come to the long wooded vale above which Penmark village stands by a stream, its church almost touching the remnants of a fair-sized Norman castle of little history.

Man has made some famous holes in the ground in Wales, especially in the north. But the slate quarries of Nantlle and the copper mines of Parys have a rival in the vast excavation for limestone at Aberthaw where the tall smoking chimneys of a cement works dominate a coast whose appearance is ruined anyway by a great power station at Breaksea Point. All this industrialization makes Aberthaw seem modern: but as a port it has a history going back to the Middle Ages and an inn claiming to be 600 years old. Just west of Aberthaw is Gileston, a village whose name perpetuates the memory of a medieval family whose arms, along with others, are carved on the fifteenth-century church door.

Four miles west of Aberthaw is one of the most ancient centres of Welsh civilization—Llantwit Major (Llanilltud Fawr), that is 'the great church of Illtud', as distinct from the many less important churches of this very active sixth-century propagandist. At Llantwit was a very early type of British monastic university which may well have carried on a tradition of culture established by the Romans who had a villa here in the second and third centuries. With the Cardiff–Neath Roman road on the north and busy sea-lanes on the south the monastery at Llantwit was in touch with the world. Llantwit Major church is one of the most unusual in Wales. It is twice the length of an average church because it is in fact two churches, the one parish, the other monastic in origin. The western church, which was on the monastic site, was rebuilt in the fifteenth century and is now used as a museum to house an outstanding collection of Celtic stones and medieval inscribed crosses. The eastern church (late thirteenth century) is notable for its elaborate fourteenth-century reredos and its wall paintings. But the most valued feature of the church is a thirteenth-century stone carving of Jesse. Llantwit is a small market town retaining its old lay-out of narrow streets centred on an old townhall.

Cowbridge (Y Bont-faen), a medievally chartered borough five miles inland, is a good nineteenth-century country town. In the Middle Ages it was castled, walled and ditched. The castle has completely vanished but parts of the wall and ditch are still to be seen as well as one of the gate-ways. There is a grammar school founded 1608. A curiosity is the rough standing stone outside a butcher's shop in the main street—a rare survival of an ancient stone within a built-up area. If you hear the eight church bells you will be listening to some of the masterpieces of the famous Chepstow foundry of the first half of the eighteenth century. Attractive villages abound near Cowbridge. St. Hilary, two miles south-east, has an agreeable combination of new houses and old (some thatched); and there are tall shading trees, flowery gardens and an interesting Norman church. A mile south-west of St. Hilary the ruins of Beaupre (call it 'Bewper') castle represent a once-magnificent late Tudor mansion now reached by a footpath along the stream from Howe Mill. The Basset family who built Beaupre have an excessively imposing monument dated 1597 in the church at Llantrithyd. Far too large for so small a church it really hits you with its bright reds, golds and blues. You come out of doors and look with relief at the soft tones of the mouldering ivy-clad ruins of the Tudor mansion next to the church.

For the western half of the Vale the best centre is Bridgend. Though trafficky and industrial it has an attractive reach along the Ogmore river where there is a humpy, two-arched bridge of the eighteenth century. Castle ruins, small but with a good Norman doorway, stand with St. Illtud's church above the town near the brink of a formidable cliff. The church has interesting cross slabs. A small sixteenth-century building on the right as you go up to the church was a hospice of the Knights of Jerusalem. It has their cross on the gate and interesting monograms and doorways inside. Bridgend castle is traditionally called the old castle, which presupposes a new one somewhere. This presumably was the twelfth to fourteenth-century castle at Coity, a good mile to the north-east. Though now only a shell it still stands tall and imposing in the centre of the village. Next to the castle is a fine medieval cruciform church with a massively timbered roof and other interesting features. It may be compared with the similar church a mile and a half south-east at Coychurch where there is a good Celtic cross and the base of another. For a hamlet that retains an air of remoteness though only two miles from the outskirts of Bridgend go to Llangan whose churchyard, half circled by beeches, is notable for its two ancient crosses, one tall and ornate on a stepped platform, the other a large wheel cross roofed against the weather.

But the architectural and historical pride of this district is the priory church at Ewenny. It stands a little south of Bridgend along a quiet streamside lane adjacent to a Georgian house built on the site of the monastic buildings. Founded in the twelfth century this was a Benedictine priory subordinate to Gloucester abbey. Its church is purely Norman work, perhaps the best in any church in Wales. The tower is decidedly military and there are other castle-like defences which make this one of the most fortified church buildings in Britain. In the church are various medieval monuments including the fine sepulchral slab of Maurice de Londres, thought to be the son of the priory's founder. Among objects of interest kept in the church is a good specimen of an ammonite, a fossil no doubt brought in long ago as a 'holy relic'. The Ewenny district has first-class potter's clay that has served local craftsmen for centuries. Ewenny ware can still be bought at roadside potteries between Bridgend and the priory.

The coast of the Vale from Llantwit Major west nearly to the Ogmore river is mercifully undeveloped. First you come to St. Donat's where a wooded glen above the shore contains a large, thirteenth century Norman castle which has been continuously lived in and adapted. The interesting mixture of styles includes some good Tudor work. This century the castle was modernized

by Hearst, an American newspaper tycoon and now houses
Atlantic College, an international, co-educational sixth-form
school. It is occasionally open to the public especially in August
and September. For centuries the castle was occupied by the
Stradling family whose memorials survive in the ancient church
amid trees below the castle. The church, which has an elegant
medieval cross, is dedicated to St. Dunwyd, a Celtic name of
which Donat is an Anglicization.

At Marcross, a mile north-west of St. Donat's, is a little
church whose twelfth-century chancel arch has unusual orna-
mentation—a simple chevron motif. From here a deep green
glen goes down to the sea at Nash Point which has the well-
defined banks of an Iron Age promontory fort. On the east side
of the cwm are two lighthouses (one dismantled). Originally the
two lights shone together, for this was one of the few ways of
distinguishing one lighthouse from another before revolving
light beams were invented. The limestone cliffs are beautifully
stratified and when the tide is out you see how their lowest beds
extend out to sea as a wave-cut platform. There are good breezy
walks along their tops and views across to Exmoor. The 'pillow
mounds' marked on the map are probably the remains of
medieval rabbit warrens.

Four miles up the coast road you come to St. Bride's Major
whose church has early monuments. From St. Bride's a road
winds down a fine bare valley northwards to Ewenny. And from
near the church a path that looks ancient goes north-west over
the down to Ogmore castle, a much photographed ruin perched
up on a motte beside a river with picturesque swans and stepping-
stones. Ogmore castle, parts of it as old as Ewenny priory church,
was built of stone at a time when most motte castles were still
being constructed in wood. Built by the same de Londres who
founded Ewenny priory this castle's best surviving feature is a
twelfth-century hooded fireplace. Below the castle the Ewenny
river soon joins the Ogmore to flow by a lovely woodland to the
coast at the popular little resort of Ogmore-by-Sea. Here are
sands for bathing and cliffs for walking along to Dunraven Bay.
At Ogmore are the Sutton limestone quarries, source of a
famous building material. A mile offshore is the infamous
Tusker Rock which comes out at low water. The coast is particularly beautiful from Ogmore to Dunraven, with caves and

blow-holes in the cliffs. On the point called Trwyn-y-witch ('witch's nose'), the embankments of an Iron Age fort are clear to see. So, usually, is the splendid herd of fallow deer in the grounds of Dunraven castle, a private house just inland.

From Ogmore castle you can cross the stepping-stones and follow the short path to Merthyr Mawr, picturesque hamlet with thatched roofs. A mile south-west the gloomy ruins of Candleston castle stand amid trees. This castle was a fifteenth-century manor house that looked seaward across wide and fertile lands that have since been lost under mountainous sand-dunes. As you wander through these dunes you will find them heavily patched by a thorny shrub with silver-green, willow-like leaves. This is the sea buckthorn, a beautiful species with many orange berries eaten by fieldfares and other thrushes. But unless checked it may eventually spread into a vast, impenetrable scrub. Beyond the buckthorn zone is something much more sinister: the central area of these dunes is an army firing range. So look out for red flags flying. Merthyr Mawr dunes are a likely spot for keen-eyed amateur archaeologists to pick up something good. For here man lived in Neolithic, Bronze and Iron Age times and beneath these sands his traces are copiously preserved. After gales have scooped up sand by the ton all sorts of treasures have sometimes come to light in the form of flint tools, arrowheads, scrapers and even brooches. So try your luck. And if unsuccessful you can console yourself by visiting the good collection of such finds that are displayed at Cardiff and Swansea museums. These impressive dunes peaking up here and there to over 200 feet are the highest in Europe except for some on the German coast. They continue all the way to Porthcawl which was a busy port last century until Barry put it out of business. This century Porthcawl has grown rapidly as a holiday resort and is particularly popular as a centre for conferences and other gatherings, none of which is more vocal than the annual miners' eisteddfod in October. Then you really do hear the people sing.

From Porthcawl the coast turns north-west and after two miles the dunes begin again. Then you have one of those violent scenic contrasts so typically Glamorgan. At Kenfig you are in a sandy wilderness fragrant with thyme and rest-harrow near a beautiful lake. And just beyond it all is a vast, malignant-looking steelworks. But though man's impact on nature here is formid-

able, in the past it has been the other way round. For just after
the end of the Middle Ages the walled and castled borough of
Kenfig was totally buried by blown sand. Records show that the
sand began to trouble the town in the fourteenth century and
continued to do so all through the fifteenth. But the end seems
to have come suddenly when a tremendous storm early in the
sixteenth century deposited a Sahara of sand on the place. How
Kenfig pool survived is a mystery. All we know is that it was
there before the dunes came, for in 1365 it was granted as a
fishery to the monks of Margam abbey. All that is now left of
Kenfig are its castle remains that stick up out of the sand close to
the railway north of the pool. You can see them from Maudlam
church which looks over the dunes from the safety of higher
ground. This church is notable for its thick, stumpy, fortress of
a tower (the district suffered terribly in the medieval wars) and
for its early Norman font with a fish-scale pattern worked all
over it. The name Maudlam was once 'Magdalene'.

Three miles north of Kenfig are the ruins of Margam abbey
founded in 1147 by the Earl of Gloucester who gave lands there
to the Cistercians. Today this abbey's church is unique in Wales
as the only Cistercian church still in use. Not that it survives in
anything like entirety. In its day it was larger and perhaps more
splendid than Tintern but the present church uses only a part of
the original structure. It has a fine Norman arch in the west front
and contains elaborate tombs of generations of two local
families, the Mansels and the Talbots. The rest of the monastic
ruins are in private grounds that contain a magnificent eighteenth-
century orangery. Close to the church is a fascinating little
museum crowded with Celtic crosses and medieval monuments,
the finest being the tenth-century cross of Conbelin, one of the
greater crosses of Wales. A Roman milestone re-cut as a Christian memorial in the sixth century is another rare exhibit. The
presence of so many early stones suggests that Margam had been
an important religious place for centuries before Norman times.
Immediately above the abbey is a hill fort with a view across the
steelworks to Port Talbot—the Iron Age of prehistory face to
face with that of today. From the hill fort the land climbs quickly
to the beautiful uplands of Mynydd Margam which have probably altered little in many centuries until the recent afforestation.
Some of the sheepwalks on which the Cistercians founded their

wealth still survive. So do traces of prehistory in the form of trackways, earthworks and burial mounds. ('Twmpath' is a favourite word here for such mounds.)

Port Talbot, with no pretensions to beauty in its docks and factories, nevertheless welcomes multitudes to its amusements and fine sands at Aberafan. North-westward the scenic contrasts continue. Briton Ferry is singularly charmless yet has beautiful woodland climbing out of it towards the hills. And Neath, unlovely as the rest, is close to a beautiful vale with attractive side-dingles. To see one of these take B4434 towards Resolven. Turn right at Melin Court up a steep hill and you are soon at the brink of a waterfall that drops in thunder into a deep ravine. But upland Glamorgan is full of such little-known beauties—streams, gorges, waterfalls, viewpoints and forests. There is much fine country, especially if you climb high, both north and south of the Neath to Merthyr road.

Neath was an important Roman station with a good road to Cardiff. Another Roman road, worth following for the fine country it goes through, climbs steeply to the north-east along the ridge called Hirfynydd which it follows for several miles through or alongside forestry plantations, eventually dropping to Coelbren Roman fort. A third Roman road from Neath went north-west to Carmarthen. Possibly a fourth climbed directly to the east for there seems to have been a large Roman marching camp three miles away at Blaen-cwm-bach. Of Roman Neath itself a few fragments of gateways survive above ground. The site is on your right by the grammar school just as you enter Neath from Swansea. Neath abbey, which was Cistercian, was described in its day as 'the fairest abbey in all Wales'. Today after centuries of neglect and then a period of use as an iron foundry the considerable portions that remain have been carefully preserved. Work from the thirteenth to the seventeenth centuries survives, the vaulted roof of the monks' dorter being particularly good.

Efforts to drain Crymlyn bog, squeezed in between Neath and Swansea, have not yet entirely succeeded. A guide book of 1840 reported that 'none but botanists traverse this morass'. So they do today for despite all the air and water pollution it still grows the sundews and other bog plants that attracted the earlier botanists. The nearby Crymlyn Burrows too remain botanically attractive. These sands buried a medieval hermitage for 600 years until it was discovered in 1898. Swansea, until the industrial revolution hit it, saw its future as a fashionable seaside resort. In those days people like Beau Nash frequented the place and his house is still preserved. Now Swansea is second in size to Cardiff and has important metallurgical and other industries. It is a city of contrasts. The seaward side, away from the docks, remains agreeably residential. But inland the lower Swansea Valley is an area of appalling industrial dereliction whose rehabilitation is going to be difficult. Much of the centre of Swansea, destroyed by bombing in World War II, has been rebuilt. There is a fine civic centre, the Guildhall, which houses the British Empire panels painted by Sir Frank Brangwyn. They are in the Brangwyn Hall which is famous for its concerts. A Festival of Music and the Arts is held in October. There is a modern theatre and a good art gallery, the Glynn Vivian. The Royal Institution of South Wales houses a fascinating museum where local geology, history, archaeology, natural history, industry and art are fully illustrated; there is beautiful local porcelain (Swansea and Nantgarw ware); models of sailing ships are another speciality. Swansea folk have one peculiarity: they eat a seaweed called laver bread so avidly that they have nearly exhausted local supplies and have to get it from Scotland. From London to Swansea you can take your car by train; then by ferry to Cork in Eire.

West of Swansea and in the utmost contrast with the industrial region stretches the Gower, an oblong peninsula twelve miles by four, an Area of Outstanding Natural Beauty rich in archaeological, historical and natural history interest except for the east coast from Swansea to Mumbles and round to Langland and Caswell Bays which are extensively built up. Oystermouth castle, though now perched above houses and holiday crowds, retains a certain dignity. The gate house and outer walls are in good order and there are substantial remains of the keep, chapel, kitchen, dungeons and well. The name Oystermouth is an English attempt to say Ystumllwynarth! From near Mumbles Head with its lighthouse, islands and famous lifeboat station there is a delightful westward cliff walk.

West of Caswell Bay the coast gets wilder. A splendid mile of cliff-top walking brings you to Pwll Du Bay with its hamlet, rock stacks and old limestone quarries. On the shore there is a beautiful contrast between the whiteness of the pebbles and the green of the woods behind. From Pwll Du you can walk up the winding, rugged and wooded valley to Bishopston. This National Trust dingle is especially lovely in spring when the wild flowers are at their best. Alternatively from Pwll Du bay you can go on round the cliffs to the headland with its hill fort and great views east and west. From there the cliffs go on in splendour, here and there hollowed by caves where the bones of prehistoric animals have been found. Bacon Hole and the even greater Minchin Hole are huge chambers in the limestone. But the whole district is full of caverns and pot-holes.

Threecliff Bay is one of Gower's special delights. A deep valley comes to the coast and the gap it makes in the cliffs has long been invaded by storm-blown sand. Dunes have piled up at Pennard Burrows, buried a medieval church and threatened a castle which now stands as a small evocative ruin with little history. The church was replaced in the Middle Ages by a building that still survives, fragmentarily Norman but much restored, at Pennard. Sand has also invaded the west side of the Pennard stream where another little medieval church had to be abandoned. On the cliff edge near its ruins you will find the banks and walling of early Norman defences. And a few hundred yards inland, near a wide green path, look out for a Neolithic tomb with entrance passage and side chamber. From the point called Great Tor is a glorious view of Threecliff Bay—the yellow sand and green saltings with a blue stream winding through; beyond are jagged cliffs pale against the sea. Great Tor itself is spectacular. Here the limestone strata, tipped over to become almost vertical, have weathered into a fine upstanding column that looks ready to fall into the waves. West from here the light-coloured cliffs, bracken slopes and yellow sands continue in beauty past Nicholaston woods and dunes to Oxwich Burrows.

Delightful country lies inland from Threecliff Bay. A walk up a glen east of Parkmill takes you through woodland rich in lime-loving flowers and ferns to the village of Ilston which has a militant church tower. Or from Parkmill you can go north-west through forestry to either Llethrid or Cillibion. In half a mile you reach Parc le Breos tomb (locally called the Giant's Grave), a well-restored Neolithic communal burial place with entrance passage and side chambers. Marvellous stalactite caves go far underground in this valley but to see them you need to be a pot-holer. West from the woods of Llethrid the ground rises to Cefn Bryn, a long sandstone spine of Devonian age exposed by the erosion of the Carboniferous Limestone that once lay over it. Perhaps Cefn Bryn is the best of inland Gower, a ferny, rushy moor with wide views. South far over the sea are Exmoor and even Dartmoor; in the south-west is Lundy Island, high, flat-topped, severely cliffed; due west along the coast you see the Tenby cliffs, Caldy Island and St. Govan's Head beyond; close in the north across the Burry River lies the Carmarthenshire coast; and round in the east are half the mountains of South Wales.

If Paleolithic Gower is hidden away in caves, the Neolithic period is clear for all to see. Here on Cefn Bryn is a burial chamber that is outstanding for its enormous, shapeless capstone. It is called Arthur's Stone but pre-dates his alleged time by over two thousand years. A road and several paths cross the width of Cefn Bryn but the best way is the green road that starts at Penmaen and follows the whole length of the ridge. On a roadside half a mile south-west of Cillibion is Broad Pool, a nature reserve of the Glamorgan Naturalists' Trust: it is rich in aquatic life and on it floats the fringed water lily.

To return to the south coast: Nicholaston church, solitary along A4118, is nineteenth-century Gothic but has an ancient, cross-carved stone built into its porch. Below are woodlands sloping down to Oxwich marshes and the shore. Oxwich with such beautiful sands is understandably popular and has a huge park for cars. But behind the dunes the marshes with their great reed beds, pools and a slow winding stream remain quiet and part of them are a National Nature Reserve rich in waterfowl, fish (especially roach and rudd) and fen plants. Oxwich has been described as Glamorgan's loveliest bay (some prefer Rhosili), for its surroundings are remarkably undeveloped all the way from Pwll Du Head to the wooded point on the west. Inland it has Cefn Bryn as a skyline and nearer you see Penrice castle peering through the trees. At the end of the beach is an old sycamore-sheltered church with a decorated medieval cross in the porch and effigies of a knight and his lady inside. For information about all this attractive region visit the Countryside Centre (next to the car park) where a fine model of Gower is on view.

Glamorgan

On the tree-covered hill behind the shore the hamlet of Penrice seems blessedly remote from the world. Its medieval church has been made cruciform by the addition of a huge south porch to balance a transept on the other side. The doorway is a wooden arch made of three crude pieces of timber set within a stone arch. Just west of the church is a motte the Normans built as soon as they overran Gower in about 1099. But as usual this early wooden castle was abandoned for a stronger site on which a large stone castle was built. Of this castle extensive walling remains but the best feature is the late thirteenth-century gatehouse on the north side. The dovecote is sixteenth century but now instead of doves there are jackdaws and kestrels. This castle stood high above a stream whose mouth was probably an anchorage. Then came those late medieval tempests that built up the dunes, blocked the stream and created the marshes behind. In the sixteenth century the Mansel family to whom Penrice castle had descended built Oxwich castle, a fortified mansion a mile to the south. This has long been a farmhouse. There are extensive high walls, a tower, a dovecote and a gate with the Mansel crest above it.

Oxwich Point is a bold promontory from which a rock-bound coast continues to the next fine curve of sands in the lee of Port-Eynon Point. Port-Eynon is a small sea-side village at the end of a main road that brings a stream of summer visitors to the hundreds of caravans or for a day on the beach. At Port-Eynon begins the finest walk in Gower along the great limestone cliffs six miles to the tip of Worms Head. All the way the cliffs are shattered and gnawed into fascinating shapes, cut into by inlets and hollowed under by caverns, many of them bone caves. Right at the start is the intriguing Culver Hole about a quarter-mile from Port-Eynon Point on the west side. It is a cleft in the cliff walled up by medieval masonry and is of uncertain purpose. No doubt it had something to do with the now vanished Port-Eynon castle but you had better try to solve the mystery yourself. You reach it from the cliff top or by walking round below at low tide. A favourite interpretation is that it was a dovecote (culver means a dove) but was this its entire purpose?

The most famous Gower cave is two miles along the coast at Paviland. Here were found not only the bones of prehistoric animals but also a ceremonial Paleolithic burial unique in the

British Isles. The body, that of a young man, had been coated with red ochre (which eventually coloured the skeleton) and there were ornaments laid beside it. This is now a sea cave but in Paleolithic times these cliffs were far inland and well above sea level. It is reachable from the beach at low tide but involves a bit of scrambling up the cliff. The flora and fauna of these cliffs are protected by the Nature Conservancy. Rare plants include attractive species like spring cinquefoil, small rest-harrow, hoary rockrose and hutchinsia, all mysteriously far from their main centres of distribution. At Mewslade Bay, where there is a sandy beach at low tide, the cliff scenery is outstanding. Great slabs of limestone are tilted at steep angles and others are wildly contorted. Then you reach Worms Head, a curving finger stretching a mile into the sea. At its tip are high cliffs that drop sheer into the water to form Glamorgan's one noteworthy sea-bird colony —guillemots, razorbills, kittiwakes, shags and fulmars. Sometimes there are puffins present too but they are not known to nest there. To reach the Worm you walk out over low-tide rocks: but allow time for getting back.

Rhosili Bay is perfect and deserves priority protection from caravans, chalets, houses, pylons, masts, power stations and all else. From its southern cliffs you look due north across the flat sands for three splendid miles with line after line of waves moving slowly shoreward and breaking in the shallows. A terrible place in storms it has been the scene of shipwrecks in every century. Behind the shore Rhosili Down (of Old Red Sandstone) rises steeply, reaching its highest point at the Beacon (632 feet). Half a mile north along this ridge are two Neolithic burial chambers traditionally called Sweyne's Howes, 'howe' being an old word for mound. The mounds have long since been dispersed by the ocean winds and the capstones of the tombs have slipped off.

Rhosili Bay ends in the north at Burry Holms which at high tide is an island. On it are the scanty ruins of a medieval religious settlement. The Iron Age also used the place, leaving behind a bank that stretches across the island. Dating from far earlier than that are the flint tools discovered on the north side. The island has long been uninhabited but is walked to in summer by bathers and picnickers. On its landward side are the dunes of Llangennith (Llangynydd) and Broughton which are wild, flowery and beautiful (though there are some caravans). And further to the north-east the Whiteford dunes stretch into the Burry River for a couple of miles and are even wilder and more beautiful. They belong to the National Trust and are also a National Nature Reserve. North of the dunes the great scatter of low-tide rocks, on which there is a lighthouse, are a glacial moraine. The village of Llangennith is on the site of a now vanished priory founded in the twelfth century by black-habited monks from Evreux in Normandy. In the parish church are several medieval slabs, an effigy and a decorated Celtic cross base. On Hardings Down that rises south of the village there are Iron Age banks and enclosures. To the north Llanmadog Hill has Bronze Age cairns, a prominent hill fort called the Bulwark and is a lovely viewpoint.

Llanmadog and Cheriton are neighbouring villages standing on ancient sea-cliffs now well back from the sea. Both the churches here are medieval, Llanmadog's having ancient memorial stones. Three miles east the rebuilt church at Llanrhidian keeps its ancient fort-like tower. To get to the church you pass between two standing stones, one plain, one oddly shaped but apparently the broken remains of a Celtic cross. A big crude limestone block in this porch has worn human and animal figures carved upon it—all very mysterious. On the slope opposite as you leave the church you see the banks of a hill fort ascending in three bold steps. The lane down from Llanrhidian is the lower road to Crofty, skirting miles of saltings. These coastal marshes are a fascinating region of vast flat horizons more typical of north Norfolk than west Wales. After an interval they begin again at Pen-clawdd and extend into the distance with a road following them all the way to Gowerton. Crofty keeps its feet out of water by huddling over a little rise at the edge of the marshes. It has been slightly industrialized and here and there are minor coaltips overgrown with vegetation. Meanwhile old ways endure and people from Crofty and Pen-clawdd still go far out into the estuary with donkeys to gather cockles. And tourists come to see them at it. At Gowerton, two miles east of Pen-clawdd, you are back again in the industrial world and the delights of Gower seem already far away.

12

CARMARTHENSHIRE
(Caerfyrddin or Sir Gaerfyrddin)

Let us begin in the north-east corner of this the largest Welsh county, up in the wide uplands that reach out north from here across a vast, sparsely peopled spread of central Wales. Traditionally it is sheep country but much of it has become conifer country. And now in the heart of it is the long, narrow Brianne reservoir (pronounced 'bree-anny'). The region is made especially lovely by the deep valleys of Towy (or Tywi), Camddwr, Doethie, Pysgotwr, Gwenffrwd and Cothi, delicious streams which, with their countless side-rills, come hastening down rocky clefts and splashing down little falls into clear green pools. The first trees they see are a scatter of crooked rowans and birches. Then the valleys widen and their steep slopes are covered with the most extensive oakwoods left in west Wales, woods that make exquisite scenery especially when coloured by autumn. Under the conical hill called Dinas, a mile or so below the reservoir the Towy receives the Doethie (pronounced 'doyth-ee-a' with the stress on the middle syllable). The Dinas, which is oak-clad to the summit, has on its west flank the cave of Twm Shon Catti ('Tom Jones (son of) Cathy'). He was a wild young man of the sixteenth century whose adventures have become legendary. But though famous, his cave would not be worth visiting if it were not for the charming walk to it. This hill, which in spring has many redstarts and pied flycatchers, is a reserve of the Royal Society for the Protection of Birds. Another wood a mile up the Doethie is a National Nature Reserve.

Carmarthenshire

Below the Doethie the valley broadens. From the west comes the Gwenffrwd down a richly oaked cwm where the R.S.P.B. has another extensive reserve. In the widening vale from Rhandirmwyn to Llandovery there is less wildness but not less beauty. On both sides the hills have abounded with traces of ancient man, chiefly cairns and standing stones, some of which survive. Relics much nearer our own time are the once extensive lead mines at Rhandirmwyn. For a notable old bridge go to Dolauhirion, a mile above Llandovery. It is a high single arch gracefully spanning twenty-eight yards over the deep swift river. Built in 1773 by Williams Edward, this bridge has circular openings in its masonry to lessen its weight and so is of the style Edwards had pioneered at Pontypridd, Glamorgan.

That Llandovery (Llanymddyfri—'the church between the rivers') was chosen as a principal station by the Romans (who may have called it Alabum or possibly Loventium) is a sure sign of its good position in the world. Their fort has now vanished except for small grassy banks west of the church of St. Mary on the hill above the town. This church is in the centre of the fort and if you examine its outside walls, especially at the east end, you will find long, narrow pieces of what looks like Roman brick. After Roman times humanity moved downhill so that when the Normans came they built their sizeable motte quite close to the river. It is still there, crowned by a pair of sorry towers and an old ash tree. From the river it is photogenic. But on the town side it is jammed against a cattle market.

West and north-west of Llandovery lies a long reach of fair country that has little fame among tourists until you get right over to the valley of the Teifi. But the early thirteenth-century abbey at Talley is justly loved not only for its elegant ruins but also for its good surroundings and two shining pools that share its peaceful hollow. Though the place may be Talley to you, a notice as you enter the village assures you that the people call it Talyllychau (or should do). Talyllychau ('the end of the lakes') is an interesting name because the *llych* is a memory of the obsolete Welsh word *llwch* (replaced by *llyn* in modern Welsh), *llwch* being the equivalent of Scottish *loch*. Not much is left of the abbey, the only one in Wales built by the Premonstratensians, a French order closely similar to the Cistercians. The pair of tall arches that now stand in isolation are all that remains of the cruciform

223

church's central tower. The rest of the ruins have long ago been used as a quarry for other buildings including Talley parish church in which there is a lavish survival of box pews. From the abbey you can go north along a high-level lane that looks down on the lakes with their water lilies, ducks, coots, dabchicks and sometimes great crested grebes. Between the lakes, which no doubt used to provide the monks with fish, is a Norman motte quite hidden in the summer trees. The road goes under a hillside of conifers margined with American oaks that are bright yellow in spring and boldly scarlet in autumn. It then curves round the head of the lakes down an avenue of fine old native oaks.

At Abergorlech an attractive village three miles west of Talley, there is a good bridge over the Cothi built in the seventeenth perhaps even the sixteenth century. Note its distorted arches and the fading inscription with one of its figures upside down: 'This bridge was mended by John Jones 179ϯ.' Downstream from here is a region dark with the vast spread of conifers near Brechfa. So from Abergorlech most people will prefer to go upstream to Pumsaint (pronounced 'Pimsant'), a place with a unique link with Roman and probably pre-Roman gold mining, the ancient mines being still there though somewhat confused with later workings. But a remarkable rock-cut aqueduct by which the Romans brought water to the mines from seven miles away up the Cothi is even now traceable in places, especially where, as a stone-lined ditch, it reaches the top of the mine to feed a former reservoir. This, one of the most important mines in Roman Britain, would clearly have been guarded by a fort. Quantities of Roman pottery that have been found nearby are a good guide to its approximate site but its exact location has not yet been determined. From time to time in the past two centuries various Roman gold ornaments have been found near these mines. Roman money has also turned up in abundance including one hoard of three thousand coins. Strongly suggestive evidence that the Normans also mined here is the presence of their motte still standing at the roadside below the mine and now covered with rowans and birches. Close to it you will find a square upright stone about three feet high, its four faces deeply saucered. It has obviously been brought down from the mine where it was hollowed by hand-held stone hammers crushing the ore. It can be regarded, if you like, as a memorial to the gold-

27. Ramsey Island, Pembrokeshire, a reserve of the Royal Society for the Protection of Birds

28. St. David's Cathedral: it stands in a hollow close to the sea-cliffs of west Pembrokeshire

29. St. Brynach's cross, Nevern church, north Pembrokeshire

hungry generations, all the pre-Romans, Romans, Saxons, Normans and moderns whose eyes have strained for the glint of yellow metal in these iron-red rocks.

The word Pumsaint means 'five saints'. And five good Celtic names they have bequeathed to us from the depths of the Dark Ages: Ceitho, Celynnin, Gwyn, Gwyno and Gwynoro. But oddly enough their church is not at Pumsaint but a mile away over the hill past the gold mine in the secluded village of Caio. The church is quite small but has a massive square tower that any medieval military architect would have been proud of; and it is built on a strategic platform of rock with a drop on both sides. A very worn Latin inscribed stone (which remembers one Regin son of Nudintus) is built into the outside wall of the north side of the tower near the ground.

For a great prospect of Carmarthenshire take the north-bound Roman road (Sarn Helen) which goes over to Llanfair Clydogau. You climb to a high ridge that looks back down the valley of the Twrch across a delightful pattern of little fields and hedges, the traditional pattern that is disappearing in many districts. Beyond are the ribboned woodlands along the Cothi; and far into the south, across the Towy, the high dark line of the Black Mountain. On this ridge above the Twrch you are almost in Cardiganshire. So if you like old boundary-marking monoliths you can make your way a mile and a half south-west to the Hirfaen Gwyddog, marked simply 'Hirfaen' on the one-inch map. This fifteen-foot standing stone, presumably prehistoric, has long been in use to mark the county boundary. But centuries before that it marked the northern limit of church lands, those of Talley abbey in the twelfth century and those of the church of St. Teilo in the tenth. In fact it is claimed that the mention by name of this stone in a tenth-century document gives it a longer historical record than any stone now surviving in Britain. It stands tapering, lichened and view-commanding where three fields meet. There is no public path to it and visitors should ask permission at the farm nearby.

Returning to Talley: the lane south-east, signposted to Felindre, leads you to several good viewpoints that look across the Towy to the Vans (Bannau Sir Gaer), the highest points in the Black Mountain range. You then drop down to A483 near Llangadog, a large and lively village, almost a town. To catch it with its hair down go on Easter Monday for its annual horse-races. Llangadog had a motte castle, Castell Meurig (destroyed 1209), whose mound survives on the streamside where it guarded a ford south of the village. The region east and south of Llangadog is, after the upper Towy country, the wildest part of Carmarthenshire. For though at first it rises gently through greenness and fertility it soon becomes high, breezy moorland. You get a cross-section of it by going south along A4069 which keeps in the valley as long as it can but is forced at last to go zig-zagging high over the tops before it plunges amid spoil-heaps on its way to Swansea. A far quieter road comes over from Trecastle in Breconshire passing south of Swansea's Usk reservoir (a good picnic spot). Above the reservoir the Usk is a mere stream-let rippling over stony shallows, and walkers can reach its source on the moorland flank in a couple of miles or so. The hill north-west of the reservoir is Mynydd Myddfai which is a worth while viewpoint but the low tumulus on its summit has clearly been rifled by treasure-hunters. Myddfai is a village whose fame as a centre of magicianry goes back to early medieval literature. In due course the generations of magicians evolved into generations of medical men—a remarkable line of physicians who persisted till the middle of the nineteenth century. Myddfai church, partly thirteenth century, has several interesting features including a hatchment.

Reverting to the road from Trecastle to Pont-ar-llechau: if as you pursue it on its bold course across the moor you detect a Roman feel about it you are not mistaken, for the faint rectangle of a small Roman fort can be seen near its highest point. It is on the direct line from Moridunum (Carmarthen) and Y Gaer (Brecon). From here you descend gently to the west with views far down wooded valleys on either side. Note the place called Talsarn, for *sarn*, in its sense of a paved way, is frequent along Roman roads. Then you cross a cattle grid and it is good-bye to peewits and ponies as you go down into a leafier land. A little south of this road is Llanddeusant ('the church of two saints') in the upper Sawdde, a valley generously patched with natural oak-woods. Towards the hills the woodlands thin into tongues up side-streams, then into hedges up open slopes, finally into scattered thorns. Above them rise the wide grassy ramparts of Black Mountain. It is all most enjoyable country whether you stay below in tree-shaded, water-loud dingles or walk up with the Sawdde to the deep, cirque-lake called Fan Fach.

Below Llanddeusant you go down a lane between high hazel hedges and are soon along the lower Sawdde at Pont-ar-llechau, the river here very beautiful and troutful in an ash-shaded gorge. Here too you come to A4069 but if it looks too trafficky and you are in no hurry you can continue along westward lanes and go to Bethlehem. The biblical names that so many Welsh places have —Bethesda, Ebenezer, Nazareth, Sodom and countless more— were originally the names of the Nonconformist chapels round which these communities formed a century or two ago. Sometimes a Welsh name got displaced in the process. Thus, so I was told there, the original name of Bethlehem was Dyffryn Ceidrych. At Bethlehem you will find the chapel dominant on a hill upstream from a sadly disused watermill. To this hamlet people flock just before Christmas to get their letters franked 'Bethlehem'. But the really splendid thing hereabouts is neither mill nor chapel but the great Iron Age stronghold of Carn Goch, one of the finest prehistoric forts in the British Isles. Carn Goch is really two forts side by side. But if you count them as one they form the largest hill fort in Wales, reaching nearly half a mile from end to end and crowning a 700-foot ridge already well defended by drops on both sides. Whatever shape the walls originally had they now consist of loosely heaped rough pebbles piled up like a storm beach and still rising to twenty feet for long distances especially on the west. It is in fact a rampart quite remarkably preserved when you see it is only a bank of loose stones and remember that it has two thousand years of wear and weather behind it. Within the fort stands a great pile of stones rather like the one on Gop Hill, Flintshire, but not so huge. Was it a look-out, as some have suggested, or was it a Bronze Age cairn?

From Carn Goch there are south-west lanes which lift you over high and open ground into the valley of the Cennen. There you see one of the most finely sited castles in all Britain, the twelfth-century castle of Carreg Cennen aloft on its limestone cliffs. Yet though so splendid, its history is rather obscure and it had less importance than nearby castles along the Towy. Though Norman in style it is likely that it was built by the astute Lord Rhys (twelfth century) who managed to hold on to much power in South Wales by working in with the Norman conquerors. It is known to have changed hands several times in the thirteenth century. In the early fifteenth it was repaired after damage by Owain Glyndŵr but it then became a bandits' stronghold and had to be dismantled by the authorities. I first saw Carreg Cennen from the west one evening when the sun was setting. The light had gone already from the crags of the gorge leaving them grey and dim. But the castle still looked at the sun and its pale walls had turned pink. Perhaps I should have left it at that and gone away with the image of a fairy castle in my mind. For what with deliberate damage and the decay of ages this castle, like so many, is far more splendid outwardly than within, being rather empty. But if I had not climbed the hill I would have missed not only the impressive gateway but also a most unusual feature—the underground passage ingeniously carved within the brink of the precipice and leading from the courtyard to an underground spring that has now become a wishing well. So if you are a wisher of wishes take a pin to drop into the water. And take a torch also for the passage ends in deep darkness.

This castle looks picturesque from several places round about, especially from the high moorland road across the gorge to the south. From there, with the midday sun squarely on it, the gleaming white ruin seems to grow naturally from its white rocks. This road parallel to the Cennen gorge runs through a hummocky, stone-walled, sheep-nibbled landscape that rises away to the Black Mountain with big cairns ominous on the distant skyline. They are survivors of a multitude of cairns that existed hereabouts from prehistoric times until the age of enlightenment stripped them of the protective awe in which country folk had always held them. The result all over Britain has been the despoliation of countless stones, cairns and mounds in the past two centuries. These Black Mountain slopes seem to have particularly suffered judging by a report in the inventory of the county's ancient monuments: 'In a field called Cae Beddau ('the field of the graves') is a stone cist. This is the sole survivor of seventy others stated to have formerly existed in the same spot.' Only remoter relics have survived. Especially fine and visible from miles around are the Bronze Age cairns (along the summit ridge) called Tair Carn Uchaf ('the three upper cairns'). A mile or so west the River Loughor (Llwchwr) has its source amid the cold shadows of a limestone cavern and goes on its south-westerly course down to Ammanford, passing on its way at Forge what is claimed to be the oldest iron-works in Wales. At Ammanford, an industrial town of 30,000 people, you reach the edge of the coalfield.

Up north in the Towy valley are a couple of once splendid castles now far gone into decay. They are high-placed castles that catch your eye as you drive along below. Dryslwyn, for instance, stands up gaunt and shattered against the sky and when you see it the whole family wants to stop the car and go scrambling up the grassy slopes to the top. Up there you find more than the two jagged fangs of wall you saw from the bottom. You see that the whole hill top has been shaped by sizeable earthworks that look decidedly Iron Age. The castle has stood there, or rather has fallen to pieces there, for seven hundred years and if we knew every detail of its past we would know more about the history of Carmarthenshire than few other spots in the county could tell, for Dryslwyn always seems to have been in the thick of life and events. Upon these fragments of wall grows an abundance of pellitory that so loves historical associations; nearby the boldly triangled leaves of Good King Henry make a patch of dark-green among the grass. Both these herbs could date back all the way to the medieval time.

The view from today's frail ruins takes in the flat-bottomed vale of the winding Towy far upstream and down. Immediately north-east you look squarely at Grongaer which is another hill fort. Three miles beyond Grongaer you glimpse the towers of old Dynevor (Dynefwr) castle looking out above its trees. Across the valley you look to a far view of the grey historic house of Gelli Aur, now a farm institute; and poised precisely above it, but four miles further on, you can see Carreg Cennen castle pale against the dark flank of Black Mountain. Just across the Towy south-west of Dryslwyn is another landmark of these parts, the large folly-tower raised just after 1805 in honour of Nelson by a local landowner called Paxton.

If the hill called Grongaer stirs in you a literary memory it is of a poem called 'Grongar Hill', a rather good landscape description by John Dyer who in the eighteenth century lived in the mansion of Aberglasney under the north-east end of the hill. Nearby you will find the tall militant tower of Llangathen, a thirteenth-century church which contains a carved Tudor table and an outsize monument of 1616 showing two figures in period costume. At Dynevor there are two castles. The one you see from Dryslwyn is a good sample of thirteenth-century building but with a lot of later additions. Like Dryslwyn it looks straight down to the Towy and is even more dramatically poised on the brink of cliffs. Long ago this castle had enormous prestige: from here much of South Wales was ruled until the coming of the Normans. Near it is the modern Dynevor castle which has gardens, spacious grounds, delightful old woodlands and a deer park with not only deer but white cattle as well. These attractive white oxen which live in a semi-wild state are thought to be closely related to the extinct aurochs whose bones are occasionally dug up in peat bogs. There is another Welsh herd at Vaynol park, Bangor, Caernarvonshire.

The history of Dynevor and that of Llandeilo are inevitably interwoven. Today Llandeilo is a pleasant-looking little market town (meet the farmers from miles around there any Monday) which keeps its feet well above Towy's floods. It is a good place from which to explore this much-castled district. Over the river here is a noble bridge of 1848 which, at 145 feet, is claimed to be the longest arch in Wales. It is the work of David Edwards, son of the William Edwards who built Dolau-hirion bridge. In Llandeilo church are the heads of two Celtic crosses; and Llanarthne church, on B4300 six miles west of Llandeilo, also has a fine ancient cross. Nearly nine miles west of Llandeilo A40 crosses the Cothi on a three-arched eighteenth-century bridge (Pont-ar-Gothi) and in a further half-dozen miles you come to Carmarthen (Caerfyrddin) where the Towy has been bridged for unknown centuries. Here the river is broad and the bridge necessarily massive. One was reported 'broken' as far back as 1223 and I daresay others had been swept away before then. Possibly even the Romans had a bridge there for Carmarthen (Moridunum) was important to them. The oldest parts of Carmarthen, which today is a very busy market town with some industry, stood well above the river. The Roman station, now bounded by Priory Street, the Avenue and East Parade, was built-over long ago but there are Roman relics in the museum and a Roman altar in the parish church of St. Peter. It may well be that Moridunum was not only a strategically important fortress commanding the approaches to south-west Wales but also a considerable Romano–British settlement.

In Norman times Carmarthen had town walls and a castle but of these there is not much to show except the castle gatehouse, a little walling and a motte. Carmarthen has military traditions and where the medieval market cross once stood they now have a statue to a general. In fact all the town's statues seem to be to the military as if Carmarthen never produced anyone of peaceful eminence. Earthen banks called the Bulwarks are defence works of the Civil War when Carmarthen was defended by Royalists and Parliamentarians in turn. Though built round several British towns at that time such defences survive today only at Carmarthen and Bristol. The stump of a long-dead oak in Priory Street, now petrified by age, is preserved with a care understandable in view of the tradition that:

> When this oak shall tumble down
> So will fall Carmarthen town.

Carmarthen's parish church contains an array of memorials and effigies going back to the early twelfth century. All journalists should make obeisance at the brass to Sir Richard Steele (1671–1729) 'first chief promoter of the periodical press of England'. The museum is full of good things from the Stone Age onwards. A prized possession is an Ogham memorial to 'Voteporix the protector', a ruler of South Wales as long ago as the early sixth century. There is a cast of the magnificent cross of Eiudon that stood at nearby Gelli Aur before it went to the National Museum at Cardiff. There are also finds from Talley abbey and medieval tiles from Whitland abbey. From more recent times come old ploughs, a stand for milking sheep, mantraps, love spoons, an 1840 printing press and an hour-glass formerly used by a local parson for timing his sermons. The most priceless of all the town's relics is now at the National Library at Aberystwyth. It is the medieval manuscript of *The Black Book of Carmarthen* which was written at the Augustinian priory (now gone). For a commanding look at this part of the Towy climb Merlin's Hill, three miles east of Carmarthen. From it you see Grongaer, Dryslwyn, Paxton's tower, Carreg Cennen and all the hills beyond. Near Merlin's Hill is Abergwili where, in the Bishop's Palace, William Salesbury of Llanrwst, Denbighshire, made the first Welsh translation of *The Book of Common Prayer* of which only one perfect copy of the first edition (1567) now survives. He did this work under the patronage of the Bishop of St. Davids, Richard Davies, to whom there is a memorial in Abergwili church.

Like the Teifi, the Towy retains a link with the very remotest past—the coracles that are still in use for salmon fishing. The tradition of burning disused coracles, still kept up, is probably as ancient as coracles themselves. Below Carmarthen the river broadens to its noble estuary that winds through several miles of gentle hills. Like all Welsh estuaries it is good birdwatching country, especially in autumn when waders are numerous (black-tailed godwits are a speciality) and in winter when the duck are in. For a quick look at this river-mouth go by train: for a dozen splendid miles the line keeps right along the edge of the estuary of the Towy, then that of the Gwendraeth as far as Kidwelly.

To go south-east from Carmarthen is to let yourself gently into the orbit of South Wales industrialism. The trunk road to Swansea (A48) leads you at first through fair farming country, then climbs to a curious semi-industrialized higher district where coal mines at villages such as Cross Hands and Tumble (Y Tymbl) have been imposed on but have not obliterated the farming pattern. The result is a region where miners comment knowingly at sheep-dog trials and where shepherds are far from ignorant about mining. North of Cross Hands is a fair, water-lilied lake called Llyn Llech Owen. South of Cross Hands the Gwili valley goes on in beauty almost to Pontardulais and is well seen from crests along B4306 south-east of Llannon.

Llanelli, by far the largest town in the county, is Carmarthenshire's chief contribution to industrial South Wales. It is famous for tin-plate factories, steel works, choral singing and rugby football. In the town centre there is a good library and at Parc Howard an art gallery and museum. The town also has a fine swimming pool; and to the north there are scenic reservoirs. Formerly a port Llanelli looks out to the Gower peninsula across a wide, shallow sea which at low tide is a place of gleaming wet mud and meandering creeks that are the feeding ground of many wading birds and wildfowl. And along the shore from Burry Port to the Gwendraeth estuary there stretches an area of sands, dunes and saltings that, despite some of it having gone to caravans, the military, a scrap-metal factory, a chicken factory and forestry, still retains some wildness and beauty which let us hope will survive.

At the head of the Gwendraeth estuary stands Kidwelly (Cydweli) an ancient town whose walls, except for a fragment, have gone. But a splendid medieval castle remains posed above the river. It is a typical thirteenth century Norman concentric castle commanding a vital river-crossing. The oldest parts are the four drum towers guarding the inner ward. The very fine main gateway came later. Having no part in the Civil War this castle escaped being slighted by Cromwell. Opposite across the river is the spired parish church, formerly that of a Benedictine monastery. In it is the tomb of Isolda (died 1274), mother of Pain de Chaworth who built the great stone castle. Most of Kidwelly is between two rivers: the Gwendraeth Fawr which flows down from the coalfield and looks as if it does; and the Gwendraeth Fach which is cleaner. Two miles south-east of Kidwelly, where B4308 crosses the Gwendraeth Fawr, you will find Pont Spwdwr, claimed to be 'by far the most ancient bridge remaining in South Wales'. It is an admirable old structure with six pointed arches though normally the river passes under one arch only.

Where, west of Kidwelly, the Towy and Gwendraeth estuaries merge, the coast road and railway are squeezed together under the church of St. Ishmael's (Llanismel). From here you look at low tide over a wide stony area that was the site of the village of Hawton (or Halkin), destroyed by a great storm probably in the early seventeenth century. There are many legendary lost villages around the Welsh coast but what is special about Hawton is that its legend has been shown to be truth. Old walls and dressed stones of its houses are still visible at the very lowest tides; and finds from the site date from medieval times to the sixteenth century. Beyond the stones stretches a waste of muddy sands where cockles are plentiful, Llansaint, the village on the hill above, being a former centre of cockle-gatherers. In the outside south wall of Llansaint church are two ancient inscribed stones, one of them upside down. From St. Ishmael's church you look across the estuary to the dunes of Laugharne, the bold headland that separates Taf from Towy, and the striking ruins of Llanstephan castle outlined against the sky. Following the coast north you are soon in Ferryside, a long ribbon of a place growing rapidly as a residential and holiday village. It has much sand and many yachts; and thundering express trains.

The triangle between Carmarthen, St. Clears and Llanstephan is a region of tranquil farming country. Llanstephan is a long-popular, delightful village with early gardens and a mainly thirteenth-century Norman castle built on the banks of an earlier motte and bailey which in turn were raised within the ramparts of an Iron Age fort. Perhaps it is best to see this castle's place in history as one end of a long strategic line of similar forts which the Normans threw from Llanstephan right across country to St. Bride's Bay in Pembrokeshire.

The winding estuary of the Taf curves through unspectacular country where fields slope easily to the tide. From wooded dingles a few miles north comes the stream called Cywyn whose last mile, before it meets the salt, is a hesitant wandering along a marshy level. Here there was not always such peace. Till the threshold of our own time it was a place of ships and men, one of the county's outlets to the world. But its past survives most solidly in two ancient churches that look at each other across the Cywyn from which both take their name. On the east side is the primitive little church of Llandeilo Abercywyn ('St. Teilo's church at the mouth of the Cywyn'), a calling place of medieval pilgrims flocking to St. David's shrine in Pembrokeshire. The adjacent farmhouse is still called Pilgrims' Rest and retains medieval features in its structure.

On the west side of the Cywyn is the other church of this ancient pair, that of Llanfihangel Abercywyn ('St. Michael's church at the mouth of the Cywyn'). It stands alone in fields above the tide line, a roofless ruin in a churchyard ringed with trees. As well as more recent gravestones there are strange, so-called pilgrims' graves in two groups, one close to the church under a very old yew, the other several yards away in the shade of a cypress. To call them the graves of unfortunates who died on pilgrimage makes an appealing story but is without foundation. More likely they are the graves of local people of distinction who first built the church, perhaps as long ago as the twelfth century. Whoever they were their graves could now hardly be in a quieter place; for life has long since moved far away up to the main road. Now there is not even a track down to the old church. To get to it go to the farm called Trefenty and ask your way from there. You may well find this abandoned little church and these pathetic graves more moving than some cathedral cluttered with pompous alabaster.

A few miles upriver from the mouth of the Taf is St. Clears, a place that in the twelfth century had the promise of greatness, for it had a castle, a Cluniac priory and the status of a borough. But time has broken the promise and St. Clears is now a village at a junction of main roads. The priory has gone. But the church is still fragmentarily Norman with a fine chancel arch; and the castle mound still dominates the houses and the tidal riverside marshes. The busy side of the Taf estuary is the western, for that way the road goes to Laugharne and on to Pendine, both popular holiday places. Laugharne (pronounced 'Larn') is a little estuary-side town (chartered in 1300) at the bottom of a leafy valley. It keeps a conscious eye on its traditions, its bounds are ceremoniously beaten every third year and it cherishes an eighteenth century town hall complete with a prison cell called the Clink. Last time I was there a notice on the town hall read: 'The Laugharne Corporation invites nominations from burgesses to fill the office of Portreeve for the ensuing six months.'

At the bottom of the largely Georgian main street you come to a wide world of saltmarshes and creeks with views to the sea which is far away most of the time but which at highest spring tides comes right across the roadway. On your left looking seawards stands a castle on a tree-clad cliff. Tall and tottery-looking, it may originally have been thirteenth century, but it was largely rebuilt in Henry VIII's time by Sir John Perrot whose hobby was doing up old castles at hair-raising expense. In the town the bookshop window, as well as the Milk Wood restaurant will remind you that here lived the gifted writer Dylan Thomas. On the estuary the now famous boathouse in which he lived survives miraculously, the miracle being that it has not been sold to America where his work enjoys a vast reputation. It was in New York that he died in 1953 aged 39. His grave is in the churchyard at Laugharne.

On your left a third of the way from Laugharne to Pendine you pass Coygan Hill, well known to archaeologists for its cave in which have been found many bones of animals long extinct in Britain. You can see some of these bones in the museums at Carmarthen and Cardiff. The top of the hill has elaborate earthworks and copious shell mounds which date back to the Bronze Age or even earlier. Alas, Coygan Hill is being quarried for its limestone, the cave has nearly gone, great tips of debris have been dumped upon the summit and all archaeological interest is rapidly disappearing. The shell mounds, like others found in Laugharne and Pembrey sand-dunes, contain relics of a cross-section of history down to at least the Dark Ages (see for instance the fascinating Viking combs in Carmarthen museum). From the top of this isolated hill you look seawards across a wide sweep of marshes and dunes that unfortunately are a military firing range. So you have to go on to Pendine to get to the shore which at low tide is perhaps the finest and firmest stretch of sand in all Wales. It was formerly used for motor speed trials and the many records broken here in the mid-twenties are documented on the wall of the Beach hotel. Along the cliffs westwards a brackeny path goes high above the sea, passing the slight banks of an Iron Age promontory fort less than half a mile from Pendine. There are splendid views onwards across the water to Tenby and also back along the Carmarthenshire coast. On the scree-covered slopes above Ragwen Point you can search for the chambered tombs and other traces of the Stone Age that have been discovered there. A mile north of Pendine the old church of Eglwys Gymyn is built within a hill fort, has Tudor wall lettering, a Dark Ages inscribed stone and other objects of interest.

On the county boundary a dozen or so miles west of Carmarthen is Whitland which, though it has little to prove it in the shape of stones and mortar, was a centre of life in medieval Wales. For here, if history speaks truth, Hywel Dda (Howell the Good), a king who ruled all Wales, had a hunting seat: and here in about 940 he held a council at which he codified a celebrated body of laws which lasted in force at least until Edward I conquered Wales three centuries later. These laws are still known in detail and shed valuable light on the social order of what otherwise would be an extremely dark age. Two centuries later along came Cistercian monks from Clairvaux, Burgundy, to found their first Welsh monastery at Whitland. They called it Alba Landa and from it soon sprang the abbeys of Cwmhir (Radnorshire), Strata Florida (Cardiganshire) and Strata Marcella (Montgomeryshire). But of Alba Landa practically nothing remains.

Carmarthenshire

North of Whitland the land climbs gently through farming country that is mainly attractive for its many valleys in whose deep windings are places of hidden beauty where wooded slopes have rocky waters chattering below their skirts. You can do a traverse by miles of these dingles across this corner of the county starting up the Gwili valley east of Carmarthen, then pressing on north-west along the lanes from Cynwyl Elfed and over the moorland watershed to descend to the Teifi down the fine valley of the Cych. Alternatively you could come up one of the other streams, taking in beautiful wooded country such as lies above Gelli-wen north of Mydrim (Meidrim). Lovers of past things will enjoy this region not for any great splendours but for oddities such as the position of the churches at Meidrim and Llanwinio, both of which appear to be built on prehistoric earthworks. On the high ground to the north we come to the barrow zone. Few districts in Wales have been more thickly endowed with these Bronze Age burial mounds often called in Welsh *crugiau* (singular *crug*). No doubt scores of them have been destroyed but survivors can be found by careful map reading, especially in the heathy, grassy country on either side of A484 a few miles north of Cynwyl Elfed. But easily the most prominent earthwork of this area is Clawdd Mawr ('great dyke'), of which two miles survive in good heart close to the west side of the highest part of A484. Anyone who has seen the dykes on Kerry Hill in Montgomeryshire may suspect that Clawdd Mawr has affinities with them. Perhaps like them it stood across a Dark Ages ridge road, its two ends deep in morass or thick forest. Or is it a relict boundary between the old kingdoms of Dyfed (modern Pembrokeshire) and Ystrad Tywi (Carmarthenshire)?

Two miles north-west of Clawdd Mawr is Penboyr church with a savagely treated little castle mound across the lane. More interesting are the multiple earth banks of the Iron Age promontory fort called Caer Blaen Minog, the finding of which in its quiet retreat among the woodlands should keep you happy a fair time. Its ramparts stand high above the dingles of Nant Bargod half a mile south-east of the church. You find your way to them up deeply tree-clad glens in whose cool shade the branches bristle with pale-green lichen beards and polypody ferns. This place can be compared with another promontory fort called Castell Pyr on the bank of the Teifi and easy to find because the road from Maesycrugiau to Llandysul passes right through it. For a fine castle mound, but no castle, go three miles south-west to see the prominent ditch-surrounded tump among the houses of Pencader. Here Henry II received the submission of Rhys ap Gruffydd in 1163. North of Pencader the land drops quickly to the Teifi which is the county boundary. This long and lovely valley with its hamlets, villages and small market towns is rather a world on its own. So although some of its places are in Carmarthenshire I have included them in my account of Cardiganshire in order to keep the Teifi region intact.

13

PEMBROKESHIRE

(Penfro or Sir Benfro)

The increasing popularity of Pembrokeshire is understandable. The Preseli mountains and most of the coast are a National Park, and there is a footpath, almost continuous, round its miles of beaches and cliffs. The open spaces of Preseli are all a delight; and everywhere in the county there is the feeling that the sea with its light and colour is never far away. In fact Pembrokeshire, though far from being an island, seems to belong to the sea as much as Anglesey does. Perhaps more so when you realize that when great tides swell up into the remotest creeks of the Cleddau river then no part of the county is more than seven miles from salt water. Go to the west coast and see how boldly Pembrokeshire thrusts three majestic peninsulas against the ocean, one near St. David's in the north, another near Dale in the centre and a third near Castlemartin in the south. On a map they look like the battered prongs of a trident but geologically they have little in common with each other.

St. David's Head is a firm shape of dark igneous rock knobbed inland with the hard dolerite of Carn Llidi and Carnedd-lleithr that have resisted the elements and stand in isolation above the plain. South of St. David's the sea has bitten deep into the softer rocks of the Coal Measures and has shaped the sandy bay of St. Bride's. Then a tougher headland reaches out towards Skomer and Skokholm islands and ends in the red sandstone promontory of St. Ann's. Beyond St. Ann's, to form the great inlet of Milford Haven the Atlantic has had things easy: for there what was already a deep river-valley has sagged even deeper to admit the sea, forming not an estuary with a shallow mouth but a deep-water fiord that allows passage to the greatest ships yet built. South of the haven the land regains its height, facing the ocean with a bold line first of sandstone then of hard limestone cliffs. So in three languages, igneous, sandstone and limestone, west Pembrokeshire speaks to the sea.

Not only by its rocks is the St. David's peninsula different. It is historically apart also, being from earliest Christian times a place of special significance for the Celtic church. For here in the sixth century came Dewi, a preacher who rose to great prominence and has become known to the world as St. David, patron saint of Wales. Gradually in the Dark Ages St. David's evolved as a centre of power and there was evidently an attempt to isolate the last few miles of the peninsula as a private domain. This seems the likeliest explanation of the three-mile-long earthwork, still intermittently traceable, that cut off the peninsula from north to south and which is marked on the map as Ffos y mynach ('the Monk's dyke'). Its slight banks are visible on the west side of the hill called Pen Berry (Penbiri) and in one or two places where it skirts Dowrog Common (a wetland of interest to naturalists) and reaches the south coast at Morfa Common. By the Middle Ages, when the militant Norman bishops established themselves there, the influence of St. David's see spread right across Pembrokeshire. It seems reasonable to suppose that the ring-motte marked as 'Castell' half a mile west of St. David's cathedral was the stronghold of the first Norman bishops. But Clegyr Boia ('Boia's rock'), further to the west, is prehistoric, its finds extending back from Iron Age to Neolithic. On the bleak and rugged headland of St. David's there is a splendour of cliff flowers. In spring the slopes are sheeted pink, yellow and white with thrift, lady's fingers, sea campion and scurvy grass; later come the deeper colours of heather, saw-wort and knapweed. The whole rock-strewn headland is cut off by the still massive strong banks of an Iron Age promontory fort which contains a few hut-circles. Contemporary with them are probably the ancient fields traceable on the nearby slopes of Carn Llidi. And for an earlier relic there is a collapsed Neolithic burial chamber. The headland is reached by a delightful path round the cliffs from Whitesand Bay, a popular bathing beach.

Pembrokeshire

People throughout the Middle Ages, kings and commoners alike, streamed down the long road to St. David's in pious pilgrimage. Not that St. David's will fill you with awe as a greater cathedral might. In fact you will pass right through the village ('Britain's smallest city') and see no sign of the cathedral nor even the top of its tower. Then suddenly there it is below you in a hollow called Glyn Rhosyn, a long, squat, cruciform church with a severe-looking tower. Yet though so plain and unimposing it looks perfectly right for its setting in this frequently gale-swept place only a mile from the wild sea cliffs that were the source of its violet stones. Inside it is beautiful. It is much lighter than many cathedrals and churches and you can savour all the nuances of colour in the stones and woodwork. The nave has perfect proportions, a fine clerestory and a richly carved oak roof of the fifteenth century. But it is the arcades on either side that take the eye for they lean outwards and you give their builders full marks for achieving an intriguing perspective until you learn that it is more likely that the arcades were originally upright and have only leaned by accident. The three centuries of medieval work in this cathedral produced a happy blending of styles. Particularly good are the fan-vaulted roof of the chapel of Bishop Vaughan; the stone screens; the bishops' throne; the presbytery screen and other oak screenwork; the rare wooden sedilia; and the stalls with their amusing misericords. There are ancient stones carved with crosses; and tombs and effigies of long-dead priests and bishops. Greatest temporal figure buried here is Edmund Tudor, father of Henry VII. The bells are hung not in the tower but in the gatehouse between the cathedral and the city. You leave the cathedral and cross a trout-darting streamlet to the honey-coloured shell of the palace. Here, where jackdaws now chatter and collared doves coo, the bishops lived in evident splendour. The palace, largely built about 1340, continued in use for several hundred years but has been derelict since the eighteenth century. Elegantly arcaded, it survives as one of the most attractive of Welsh medieval ruins.

At the seaward approaches to St. David's various chapels stood strategically at landing places where they could receive the thank-offerings of pilgrims who had arrived safely. One, at Whitesand Bay, has disappeared completely. But half a mile south of the cathedral the chapel of St. Non, or Nona, by tradition the mother of St. David, survives as a scanty ruin above the shore; nearby her well is still kept in order. On the shore two miles west of the city are the strongly built, roofless walls of the chapel of St. Justinian, said to have been a colleague of St. David. His chapel stands opposite Ramsey Island which itself had two medieval chapels.

Ramsey, a two-mile-long island with magnificent cliffs, is given shapeliness by its two hills of igneous rock which are topped by probably Bronze Age cairns. It looks especially good from St. David's Head which has a full view of the island and of Ramsey Sound, a passage where the spring tides flow like a mighty river, roaring through a line of dangerous rocks called the Bitches. Geologically this small island has surprising variety. For while most of its southern half continues the igneous rocks of St. David's, much of the northern part belongs to the Ordovician sedimentary beds of the north coast of Pembrokeshire. The result is that the southern half of Ramsey is poor-soiled and heathy while the northern, where the one farmhouse is, has fertility. So for centuries tithes were paid to the bishops of St. David's. At the north end some of the rocks are rich in fossils, especially trilobites and brachiopods.

Ramsey—the name is Norse, perhaps meaning the island of some Viking leader called Hrafn—is a reserve of the Royal Society for the Protection of Birds. It is a great place for choughs and in the summer its cliffs have nesting colonies of kittiwakes, guillemots, razorbills and other species. Its most magnificent side is to the open sea: there the cliffs are highest and are undermined by deep caves. In autumn grey seals come to breed in these caves and on the island's stony beaches in greater numbers than anywhere else in Wales. From Ramsey you look north and west to a charming group of islets called the Bishops and Clerks, charming that is when they stand in quiet summer seas with not a hint of white water about them. In winter they are a terrible hazard (hence the light on South Bishop).

All the coast near St. David's is great cliff-walking country, the path continuing from Whitesand Bay along Ramsey Sound and round the corner to Porth Lisgi and St. Non's. In the next two bays, Caerfai and Caerbwdi, much of the cathedral's colourful stone was quarried. From the rocky cove at Porth-y-rhaw you get a superb view back along the wild cliffs to the southern

tip of Ramsey. Nearby you pass the banks of an Iron Age cliff
fort and soon reach Solva where a winding creek makes a first-
class anchorage that was long a centre of coastwise trade and is
now a yachtsman's haven. From Solva the cliff path continues
east another three miles to Newgale. A little inland from here
'Pointz Castle' is a grand name for what is now only a scrub-
covered mound next to some farm buildings. It was presumably
built to safeguard the small domain of some twelfth century
Norman subservient to the powerful St. David's bishops. Nearby Brawdy has an ancient but much restored parish church with
three Dark Ages stones in its porch but their inscriptions are
obscure, two being in Ogham. For many years there has been
an extensive airfield near by.

St. Bride's Bay, a lovely curve of the coast, begins in the north
with the popular Newgale sands. Where they now are a prehistoric forest flourished and the stumps of trees are sometimes
uncovered by scouring tides, as Giraldus Cambrensis noted
when he passed up this coast in 1188. It is strange that these
great sands, though exposed to the prevailing winds, have produced no dunes at their rear. To the south the shore becomes
cliffy for a while then again the rocks give way to sandy inlets
and wider bathing beaches. Inevitably caravans and chalets have
multiplied. Nolton Haven is a cliff-sided cove that looks along
the southern arm of the bay to a long level silhouette of Skomer
Island. A mile south Druidston had nothing to do with druids.
Locally pronounced 'Drewson' it started life as Drue's town,
Alfred Drue being the twelfth-century Norman knight who
first settled there. If hereabouts you come to very dark cliffs you
have found where the Coal Measures meet the sea. In the past
coal has been worked in a small way and exported from Little
Haven.

Nearly two miles inland from the northern end of St. Bride's
Bay you will find Roch castle which, though not open to the
public, is easy enough to see on its rock above the road. Though
probably only a twelfth-century peel tower it was a significant
one. For it anchored the western end of a line of forts that the
Anglo-Normans built right across Pembrokeshire and which
effectively divided the county between the north, which was left
to the Welsh, and the south which was settled by English, Normans and especially by a host of Flemish refugees driven from

their homeland either by war or floods. What is remarkable is that this ancient demarcation line, long known as the Landsker, still has reality. The Welsh language and place-names still dominate north of it and are largely absent south of it in what has since the twelfth century been called Little England beyond Wales. The castles of the Landsker besides Roch were at Haverfordwest, Picton, Wiston, Llawhaden, Carew, Narberth and Amroth.

Keeston castle (so-called) a mile and a half south-east had nothing to do with the Landsker, pre-dating it by some 1,200 years. It is an Iron Age fort defended by three concentric banks which have faded away on the side nearest the village. There are also large Iron Age defences high above deep dingles at Walwyn's Castle, close to the tall-towered church. And, despite the name, Romans Castle, a mile and a half east, is likewise a circle of Iron Age banks. For a church with a view over land and sea go to Walton West, high above the southern corner of the bay. In the nave is a cross-carved stone found in the churchyard this century by a grave-digger. About a yard tall it is obviously a sea-worn stone off the beach and owes its good condition to having been buried for centuries. A lane from here swoops you into Little Haven from where it is a mile north to the rapidly growing resort of Broad Haven.

From Little Haven a cliff-edge path takes you on into the west. Soon you come to Goultrop on whose cliffs deciduous woodland lives in rare intimacy with the sea. Further west along the headlands you will see breeding colonies of gulls, fulmars and cormorants; stonechats call from the gorse; and choughs often pass in lovely bouncing flight. On these cliffs are several raths (the Pembrokeshire word for earthworks) which are mostly Iron Age promontory forts. Far more ancient are the traces of man found in the earth of Nab Head where Mesolithic chipped flints and pierced beads have been found. From Nab Head to Musselwick sands the cliffs get more and more colourful. Steeply tilted strata of near-black rocks alternate with beds some of palest grey, some of rich purple-red. Then the bedding plane changes and for a few hundred yards the rocks are tidily horizontal until suddenly they buckle in chaos. But everywhere it is the beautiful purple rocks that predominate, coming to brilliant life when the sunlight is on them and a blue sea is washing below. Along these cliff tops you may think some disease has struck down the broom bushes. They lie with their branches on the ground, spread out like the spokes of a wheel. But fear not: this is the local botanical curiosity—the prostrate broom. Not a separate species, just an odd variety.

Soon you come to the last cove along the bay, sheltered Martinshaven, departure-point in summer for the daily boat to Skomer, largest and most birdful of all the Welsh islands. Skomer is a Scandinavian name dating back to the later Dark Ages when the Vikings, centred on Dublin, were supreme along Irish Sea coasts. Perhaps a thousand years earlier the island had been intensively cultivated by Iron Age settlers whose field outlines, lynchets and hut sites still copiously endure near the cliffs. There is also one standing stone, traditionally called Harold's Stone, of unknown antiquity. Possibly it marks a Bronze Age burial. After the Vikings came the Normans who characteristically spurned the island agriculturally and turned it into a rabbit warren. Only in comparatively recent times has it been properly farmed again but now the farm is once more in ruins and the island is a National Nature Reserve annually visited by hundreds of people who get much delight from seeing the multitudes of kittiwakes, guillemots, razorbills and puffins that nest on the island's great cliffs. And if you are there after dark (a few chalets are available) you will be entertained by the thousands of shearwaters that nest there.

Skomer continues the mainland's dark igneous rocks. So does Grassholm, a much smaller island twelve miles further into the Atlantic and famous for its vast colony of gannets which cluster so thickly on the slopes that they make a white patch visible from the mainland. Grassholm is a reserve of the R.S.P.B. but can be landed on only in really calm weather. If you can manage a landing you will see the finest mass bird spectacle in all Wales. Grassholm is not the farthest land west. Beyond are low-tide rocks called the Hats and the Barrels and, even further out, fifteen miles from Skomer, are the Smalls, lighthouse-crowned and savaged by awesome seas—the westernmost fragment of Wales. Skomer's near neighbour on the south is the bleak island of Skokholm whose red cliffs are in contrast with Skomer's dark rocks, for Skokholm continues the sandstone rocks of St. Ann's Head. Like the other islands it is a splendid sea bird sanctuary, its former farmhouse now being an ornithological station where you can stay and learn about birds. It is noted especially for its colony of storm petrels, its vast population of shearwaters, thousands of which are ringed each season, and for its rare migrants.

Back on the mainland the coast path continues south-east from Martinshaven following the contortions of cliffs and inlets to Gateholm, a high-tide island on which archaeologists have found the remains of a large Celtic village thought to have been occupied during Roman times. The island can also be reached from Marloes, a once remote village that has an alien-looking clock tower commemorating a former landowner, Baron Kensington. From Marloes sands the cliff path goes south to Dale's west bay, an exposed beach pounded by breakers in high winds. On nearby Great Castle Head the 'castle' was an Iron Age promontory fort whose banks still exist. Flints of much earlier man have also been found there. The peninsula continues south with fine views of Skokholm to St. Ann's Head, a high cliff top known for its gales, its virtually frost-free climate and the wild tide-races that fret the sea below. From here you look to oceanic horizons. On St. Ann's there has been a lighthouse for centuries, perhaps right back to medieval times when a chapel dedicated to St. Ann stood here, a chapel whose custodian had the job of keeping a nightly beacon flaming.

Dale, which shelters in the lee of this great headland, is in summer a yachtman's village. It is also a centre for naturalists, the solidly-built early nineteenth-century fort on Dale Point being a field-studies centre whose courses are open on a weekly basis to school and college groups or private individuals. Birdwatchers should look at the little estuary close to the village: over the years it has produced some notable rarities. St. Ishmael's, east of Dale, has an ancient church with early crosses and a broken medieval grave slab. The churchyard is a quiet dell full of interesting trees. A path takes you from the village to another Great Castle Head. It has a lighthouse, a long Iron Age embankment and views of the vast oil-refinery west of Milford town. From this prospect you can escape into the unspoilt beauty of Sandyhaven inlet, a sheltered river-mouth with trees beautifully draping the water's edge.

Milford Haven was a planned town of the end of the eighteenth century, the speculator being Sir William Hamilton whose second wife, Emma, thirty-five years his junior, was Nelson's special girl-friend. Nelson visited Milford at the height of his fame and the place has never forgotten it. Among the first townsfolk was a colony of Quaker whalers from Nantucket Island, Massachusetts, who were invited to settle here in 1790. By deep-sea fishing, trade with Ireland and Admiralty ship-building contracts Milford prospered rapidly and one time looked capable of putting Liverpool out of business. But the pace was not kept up. Of its three main enterprises the fishing has endured longest but even that is not what it was. Now, with the coming of the oil terminals, Milford has recovered something of its old prestige. The nineteenth-century waterfront, with Hamilton Terrace climbing above the busy harbour, is the most attractive part of the town. Various oddments of Nelsoniana are preserved in the church of St. Katherine whose foundation stone was laid by Hamilton in 1801. A mile north stood the Benedictine priory of Pill, twelfth-century daughter-house of St. Dogmael's priory near Cardigan. Of Pill priory one tall medieval arch remains but is cluttered round by cottages.

The great spring tides that pour into the haven past St. Ann's Head do not spend themselves before they have brought many feet of water to the quay at Haverfordwest twenty winding miles inland. How at home the Norsemen must have felt in such a land-locked water (the 'ford' in Milford is presumably derived from 'fiord'). The trade of all ages has gone up and down this haven and the narrow Cleddau estuary. Only in this century has it ceased and the anchorages been given over to pleasure craft. Neyland, four miles east of Milford, was the terminal for the Irish mail-boats until they began to use Fishguard in 1906. From Neyland an attractively wooded tidal creek runs nearly up to Rosemarket—a deceptive name, for the 'Rose' was originally the Welsh 'Rhos', meaning a heath, and no doubt referred to some local patch of open ground where fairs were held. So look with suspicion on any Welsh place called 'Rose': Rose Cottage, Rose Hill, Rose Pool, all may disguise a 'Rhos'.

A mile or so east of Neyland, near the new bridge across the haven, Burton church has a fine altar tomb and lancet windows. Burial chamber enthusiasts will find a good specimen two miles north. It has a massive purplish capstone on three supports and stands in a hedge behind farm buildings a few hundred yards south of Sardis. From Burton church a track winds round to Benton woods and then descends to Rhoos ferry down a long shadowy dingle full of soft shield-ferns and hartstongues. The wide pool in the river below is active with small (and some large) boats. Trees come beautifully to the tide's edge all round. Some of these deciduous woodlands, rich in wildlife, are in the care of the Forestry Commission whose conifers continue upstream nearly to Llangwm which, like Hook to the north, has long been linked with the estuary trade in agricultural produce and anthracite. But the mines no longer work and all farm transport has long since taken to the roads. So as everywhere else along the Cleddau the old quays and havens are now used mostly by yachtsmen. Llangwm, once famous for oysters which went to the London markets, was described last century as 'a village of low straggling houses interspersed with trees amidst mountains of oyster shells'. It is very different now. The much-restored church has cross-incised stones and a canopied tomb with effigies. From near Llangwm there is a beautiful view up the Cleddau to the demesne of Picton Castle which is thirteenth century but modernized as a private residence.

At the head of the Western Cleddau, Haverfordwest is the focus of all roads. It was important to the Vikings who gave it its name, to the Normans who fortified it and to the Flemings who later peopled it. Of its thirteenth-century castle only the shell now stands. In Quay Street at the bottom of this steeply sloping town are still the warehouses of the old shipping trade. A short way downstream stand tall medieval priory ruins; and on the opposite bank is a riverside walk curiously called Fortune's Frolic. The castle, housing the county museum, is half-way up the town and higher still is the thirteenth-century English-type church of St. Mary which has a noble fifteenth-century oak roof, carved bench-ends, an unusual holy water stoup and some amusingly decorated capitals.

The eastern branch of the Cleddau flows from the Preseli mountains past Llawhaden castle and under A40 at Canaston bridge, an ancient crossing place. Immediately below, the stream meets the highest tides at Blackpool mill; and there it is highly possible that the famous blue stones, taken from Preseli to help build Stonehenge, were launched (presumably slung below rafts) and then carried down Milford Haven and up the Bristol Channel. Blackpool mill is a strikingly large building to discover suddenly in its rural setting. It has a long history as a flour-mill and is now open to the public as a museum, complete with café. The river here and its bridge of 1830 are most attractive. Below the mill the tidal Cleddau flows past the conifer plantations of the Slebech estate where in the Middle Ages the Knights of St. John had one of their rare Welsh hospices, this one evidently catering for travellers going from southern England to St. David's or Ireland. The tree-surrounded ruins of their church close to Slebech House can be reached along two miles of woodland track from Blackpool bridge. Across the Cleddau from the church, hidden among trees in private ground, are the collapsed walls of the so-called Sisters' House, locally referred to as 'Minwear Abbey'. Perhaps this is the site of the hospice itself? When last century the medieval church was replaced by the high-steepled one on the main road a mile north, two well-carved effigies of a sixteenth-century knight and his long-tressed lady were moved to the new church where they still remain. The position of the abandoned church quiet among trees at the edge of estuarine tides is immeasurably more delightful than that of its dull successor on the side of A40. Another well-placed church ruin, Newton old parish church stands solitary amid fields a mile south of Canaston bridge. Lost in a tangle of thickets this roofless building with no road to it is quite unrestored and medieval in atmosphere. Half a mile north-east is the site of Newhouse which was a moated manor-house. Ask at Newhouse farm for permission to visit these antiquities.

If you take the lane south-west from Blackpool mill you keep to the south side of the Cleddau. You go through more forestry plantations, pass a good viewpoint and come to Minwear (pronounced 'Minner') church, a medieval building with a stone screen that is massively oversized in such a small church. The ancient circular font has four worn human faces as decoration. On the small square tower grows a little pellitory-of-the-wall. Landshipping Quay comes next, a hamlet at the water's edge. Fairly touristy in summer this is a quiet spot all the rest of the year, the road dead-ending there. Standing at the head of a short tidal creek with woods all round, it shares in the district's not very distant memories of sea trade and small coal mines. Cress-

well Quay a few miles south-east is similarly placed on a pill
(that is a creek) which is waterless except at high tide. From there
if you go down alongside the Cresswell river to West Williamston you come to one of the strangest bits of landscape you will
find anywhere in Wales. For here is a complexity of abandoned
limestone quarries which had access to the sea along a network
of short canals cut through the salt marshes. Today much of the
place is overgrown with dense scrub and the result is a singular
wilderness of woodland, limestone and winding waterways.
Good country for naturalists. In former times boats used to go
from West Williamston with a cargo of rock limestone and local
anthracite. These were landed at kilns scattered all along the
nearby coasts of Wales and across the Bristol Channel. Thus was
lime supplied to some of the remotest farms. Where the broad
Cresswell river joins the Cleddau at a lovely spot opposite Benton castle (medieval but now a modernized private house) is the
old Lawrenny ferry now developed as a yachting centre.

Towering above tidal water three miles south-east of Lawrenny, Carew is one of the most picturesque castles of Wales,
especially when reflected in the mirror of a brimming tide. All
the same it looks a bit odd, this castle that faces you on one side
with the authentic curtain wall and drum towers of about the
year 1300, and on the other with a façade that is pure Tudor. It
was long residential, being made into a stately home in the
fifteenth century by Sir Rhys ap Thomas who lived here in
splendour with his great hall and musicians' gallery. The Tudor
reconstructions were by Sir John Perrot, the same irrepressible
doer-up of old castles who modernized the one at Laugharne,
Carmarthenshire. On the roadside near the castle is one of the
most decorated of Celtic crosses; it commemorates an eleventh-
century Welsh prince. The parish church has medieval effigies
and later monuments, several being of the de Carew family who
held the castle for many centuries. Just down the creek from the
castle is a disused but interesting water-mill built on a dam: the
impounded tides turned the mill wheel as they ebbed. Further
downriver was another medieval castle at Upton but what is
left of it has become a private house.

Greatest of all Pembrokeshire castles is the one whose towers
and walls look north across a tidal creek at Pembroke. Built in
the thirteenth century it was long the centre of power in Pem-

brokeshire and never for a day fell into the hands of the Welsh though it had some narrow escapes. The most famous person associated with it was Henry VII, born there in January 1457. Twenty-eight years later when he returned from abroad with an invading army it was in Milford Haven that he landed and Pembroke was among the first towns to speed him on his way to Bosworth Field and the English throne. The castle was the scene of one of the longest sieges of the Civil War but fell to the Cromwellians in July 1648. They slighted it but not with their usual fury. So although since then its walls have been persistently quarried for local housing, what remains is not quite an empty shell. Interesting features of the castle are the gatehouse, the great round keep with immensely thick walls (and a fine view from the top) and the unique Wogan cave, a natural cavern in the limestone below and reached down a narrow stairway. This cave opens on to the river and was the castle's emergency exit. Today it houses a colony of lesser horse-shoe bats. Perhaps it always did.

Pembroke town had medieval walls but their line is now hardly traceable. The church of St. Mary close to the castle has a medieval tomb and a few monuments. Not far is Monkton where stood a Benedictine priory now mostly gone but whose church has been restored. It contains several memorials of local families and a fifteenth-century tomb. Three miles south-east of Pembroke is Orielton, a mansion with beautiful woodlands and pools on one of which is an ancient duck-decoy originally intended to trap wildfowl for food but lately used only to catch them for ringing. Giraldus in the twelfth century described the house then at Orielton as haunted by 'unclean spirits'. Since then things have improved and today Orielton is a field studies centre for naturalists. Two miles east of Pembroke at Lamphey (Llandyfai) the medieval bishops of St. David's had a palace of which substantial fragments remain to hint of former splendour. It is approached down a quiet shady drive at the end of which you get an exotic welcome from palms, bamboos and a well-grown gingko by the entrance gate. Note especially the strong gatehouse tower with arcading reminiscent of the palace at St. David's. Outside the palace walls is a marsh that looks like the remains of a medieval fish-pond.

The coast immediately west of Pembroke is dominated by oil-installations. But wildness and beauty survive west of Angle Bay. Angle used to be a very remote fisherfolk's hamlet. Today it is well known to holiday-makers, especially yachtsmen looking for a sheltered anchorage. The beach near the village is stony and bathers are happier at the sandy bay a mile west. Thorn Island, like Dale, has a fort built to guard the Admiralty dockyards. The rocky coast curves round for three miles to the long, dune-backed shore of Freshwater West where oceanic rollers pound the shore almost unceasingly, making bathing really imprudent. The dunes at Brownslade Burrows have yielded quantities of Neolithic tools. Castlemartin has an attractive old church with a ruined rectory nearby. A record of 1602 includes Castlemartin among 'some whole parishes inhabited by the Irishe, haveinge not one Englishe or Welshe but the parson'. South of Castlemartin through country that has long been used as a military training ground you come to Flimston where there is a restored medieval chapel with glacial boulders for gravestones. From there you continue to the twin Elegug Stacks, central feature of one of the finest lines of cliffs in Britain. The stacks are magnificent in spring when all the elegugs (guillemots), razorbills and kittiwakes are massed on them for breeding. Nearby is a famous natural arch standing off the cliff face and called the Green Bridge of Wales. Further west the cliffs go on in splendour all the way to Linney Head.

The walk east from Elegug Stacks along these vertical limestone cliffs is also superb, especially if a big sea is running. You soon find yourself looking down into a vast blow-hole in which the sea boils below at high tide; and in gales it comes bursting up with a booming that carries far. Nearby are the worn but unmistakable banks of a promontory fort and there is another half a mile further on. The path goes out to St. Govan's but most people get to that fine headland down the lane from Bosherston. Where this lane meets the cliffs is the unique St. Govan's chapel reached by descending fifty-two steps down a steep, narrow gully in the cliffs. The tiny medieval chapel quite blocking this cleft was for the use of pilgrims visiting the curative well of Govan, a sixth-century holy man. But the well is now dry. The cliff flowers here are beautiful: cowslips, early purple orchids and squills. And even on exposed stack rocks there are notable specimens of sea mallow standing tall and defiant of all the winds that blow. Dammed by a natural bar of sand the ponds at Bosherston form three exquisite finger-shaped lakes set among limestone rocks and woods. In spring and early summer wild flowers are everywhere, the water is patched with lavish sheets of lilies and there is an idyllic walk across delightful bridges down to the unspoilt sands of Broad Haven. In the churchyard at Bosherston is a medieval stone cross: and 500 yards east, between two of the ponds, is an Iron Age promontory fort. Much of this country is on the Stackpole estate and the name is frequent on the map. Stackpole (or Cheriton) church, remarkable for its tall, oddly placed tower, is visited for its monuments, medieval and later. Stackpole Head is a high square-ended promontory hollowed under by a natural arch that is spectacular when stormy seas burst through it. Stackpole Quay has a stone jetty and once exported limestone from a quarry there. Barafundle Bay, just south, is a delight.

The shore continues in beauty except for the popular bathing beach at Freshwater East which is up to the eyebrows in shacks. At Manorbier the fine castle has looked down a green valley to the sea since at least the thirteenth century but its part in history was small. In a previous castle on the site Gerald de Barri, usually called Giraldus Cambrensis or Gerallt Cymro, was born in about 1146. The name Manorbier was presumably once 'Manor de Barri'; and no doubt the de Barri family built the church which occupies another strong site on the hill opposite the castle. Inside it is fascinating to see how the original Norman nave had aisles added either side by cutting odd-sized arches through the very thick walls. Though it is not rare for a chancel to be out of line with the nave there can be few as out of true as this one. The tower too is oddly placed on the north side and is entered from a high gallery of fourteenth-century oak. South of Manorbier beach is the headland called the Priest's Nose, which has a collapsed burial chamber at the side of the path. Beyond rise the higher cliffs of Old Castle Head, so called from its Iron Age fort. Further east lie the fine headlands of Lydstep Point (National Trust) and Proud Giltar which between them shelter Lydstep Haven, a popular caravan and bathing beach. The cliffs here have long been famous for their caves and there is an exhilarating cliff walk to the end of Giltar Point, the nearest land to Caldy Island.

Pembrokeshire

Caldy is beautifully seen from the main road near Lydstep. It appears as a long, slightly domed island standing on cliffs that are red sandstone in the south and white limestone in the north. You can see various monastic buildings and an automatic lighthouse. The island has long been a treasure house for archaeologists who in its limestone caves have found copious remains of prehistoric animals. These you can see for yourself in Tenby museum's fascinating collection of teeth and other bones of hyenas, rhinos, lions, bears, reindeer and other long-extinct species. Man too was early and persistent on the Caldy scene: large number of his tools and other remains attest his presence there from the Middle Stone Age onwards. Caldy became a Christian centre in about the sixth century and presumably remained a monastic site all through the Dark Ages. An Ogham stone from about the sixth century (and inscribed in Latin about three hundred years later) is preserved in the priory church. This is a vaulted, cobble-floored building with very thick walls. Its battlemented tower is topped by a worn spire wildly out of perpendicular. Both this church and the village church belong to the Middle Ages when Caldy monastery was a dependent of the powerful Benedictine house at St. Dogmael's near Cardigan. So it remained until the Dissolution after which the island passed into secular hands for several centuries. There is now a Cistercian monastery of about thirty monks who flourish by dint of farming and a summer flow of cash from tourists. In the season a stream of small boats plies between Tenby harbour and Caldy. They land you at Priory Bay where bathing and picnicking are allowed. Beyond that you are expected to keep to the paths either to the monastery or to the lovely cliffs with their many flowers, butterflies and birds. At the north-western tip of Caldy is a high-tide island called St. Margaret's, a bird reserve of the West Wales Naturalists' Trust.

The nearest mainland village to Caldy is Penally whose church has a worn, decorated Celtic cross standing by the shaft of another; a thirteenth-century tomb; and a fine view across the Burrows to the sea. Alongside the Burrows a mile of yellow sands takes you to Tenby, a town with beautiful beaches; a picturesque old harbour surrounded by attractive houses; and lovely views across to Caldy. Though so deep within Wales modern Tenby developed as an English-style Regency resort and remains very English. Of its sizeable twelfth-century castle only a fragment is left. Connected with it were the town walls which have survived remarkably complete with round towers at intervals, the best being the Five Arches. But the demolition of ancient housing has been thorough. The only survivals seem to be the Tudor Merchant's House on Quay Hill and Plantagenet House next-door, both National Trust. St. Mary's church, one of the biggest in Wales, has a very tall spire and a handsome fifteenth-century oak ceiling decorated with bosses carved with figures that include some oddities. There are many monuments, the most colourful being an elaborate Jacobean tomb. There is also a memorial to a Tenby man of the sixteenth century, Robert Recorde, a pioneer of mathematics. He invented the equals sign, was the first to work out square roots and was also the first in Britain to adopt the signs for plus and minus. Some of the books he wrote are in the museum on Castle Hill whose exhibits show many faces of Tenby's history as a port and a resort and there are cases of prehistoric material from all over Pembrokeshire. Sea shells and shore life are also a speciality.

Tenby's Welsh name is Dinbych y pysgod ('Denbigh of the fish') for there has been a great fishery here. Today holiday fishermen trail spinners to catch a few mackerel and the more adventurous use a whole mackerel as bait for shark and tope. There is a centre for this big-game fishing along the coast at Saundersfoot which once mined and exported anthracite (hence the harbour) but is now a resort popular for its sheltered beach. The coast continues as a sequence of shingle and sands below cliffs for many miles beyond Amroth where Pembrokeshire ends and Carmarthenshire begins at the mouth of a pebbly stream. Amroth castle is a nineteenth-century house on the site of the vanished medieval castle. At low tide you can sometimes see traces of a submerged forest that has yielded bones of now extinct animals and flakes of primitive tools.

Pembrokeshire north from Tenby to the Preseli hills and east from Slebech to Whitland, is an unspectacular hinterland that feels comparatively little of the impact of tourism. This does not mean it lacks interest, only that it has not the magnetic attractions of the coast. A good centre is Narberth whose old name was Castell yn Arberth where the Normans built a strong castle to make sure the Welsh were confined to the infertile slopes of

Preseli. And as a further discouragement to the Welsh they garrisoned it with thrusting Flemings. Not that the Normans were the first to put Narberth (or Arberth) on the map. In fact the first sentence of the *Mabinogion* refers to it as 'a chief court' of the prince of Dyfed, the Dark Ages name for Pembrokeshire. Only fragments of the Norman castle now stand and these you see on your right as you climb up to the town. The castle looks south over the country it once dominated and whose place-names are mostly English like Templeton, or heavily Anglicized like Ludchurch which presumably was Eglwys-lwyd ('grey church'), a medieval building now hemmed round by flooded limestone quarries. Templeton hints at its own story: it was a holding of the Knights Templar who probably had a hospice there under the protection of the curiously named Sentence Castle. East of Narbeth in the Marlais valley another historic place-name is Llanddewi Velfrey which goes back to the Dark Ages when the name of this whole district was Felffre. Earlier antiquities are also evident, notably a pair of Iron Age forts on the hills just outside Llanddewi Velfrey.

Three miles north-west of Narberth is the deeply moated castle of Llawhaden built and often altered during the Middle Ages by the bishops of St. David's, first to safeguard their far-flung estates, later as a baronial residence in an age when the princes of the church really lived like princes. The bishops abandoned it in the sixteenth century and it is now an attractive ruin, its warm-brown stone coloured with yellow and white lichens. With fair views over fields and woods it is defended on the east by a deep reach of the Cleddau on whose bank is a curious church with two towers. The outer tower was the first and when the church was moved a few yards further from the river in the fourteenth century the new tower was built against the old. On high ground three miles west of Llawhaden was the Landsker castle of Wiston which began life as a chartered town but is now a minute hamlet. The castle is likewise diminished, surviving only as the thick-walled stump of a round keep on top of a prominent mound. From here if you carry on west along the lanes you reach Rudbaxton church, famous for its outsize seventeenth-century memorial to a family called Howard. In this colourful but inartistic monument five tall figures stand facing you theatrically. Four hold skulls to signify they are dead, but the mother of the family has an hour-glass to indicate that for her the sands have not all run out.

A40 which passes close to Rudbaxton goes north to Treffgarne in a deep wooded dingle. This locality has historic interest because the family of Owain Glyndŵr's mother owned the manor of Treffgarne in the fourteenth century. Modern research has shown that Treffgarne Owen near Brawdy, long claimed as Glyndŵr's birthplace, had in fact no connection with him or his family. The rocky outcrops above Treffgarne make striking scenery and at one spot these igneous rocks (rhyolites) have weathered into a huge whimsical sculpture called Maiden Castle. Where the river divides at Wolf's Castle a motte and bailey was built between the streams. The eastern tributary comes down a tree-filled valley from Sealyham Hall where the dogs of that name originated. The stream here, the Anghof, comes directly off Preseli past the moorland village of Puncheston whose school looks most odd ringed round by the large earthworks of an Iron Age fort. Nearby Castlebythe has an abandoned church and a conspicuous castle mound within the hamlet and a less obvious one, Castle-fuwch, on a neighbouring slope. Two miles southeast Henry's Moat was clearly 'Henry's motte' but it may be less obvious that 'Henry' is a corruption of Hendre ('the old homestead'). The motte is next-door to the church. Castle Flemish, near Wallis woollen mill, is a Roman fortlet with an east-west Roman road through it. In the valley of the Syfynwy close to Henry's Moat is Llys-y-frân reservoir.

Because Preseli is Pembrokeshire's only mountain its shapely summits are visible from all over the county. When you get up there you find they are treeless, grassy domes with patches of heather and gorse which mix their purple and yellow flowers most handsomely in late summer. Several roads edge round Preseli but only B4329 goes boldly over the ridge and reaches 1,300 feet. From this high point you can take to foot or horse and go east from summit to summit, coming down to Crymych seven miles away. But to include Preseli's highest point, Foel Cwmcerwyn (1,760 feet) you must detour south after just over a mile, keeping above forestry plantations. Because Preseli stands back from the rest of the Welsh mountains the views from the top are among the greatest in Wales. It looks down on Pembrokeshire's thousands of little fields, a marvellous map-like scene with the sea nearly all round and Milford Haven reaching into the land. Further away you look to a huge slice of Wales, especially north to Snowdon and across the bay to Lleyn and Bardsey Island; and sometimes you see west to Ireland or south as far as Devon.

Preseli's ridge road is ancient. Past antiquarians have variously described it as Neolithic, Bronze Age, Iron Age, Roman and Flemish. It was probably all these except Flemish, for Flemish is a dangerous word, being often used by our forbears as meaning simply 'foreign'. Preseli's prehistoric story is a marvellous one not only because in the Bronze Age the blue stones went from here to Stonehenge but because the whole district is so rich in stones, mounds, hill forts and ancient roads. Perhaps nowhere in Wales is a Bronze Age landscape so well preserved. And when you are up among those weird-shaped rocks of Carnmenyn (or Carnmeini) you can easily persuade yourself that many Bronze Age objects lie waiting discovery just below the turf: for instance the original site of what we might call Preseli Henge. For many archaeologists assume that the blue stones stood as a mega-lithic monument on Preseli before being removed to Wiltshire. If so the holes in which they stood may come to light some day. And with them no doubt other finds of interest.

It is evident that the people who migrated from Preseli to Salisbury Plain (if this is what happened) attached enormous religious importance to these mighty chunks of white-spotted blue stones (which seldom look blue). For they weigh several tons each and had to be sledged all down Preseli's flank perhaps to Blackpool, then rafted down Milford Haven, around Linney Head and up the Bristol Channel and the Avon and thence over-land to Stonehenge. But such prehistoric moving of great stones is not unique, not even at Stonehenge where some of the biggest monoliths were hauled eighteen miles from Marlborough Downs. Similar stone-shifting has been recorded on the Conti-nent. And in ancient Egypt the megalith builders transported stone hundreds of miles down the Nile from Asswan to build pyramids near Cairo. It is also fascinating that although the Preseli origin of Stonehenge's blue stones was not demonstrated until this century a folk memory of the move may have persisted until the Middle Ages. For in the twelfth century Geoffrey of Monmouth, perhaps not inventing for once, stated that some of the Stonehenge stones were believed to have come from Ireland. If we grant that the Preseli ridge road was part of a Bronze Age trade route from Ireland it becomes pardonable that confusion between Preseli and Ireland as the origin of the stones might arise as the folk memory passed down the generations. Also in certain Arthurian chronicles there are vague references to the transporting of highly revered stones across the sea.

Preseli's blue stone material has earlier than Bronze Age connections: Neolithic hand axes made of this white-spotted dolerite peculiar to Preseli have been found both nearby and elsewhere in Wales as well as in Ireland. So there is something else to be looked for—the site of a hand-axe factory. A good Neolithic site is Bedd yr Afanc, a chambered tomb of the long barrow type. It is close to Brynberian on B4329. The name, meaning 'grave of the afanc', a mythical beast, is a fanciful attempt to 'explain' a mystery. A Bronze Age stone circle survives a mile south-west of Mynachlogddu church. With sixteen stones it is one of the most complete in Wales. The parish name Mynachlogddu ('black monastery') presumably means that the land here belonged to St. Dogmael's, an abbey of black-habited monks. On Foeldrygarn (or Moel Trygarn) ('the hill of three cairns') the Bronze and Iron Ages come together. For here on this east end of Preseli that looks down on Crymych the ramparts of one of the best hill forts in Wales enclose three fine Bronze Age cairns as well as the remains of scores of Iron Age huts. Finds from here: beads, spindle whorls, pottery fragments—can be seen in Tenby museum. In the bogs on Preseli's flanks plant-seekers should look out for the pale butterwort curiously absent from the rest of Wales.

In the north the Pembrokeshire coast begins at the mouth of the Teifi, though its grasp of the estuary is very small, for the lords of Ceredigion, no doubt because Cardigan castle was so near and so important, early got possession of most of both sides of the estuary. But St. Dogmael's remained in Pembrokeshire because its Benedictine priory was an integral part of the Pembrokeshire lordship of Cemaes (or Cemais). The abbey ruins are sparse but the outlines of its various buildings are recognizable, there is a collection of carved stones and there is a stone cadaver. For the Dark Ages go to the parish church where there are ancient inscribed stones. For a bathe go to Poppit sands. For sea breezes go past Poppit and stroll for miles along the wild cliffs south from Cemaes Head. Look out for grey seals—they have a special love of this coast. A mile inland is Moylgrove, a hamlet that hides its charms within a deep valley. For antiquarians there is a promontory fort at Castelltreruffydd (take it gently: 'cas-teth-tray-riff-ith'). And there are burial chambers a mile south (Llech-y-tribedd) and two miles south-west (Trellyfaint), both with large capstones. The Trellyfaint capstone is pocked with several cup marks—shallow depressions among the golden lichens.

Much of this high land above the sea drains south to the Nyfer stream along whose wooded banks you come to one of the most beautiful of the old stone carvings of Wales—the high cross of Nevern. Called St. Brynach's cross because it stands outside a church of that dedication, it was in fact made to commemorate some obviously much revered chief of about the tenth century whose name is indecipherable. The decoration consists of interlaced ribbon patterns of Irish type. It stands in the shade of yews, and photographers who want the sun on it should go there in the morning. The church has other interesting stones including a Latin and Ogham memorial to one Vitalianus.

Inevitably Nevern, medievally important, was a calling place of pilgrims going to St. David's; and up the lane a hundred yards west of the church they carved a cross on a rock before which they knelt. On the wooded hill above the church the lords of Cemaes built their first motte castle: its banks and mounds high above a dingle are still clear to see. From its leafy place it looks inland to the lower slopes of Preseli and it is up there, two miles south-east, that you will find the tall burial chamber of Pentre Ifan set against a background of moorland and rock. Today its stones stand gaunt and unclothed and to reconstruct it as the mausoleum it was 5,000 years ago, you have to imagine it covered by a high mound some forty-five yards long.

Newport, a little west of Nevern, was a medieval chartered town from whose castle the barons of Cemaes dictated to a large reach of country. The barony of Cemaes still exists and by a remarkable survival of custom it still annually appoints Newport's mayor who presides over a court leet. A little courthouse of the sixteenth century stands at Felindre, a mile or so upstream from Nevern. It was the lords of Cemaes who, when the motte at

Nevern no longer served their purpose, built the stone castle at Newport. Its ruins are visible above the south side of the town but are partly converted into a private residence—a curious mixture of house and jagged battlements. Newport today is a holiday town popular for yachting and bathing. It has a little estuary and, beyond it, wide sands and dunes. To see the whole district at once climb one of the lanes up Carn Ingli. The town lies immediately below, and beyond it the lovely bay is embraced by fine headlands east and west. Carn Ingli is a rough, open hill with rushes, gorse, sparse heather and scattered rocks. It is topped by a massive igneous outcrop around which the Iron Age built a strong hill fort that still encloses many hut remains. From Carn Ingli a stream flows north-west to Newport Bay. Where the main road crosses it a mile or so west of Newport there are five Neolithic burial chambers clustered in a field. Though all are ruined they make an impressive group. West from Newport the coast path passes Cwm-yr-eglwys, a sheltered bathing beach with caravans and yachts. Here at the sea's edge stands the west wall only of the former parish church: the rest was felled by a great sea in 1859. From here the path circles the high cliffs of Dinas Head which shelters Newport Bay from the westerlies and Fishguard Bay from the easterlies. The top of this fine promontory has far views of cliff scenery up and down the coasts of Cardigan Bay.

Fishguard (Abergwaun) with its deep and sheltered harbour, at one time aspired to become an ocean terminal. This was after 1906 when its expensive breakwater had been completed. The plan was that Liverpool-bound liners would call here to disembark mail and passengers who would then reach London a day earlier than by going via Liverpool. But the harbour facilities proved inadequate for these great vessels and Fishguard soon had to be content with playing host to the Irish boats only, a function it still continues. To connect with these boats you can take your car from London to Fishguard by train. Fishguard is in two parts, upper and lower: the upper town is where the shops are; the lower is down on a creek, smells of seaweed, has lots of small craft and an air of sea-longing. The Gwaun valley south-east of Fishguard climbs gently towards Preseli. It has beautiful oakwoods, one of which is a reserve of the West Wales Naturalists' Trust. This is a valley where old ways endure and there are people in it who still celebrate New Year in the middle of January, not yet having accepted the change from the old calendar to the new which came into force in 1752. A lonely, little-used church half a mile downstream from Pontfaen has four ancient cross-carved stones outside.

West of Fishguard the coast bulges seawards to form the great promontory whose tip is Strumble Head. All these wild, wind-swept cliffs make exciting scenery especially when big seas spume in whiteness along their feet. And on calm summer days they are altogether beautiful with their lichened rocks and many flowers and sea birds. At Pwllderi a youth hostel perches above an often stormy cove with dramatic sea-bird cliffs all round. At Llanwnda Britain was last invaded. Here in 1797 a farcically small force of French landed on Carregwastad Point. They were easily rounded up and almost immediately the yarn spread that they were de-feated because they mistook a crowd of red-dressed Welsh women for soldiery and so surrendered in the belief that they were outnumbered. But as historians have been able to show there is not a word of truth in the tale which, however, is bound to go on being repeated for centuries. On the Strumble penin-sula you will find the remains of several Neolithic burial chambers, a few Bronze Age cairns and stones and one or two Iron Age camps notably the one at Garn-fawr above Pwllderi. For the Middle Ages go to Llanwnda church high above the landing place of the French. It is a rebuild but retains ancient roof timbers, carved crosses and, outside, a crudely carved face in the east wall. St. Nicholas church, three miles south-west, also has inscribed stones. There is a burial chamber half a mile south-east of this church and another a mile and a half north-east. Each has a standing stone within a few hundred yards, perhaps once connected with it ceremonially.

A487 on its way to St. David's passes a village conspicuous on a hill to the north. This is Mathri (or Mathry), a place that used to be the centre of all things hereabouts, both its church and chartered fair being important. The church is of last century but has two ancient stones. Away on the coast at Abercastle is one of the most finely situated of all Welsh burial chambers. Standing near Longhouse farm it looks over a beautiful deep inlet to Strumble Head. The coast continues superbly all the way to St. David's Head, a region of small hamlets and scattered farms.

Along the shore there is an alternation of igneous and sedimentary rocks: the headlands are where the igneous rocks defy the sea and the many coves and inlets are where the softer sedimentaries have yielded. Several of these little beaches are reachable only along peaceful cliff paths through the gorse. There are roads down to Porthgain and Abereiddi because these coves have had large slate quarries. At Abereiddi the bedding planes of the dark Ordovician rocks are famous for graptolites, delicate and ancient fossils that look like tuning-forks. Find them on the stones of the beach. For sand follow the path to Traethllyfn half a mile north-east. All this quiet coast is still as far from the stream of modern traffic as it always has been. The many who came to St. David's in the Middle Ages used the same route as today's main road. Presumably it was pilgrims who left their sign on the south side of the road half a mile north-east of Croesgoch—a rough cross inside a circle carved upon a rock. It is known as Mesur-y-dorth ('loaf measure') and so called, says tradition, because the circle round this cross came to be used locally as a standard measure for the official size of a loaf of bread.

Today pilgrims to St. David's are few, their place having been taken by tourists. These all visit the cathedral but they wish to see much else besides. And increasingly they are realizing that the more they understand about the places they visit the more delight they get out of them. So visitors to Pembrokeshire are lucky—at Broad Haven they can seek the aid of the Countryside Unit, an organization which provides guides and itineraries so that anyone, including the family on holiday, can get an introduction to the geology, topography, natural history, ancient monuments and footpaths of Pembrokeshire. Field excursions and lectures are also available. Let us hope such a service will soon be extended to the rest of Wales so that everywhere people will be helped towards a heightened appreciation of the landscape about them. A landscape reflects the lives of its people and as their social patterns change so inevitably the landscape does also. The better we understand the processes involved in a changing landscape the better we shall be able to control them intelligently and with sensitivity, avoiding the mistakes of the past. That way the Welsh countryside could lose the few scars it has and be an ever more joyous place to go exploring.

APPENDIX 1

Maps

The Welsh counties are covered by the following sheets of the one-inch Ordnance map.

Anglesey:	Sheet 106	
Caernarvon:	„	107, 115, 116
Denbigh:	„	107, 108, 109, 117
Flint:	„	108, 109, 118
Montgomery:	„	117, 118, 127, 128, 129
Merioneth:	„	108, 116, 117, 127
Cardigan:	„	127, 139, 140
Radnor:	„	127, 128, 129, 141
Brecon:	„	140, 141, 142, 153, 154
Monmouth:	„	141, 142, 154, 155
Glamorgan:	„	141, 152, 153, 154
Carmarthen:	„	139, 140, 152, 153
Pembroke:	„	138, 139, 151, 152

Some of the words occurring in Welsh place-names

(many others may be found in dictionaries)

aber, mouth, confluence
aderyn (pl. *adar*), bird
ael, brow
afon, river, stream
allt, hillside (usually wooded)
annedd, dwelling
aran, mountain
ardd, garden
arth, hill

bach, small
Badrig, Patrick
bala, outlet, stream
ban (pl. *bannau*), mountain
banc, hill
bangor, monastery
bedd (pl. *beddau*), grave
bedwen (pl. *bedw*), birch
benglog, skull
ber, short
bera, hill
bere, kite, buzzard
betws, oratory
beudy, cowshed
blaen (pl. *blaenau*), head of valley
bochlwyd, grey-cheeked

bod, dwelling
boeth, warm
bont, bridge
borth, landing place
braich, arm, ridge
bran, crow
bras, prominent
bren, wood
brith, speckled
bro, vale
bron, rounded hill
brwynog, rushy
bryn, hill
buarth, cattle fold
buches, cattle fold
bugail, shepherd
bwlch (pl. *bylchau*), a pass
bychan, small
byr, short

caban, hut
cadair (*cader*), chair, stronghold
cadno, fox
cae, field
caer, fort
cafn, trough
cam, crooked

Words occurring in Welsh place-names

canol, middle
cau, a hollow
capel, chapel
carn, carnedd (pl. carneddau),
  heap of stones, mountain
carreg (pl. cerrig), rock
caseg, mare
cas, castell, castle
cefn, ridge
celli, copse
celyn, holly
cemais, river bends
cerrig, rocks
cesail, a hollow
ceunant, ravine
cidwm, wolf
cigfran, raven
cil, nook
clawdd, bank, dyke
clegyr, rocks
clip (pl. clipiau), steep hill
cloddiau, banks, dykes
clogwyn, cliff
clun, meadow
clwyd, gate
clyd, sheltered
cnwc, hillock
coch, red
coed (pl. coedydd), woodland
comin, comins, a common
congl, corner
cornel, corner
cors, bog
craig (pl. creigiau), rock
crib (pl. cribau), ridge
cribin, serrated ridge
croes, cross
crug (pl. crugiau), mound
cul, narrow
cwm, valley, cirque

cwrt, court
cyfyng, narrow
cyfrwy, saddle
cymer (pl. cymerau), meeting of
  rivers
cytiau, huts

darren, hill
ddeufaen, two stones
ddol, meadow
ddu, black
ddwr, water
ddysgl, dish
deg, fair
derwen (pl. derw), oak
deu (dau), two
Dewi (Ddewi), David
diffwys, precipice
dinas, fort
dir, land
diserth, a retreat
disgwylfa, viewpoint
dol (pl. dolau), meadow
domen, mound
draws, across
dre, dref, hamlet, home, town
Drindod, Trinity
drum, ridge
drws, pass
du, black
dulas, dark stream
dwr, water
dwy, two
dyffryn, valley
dywarchen, turf

efail, smithy
eglwys, church
eiddew, ivy
eira, snow

266

Words occurring in Welsh place-names

eithin, gorse
elen, elain, young deer
Emrys, Ambrosius
enlli, tide race
eos, nightingale
epynt, horse track
erch, gloomy
erw, acre
esgair, ridge

fach, small
Fair, Mary
fan, place
Faldwyn, Baldwin
fawn, peat
fawnog, peaty
fawr, large
fechan, small
fedwen (pl. fedw), birch
felin, mill
felyn, yellow
ffair, a fair
ffin, boundary
ffordd, road
ffos, ditch
Ffraid, Bridget
ffridd, mountain pasture
ffrwd, waterfall
ffynnon, spring, well
figyn (fign), bog
Fihangel, Michael
filiast, greyhound
foel, bare hill
for, sea
fraith, speckled, pied
fran, crow
fras, prominent
fron, rounded hill
fuches, cattle fold
fynach, monk

fynydd, mountain

gadair (gader), chair, stronghold
gaer, fort
gafr, goat
gallt, hillside (usually wooded)
gam, crooked
gardd, garden
garn, garnedd, heap of stones, mountain
garth, hill
garw, rough
gau, a hollow
gelli, copse
gesail, a hollow
gigfran, raven
gil, nook
glan, bank
glas (pl. gleision), green, blue
glyder, gluder, heap
glyn, glen
goch, red
goetre, woodland house
gors, bog
grach, scabby
graeanog, gravelly
graig, rock
gribin, serrated ridge
groes, cross
gron, round
grug, heather
gwalch, falcon
gwastad, level place
gwaun, moor
gwen, gwyn, white
gwern, marsh
gwernen (pl. gwern), alder
Gwrtheyrn, Vortigern
Gwyddelod, Irishmen
gwylfa, viewpoint

Words occurring in Welsh place-names

gwynt, wind
gyrn, peak

hafod, hafoty, summer dwelling
haul, sun
hebog, falcon
helygen (pl. helyg), willow
hen, old
hendre, winter dwelling
heol, road
hir (pl. hirion), long
hydd, stag
hyll, ugly

Iago, James
is, below
isaf, lowest

las, green, blue
lladron, robbers
llam, a leap
llan, church, village
llannerch, glade
llawr, flat valley bottom
llech, slate
llechog, slaty
llechwedd, hillside
llefn, smooth
llethr, slope
llety, shelter, lodging
llithrig, slippery
lloer, moon
lluest, bothy, summer dwelling
llwch, lake
llwyd, grey
llwyn, grove
llwynog, fox
llyfn, smooth
llyn (pl. llynnoedd or llynnau),
  lake

llys, hall, court

maen (pl. meini), stone
maenor, manor
maerdy, dairy
maes, field
Mair, Mary
march (pl. meirch), stallion
mawn, peat
mawnog, peat
mawr, large
meillionen, clover
mel, honey
melin, mill
melyn, yellow
merthyr, church
mign, migyn, bog
migneint, boggy hollows
Mihangel, Michael
min, edge
moch, pigs
moel, bare hill
moelrhoniaid, seals
mor, sea
morfa, coastal marsh
morwynion, maidens
mur (pl. muriau), wall
mwdwl, heap
mwyn, mineral, ore
mynach, monk
mynachdy, mynachlog, monastery or monastic property
mynydd, mountain

nadroedd, snakes
nant, stream, valley
neuadd, hall
newydd, new

odyn, kiln

Words occurring in Welsh place-names

oer, cold
ogof, ogo, cave
onnen (pl. onn), ash

pair, cauldron
pandy, fulling mill
pant, valley, hollow
pellaf, farthest
pen, top
penmaen, rocky promontory
pennant, head of a glen
penrhyn, cape
pentre, pentref, village
perfedd, middle
person, parson
pistyll, waterfall
plas, mansion
poeth, warm
pont, bridge
porth, landing place
pren, wood
pwll, pit, pool

'r, the, of the
rhaeadr, waterfall
rhandir, shared land, district
rhedyn, bracken
rhiw, hill
rhos, marsh, moor
rhudd, red
rhwng, between
rhyd, ford
Ro-wen, white pebbles

Sais, Englishman
saeth (pl. saethau), arrow
sarn, road, especially a paved road
sir, shire
sych, dry

tafarn, tavern
tai, houses
tair, three
tal, end
talcen, brow
tan, under
tarren, hill
tarw, bull
teg, fair
tir, land
tomen, mound
ton, grassland
traeth, shore
trallwng, wet valley bottom
traws, across
tre, tref, hamlet, home, town
tri, three
troed, foot
tros, over
trum (pl. trumau), ridge
trwyn, promontory
Trystion (stream name), noisy
twlc, knoll
twll, hole
twmp, twmpath, mound
twr, tower
twyn, hill
ty, tyn, house
tyddyn, small-holding
tywarchen, turf
tywyn, sea shore

uchaf, highest
uwch, above

waen, moor
wen, wyn, white
wig, a retreat
wrach (gwrach), witch

Words occurring in Welsh place-names

wyddfa (*gwyddfa*), mound, grave

wylfa, viewpoint

y, the, of the

yn, in

ynys, island, riverside meadow

yr, the, of the

ysbyty, hospice

ysgol (pl. *ysgolion*), school, ladder

ysgubor, barn

ystrad, valley floor

ystum, bend in river

Ystwyth (river name), winding

APPENDIX 3

Notes on the pronunciation of Welsh place-names

1. The stressed syllable is normally the last but one:
    e.g. gann in Degannwy
        the second er in Abertillery (or Abertyleri)
        pi in Llwynypia
        Llan in Llanbedr
   A frequent exception is where a name is really two words that have joined:
    e.g. Ynys-las (stress las)
        Ynys-hir (stress hir)
        Bryn-mawr (stress mawr)

2. There are no mute letters:
    e.g. Pentre is 'pentray'
        Bere is 'beray'

3. c is like English k.
        So Cenarth is 'kenarth'
        Cefn is 'kevn'
        Cilan is 'kilan'

4. dd is like English th in 'the' (not as in 'thin').
        So Cae Ddafydd is 'ky thavith'

5. f is English v.
        So Taf is 'tav'
        Fan is 'van'

6. Ff is like English f.

Pronunciation of Welsh place-names

7. g is always hard, as in 'gate'.
Practise with Gelli and Cilgerran.

8. Ll cannot be put into English. But you can make yourself understood by 'Thl' with lots of breath and saliva in it.

9. u is rather like English short i.
So Capel Curig is 'kapel kirrig'

10. w is like English oo in 'book'.
So Cwm is short and clipped not long as in English 'coomb'.

11. y has two sounds according to its place in the word.
In the middle of a word it is something like English short u. But in the last syllable it is like English short i
So Mynydd is 'munnith'
Ystwyth is 'ustwith'
Ynys is 'unnis'

12. Other letters are more or less as in English.

Armed with these very approximate pronunciations you will not sound like a Welshman but at least you'll have made the effort. Too many visitors do not even try to pronounce these ancient and beautiful names.

APPENDIX 4

Glossary

A miscellaneous list defining some of the terms used in this book.

bailey; a space round a motte (q.v.) enclosed by outer defences; but not all mottes had baileys.

barrow; *see* cairn.

bastide; a typical Norman town with a grid-iron street plan.

Bishop's Bible; the first Bible in Welsh, translated by Bishop Morgan and published in 1588.

Bronze Age; lasted in Wales from just before 1800 B.C. to just after 500 B.C.

burial chamber; a communal grave of the Neolithic period consisting of massive upright stone slabs covered by a capstone and then a mound of earth or stones. Usually the mound has long ago disappeared. 'Dolmen' and 'cromlech', good old words for this type of burial chamber, are unfortunately going out of use.

cadaver; an effigy in the form of a skeleton.

cairn; a pile of stones, often serving as a memorial to the dead. Nearly all cairns on the Welsh uplands are circular and covered Bronze Age burials. A few long cairns survive from the Neolithic Period, e.g. Carneddau Hengwm, near Barmouth.

Cambrian; the oldest system of fossil-bearing rocks, formed between about 500 and 400 million years ago. They underly the Ordovician system and in Wales outcrop chiefly in the Bethesda-Llanberis slate area of Caerns., and in the Rhinog range, Mer.

capital; head of a pillar, sometimes amusingly decorated as in Haverfordwest church, Pembs.

Carboniferous; the system of rocks overlying the Devonian system and underlying the Permian. It was formed between about 280 and 210 million years ago. The Coal Measures and much of the limestones of Wales belong to this system.

Celtic cross; the wheel-headed type of cross universal in the Celtic world of the Dark and Middle Ages.

Celts; peoples who migrated to Britain from southern Germany about 500 B.C. and are associated with the inauguration of the Iron Age. Their language survives as Welsh, Gaelic and Breton.

chalybeate; a term used to describe spa waters rich in iron salts. The chalybeate water at Trefriw, Caerns., is particularly strong.

chevaux de frise; pointed stones set in the earth as defences. Commonest in west Ireland they occur at two Welsh hill forts: prominently at Pen-y-gaer, Caerns., and slightly at Craig Gwrtheyrn, Carms.

Chi-rho; on early Celtic Christian monuments these first two letters of Christ's name in Greek stood for Christianity before the cross came into general use.

cirque; *see* corrie lake.

Cistercians; an order of white-robed monks originating at Cîteaux, eastern France, in 1098. They spread to England in 1128 and Wales (Whitland, Carms.) in 1143.

corrie lake; lake in a semi-circular hollow (cirque) carved in a mountainside by glacial action. Typically a corrie lake is bounded by moraines on the side away from the mountain.

cross-slab; the stone cover of a tomb incised with a cross and sometimes other decorations.

cruck-built; describes houses in which the ridge beam is supported on wooden arches, each consisting of two upright timbers naturally incurving to meet overhead. The style is very ancient and commonest on the west (i.e. Celtic) side of Britain.

cup-marks; small hollows chipped in the faces of ancient stones. Of uncertain age and unknown purpose they appear in Wales on the capstones of Neolithic burial chambers near Clynnog-fawr, Caerns., and Newport, Pembs. But they may have been post-Neolithic additions and are guessed to be a form of Bronze Age religious art. They are found from Scandinavia to North Africa.

Glossary

Cytiau Gwyddelod; 'Irishmen's Huts'—a name traditionally given to prehistoric hut remains in Wales. Most are of the Iron Age. An alternative name is Muriau Gwyddelod, 'Irishmen's Walls'. There is no real justification for calling them Irish.

dog tongs; an instrument for breaking up dog fights in the days when squires and farmers habitually brought their dogs to church.

dorter; a monastic dormitory.

drovers' roads; these were cross-country tracks used for walking cattle to the English markets. Some have become modern roads, others survive as green roads over the hills. Cattle were shod for these long treks; so too were geese.

Dyfed; one of the four Dark Ages kingdoms of Wales consisting of Pembrokeshire and west Carmarthenshire.

Er cof am; words on Welsh tombstones meaning 'In memory of'.

erratic boulder; a boulder deposited by a glacier at the end of the Great Ice Age.

fault; a fracture in rocks causing them to be displaced sometimes for several miles thus greatly affecting scenery. The fault from Bala to the coast is the largest in Wales.

Fenton, Richard; the eighteenth-century historian of Pembrokeshire. He lived in the Gwaun valley, Fishguard.

forest; originally a medieval term meaning royal hunting country. So it often refers to rather treeless moorlands such as Fforest Fawr (Great Forest) in Breconshire, Radnor Forest, etc.

fulling mill; a type of watermill once very common in the Welsh countryside (where it was usually called 'pandy'). Fulling was a process of cleansing and thickening cloth.

Giraldus Cambrensis (Gerallt Cymro or Gerald the Welshman); a famous twelfth-century churchman born in Manorbier castle, Pembrokeshire. His writings shed a lively light on the Wales of his time. His *Itinerary* describes a Welsh journey he made in 1188 to recruit for the Third Crusade.

Gwent; one of the four Dark Ages kingdoms of Wales consisting roughly of what is now Monmouthshire.

Gwynedd; one of the four Dark Ages kingdoms of Wales

consisting of Anglesey, Caernarvonshire, Merioneth and parts of Denbighshire and Flintshire.

hatchment; a tablet, often diamond-shaped, depicting a deceased person's armorial bearings. The custom of hanging hatchments in churches, where many still survive, lasted from the seventeenth to the nineteenth century.

hill fort; embankments of earth or stone built to defend hill tops. Nearly all are Iron Age.

igneous; describes rocks which consolidated from a molten state (as distinct from sedimentary rocks).

I.H.S.; Greek symbol meaning Jesus and often carved on memorials.

Iron Age; lasted in Wales from about 500 B.C. to about the first century.

Jesse, tree of; a familiar theme of medieval church carvings and windows. They usually show Jesse lying on his side with a vine growing out of him bearing many Old Testament kings and prophets on its branches arranged in a hierarchy with Christ at the top. A particularly fine Jesse window is in Llanrhaeadr church, Denbighshire. There is a famous Jesse niche in Llantwit Major church, Glam.

Knights Templar; a crusading military order founded *c.* 1118 to protect pilgrims' routes to holy places.

Leland, John; an official antiquary who in the reign of Henry VIII travelled through Britain making an inventory of valuable books, manuscripts and antiquities in colleges, cathedrals, monasteries, etc. His *Itinerary* is a valuable source of antiquarian and topographical information.

Lhuyd (or Llwyd), Edward; an eminent Welsh naturalist, antiquarian and philologist (1660–1709). He became the second director of the Ashmolean Museum, Oxford.

lynchet; a low bank marking the outline of prehistoric fields.

Mabinogion; a remarkable collection of medieval Welsh tales whose earliest surviving texts date mainly from the fourteenth century. But the matter of the tales clearly goes back to the Dark Ages and even to the Roman period.

megalith; a large stone monument of the type introduced by Neolithic man.

Mesolithic; the Middle Stone Age which in Britain lasted from about 12,000 to 3,000 B.C. It followed the Paleolithic (or

Old Stone Age) and preceded the Neolithic (or New Stone Age).

misericord; a projection, often elaborately carved, on the underside of a choir stall seat.

motte; a castle mound. Many were built in Wales, especially in the eleventh and twelfth centuries. Most still survive in varying states of preservation. A word introduced by the Normans, motte has become 'moat' at places such as Moat castle, Mont., and The Moat, Bugeildy, Rads.

multivallate (of hill forts); having several lines of earthworks.

Muriau Gwyddelod; *see* Cytiau.

Neolithic; the New Stone Age which in Britain lasted from about 3,000 to 1,800 B.C. It followed the Mesolithic Age and preceded the Bronze Age.

Ogham (Ogam); a script of the early Dark Ages originating in Ireland and brought by the Irish to Scotland, the Isle of Man, Wales and Cornwall. Consisting of long and short lines carved on the edges of stones, it was used on memorials. In Wales Ogham stones are commonest in Pembs.

Old Red Sandstone; sandstone formed in the Devonian Period (about 320 to 280 million years ago) and well developed in the Brecon Beacons.

Ordovician; the system of rocks overlying the Cambrian system and underlying the Silurian. Formed between about 400 to 350 million years ago it forms the bulk of rocks in the Snowdonia National Park.

passage grave; a Neolithic chambered tomb, covered by a circular mound and entered by a long narrow passage.

peel tower: a small defensive tower of a type common on the English-Scottish border and in Ireland but much less common in Wales.

Pennant, Thomas; a famous zoologist and traveller of the eighteenth century who lived in Flintshire and is now remembered for his *Tours in Wales*.

pillow mounds; mounds, usually in groups, which were built as rabbit warrens often as long ago as the Middle Ages.

piscina; stone basin with sink-hole for pouring away water used ceremonially in church. Usually in the south chancel wall.

Powys; one of the four Dark Ages Kingdoms of Wales con-

277

sisting of Montgomeryshire, Radnorshire and part of Denbighshire.

Pre-Cambrian; a term describing the most ancient rocks formed prior to about 600 million years ago. In Wales they are chiefly found in Anglesey, Caernarvonshire and Pembrokeshire. They are virtually devoid of fossils.

promontory fort; a fort, usually of the Iron Age, on a coastal promontory or the spur of a hill, defended on one side by banks.

reredos; an ornamental screen behind an altar.

river capture; the diversion of one river (A) into another (B) caused by B cutting back into A's course. If the two rivers were at right angles to each other the result is 'an elbow of river capture' as at Devil's Bridge, Cards.

Roman period; about A.D. 50–400.

rood loft; a gallery in a church on top of the rood screen (q.v.). Common in medieval churches, few now survive; but the steps built in the walls to reach the loft are still common.

rood screen; the division between the nave and chancel of a medieval church. Such screens of elaborately carved oak survive almost perfect in a few Welsh churches such as Llananno, Rads., Llanegryn, Mer. and others; but most were cleared away by Victorian restorers. Above the screen was the rood, a figure of Christ crucified, but roods were destroyed at the Reformation.

St. Christopher; the patron saint of travellers. He was often painted on the walls of medieval churches usually opposite the south door so as to greet people as they entered.

St. John; in the Middle Ages the Order of St. John of Jerusalem set up hospices through W. Europe to shelter pilgrims and other travellers. In Wales they had such refuges at Slebech, Pembs., Bridgend, Glam., and Ysbyty Ifan, Denbs.

sedilia; a set of seats in a church (usually three in the south wall of the chancel) often canopied and ornate.

sessile oak; the commonest species of oak in Wales: so called because its acorns are sessile (i.e. stalk-less) on the twigs. Preferring well-drained soils it flourishes on hillsides.

Silurian; the system of rocks overlying the Ordovician system and underlying the Devonian. Formed between about 350 and 320 million years ago it is predominant in much of the counties of Denbs., Mont., Rads., and Cards.

Glossary

slight; to slight a castle meant to dismantle it. It is used especially of the Cromwellians' treatment of castles after the Civil War.

spindle whorls; pierced stone or pottery disks which act as fly-wheels in primitive methods of spinning. They are found on prehistoric sites from the Neolithic Period onwards.

Stone Age; *see* Mesolithic and Neolithic.

torc (torque); gold torcs are necklaces or waist-bands made of twisted bars. They are associated with the Bronze Age, the gold mostly coming from the Wicklow mountains, Ireland.

Triassic; the system of rocks overlying the Permian system and underlying the Jurassic. It was formed between about 170 and 145 million years ago. It is well developed on the Glamorgan coast.

triptych; a picture or carving in three panels side by side.

tympanum; a triangular space between a lintel and an arch above it. Also the triangle between a rood loft and the roof of a church, such as survives at Llaneleu church, Brecs.

X.P.C.; Greek symbol meaning Christ, sometimes carved on memorials.

APPENDIX 5

National Nature Reserves and other Nature Reserves in Wales

Permits to visit National Nature Reserves in North Wales are obtainable from Nature Conservancy, Penrhos Road, Bangor, Caerns. In South Wales from the Nature Conservancy, Plas Gogerddan, Aberystwyth, Cards.

Apart from National Nature Reserves there are many reserves run by Naturalists' Trusts. Most are open to members only and inquiries should be addressed to:

North Wales Naturalists' Trust, Llys Gwynedd, Ffordd Gwynedd, Bangor, Caernarvonshire.

(Anglesey, Caernarvon, Denbigh, Flint, Montgomery and north Merioneth.)

West Wales Naturalists' Trust, 4 Victoria Place, Haverfordwest, Pembrokeshire.

(Pembroke, Carmarthen, Cardigan and south Merioneth.)

Herefordshire and Radnorshire Nature Trust, Martins Bank House, 21 Broad Street, Hereford.

Brecknock County Naturalists' Trust, Brynheulog, Cefn Coed, near Merthyr Tydfil.

Monmouthshire Naturalists' Trust, 40 Melbourne Way, Newport.

Glamorgan County Naturalists' Trust, 22 Lon Mefus, Tycoch, Swansea.

The Royal Society for the Protection of Birds, The Lodge, Sandy, Beds., has Welsh Reserves at:

Grassholm Island, W. Pembs.—a vast gannetry.

Ramsey Island, W. Pembs.—sea birds, choughs and grey seals.

Gwenffrwd, N. Carms.—moorlands and oakwoods.

Ynys-hir, N. Cards.—estuary, marshes and woodlands.

Nature Reserves etc.

The National Trust for Places of Historic Interest or Natural
Beauty, 42 Queen Anne's Gate, London, S.W.1, owns many
properties in Wales.

The Council for the Promotion of Field Studies has centres at
Dale Fort (Pemb.), Orielton (Pemb.), Rhyd-y-Creuau
(Denb.) and Preston Montford (Shrops.).

See overleaf for a list of National Nature Reserves in Wales.

County	Reserve	Where is it?	Acre-age	Nature	Is permit required?
Anglesey	Newborough and Llanddwyn	S. tip of Anglesey	1,565	Dunes and rocky coast	Yes, away from public road
Caernarvon	Coed Gorswen	4 m. s. of Conway	33	Base-rich woodland	Yes, away from public path
,,	Coed Dolgarrog	7 m. s. of Conway	170	Steep woodland	Yes, away from public path
,,	Cwm Glas, Crafnant	1½ m. n.e. of Capel Curig	38	Base-rich rocks and woods	Yes, for the enclosed woodland
,,	Cwm Idwal	5 m. w. of Capel Curig	984	Corrie and lake	No
,,	Snowdon	11 m. s. of Bangor	4,145	Mountain	No
,,	Coed Tremadoc	1½ m. n.e. of Portmadoc	49	Cliff, woodland, scree	Yes
Merioneth	Coed Cymerau	1 m. n.w. of Ffestiniog	65	Sessile oakwood	Yes, away from public footpath
,,	Coedydd Maentwrog	½ m. n. of Maentwrog	180	Woodland	No
,,	Morfa Harlech	2 m. n.w. of Harlech	1,214	Shore and dunes	Yes
,,	Coed Camlyn	½ m. s. of Maentwrog	57	Sessile oakwood	Yes
,,	Coed y Rhygen	W. side of Trawsfynydd Reservoir	52	Oak/birch woodland	Yes
,,	Morfa Dyffryn	4 m. s.w. of Harlech	500	Shore and dunes	Yes, away from public footpath
,,	Rhinog	5 m. e. of Harlech	991	Mountain	No
,,	Coed Ganllwyd	5 m. n. of Dolgellau	59	Woodland	No
,,	Cadair Idris	3 m. s. of Dolgellau	969	Mountain and woodland	Yes, for the enclosed woodland

County	Reserve	Where is it?	Acre-age	Nature	Is permit required?
Cardigan	Dovey Estuary	8 m. n. of Aberystwyth	about 3,500	Tidal rivermouth	Yes, for shooting
,,	Cors Fochno	6 m. n.e. of Aberystwyth	about 180	Peat bog	Yes
,,	Coed Rheidol (includes Forest Reserve)	10 m. e. of Aberystwyth	115	Sessile oakwood	Yes, away from public footpath
,,	Cors Tregaron	12 m. s.e. of Aberystwyth	1,898	Peat bog	Yes, away from public footpath
Brecon	Nant Irfon	5 m. n. of Llanwrtyd Wells	216	Moor and woodland	Yes
,,	Craig Cerrig Gleisiad	6 m. s.w. of Brecon	698	Sandstone cliff	Yes
,,	Craig y Cilau	2 m. s.w. of Crickhowell	157	Limestone with trees and caves	Yes, for caves
,,	Cwm Clydach	6 m. s.w. of Abergavenny	50	Gorge with beechwoods	No
,,	Penmoelallt (Forest Reserve)	3 m. n. of Merthyr Tydfil	17	Woodland on limestone	Yes, away from paths
Monmouth	Blackcliff and Wyndcliff (Forest Reserve)	2 m. n. of Chepstow	200	Woodland on limestone	Yes, away from paths
Glamorgan	Whiteford	West end of Gower	1,933	Shore and dunes	Yes, away from shore
,,	Gower coast	s.e. coast of Gower	116	Limestone sea cliffs	No
,,	Oxwich	3 m. e. of Port Eynon	542	Dunes, marshes, pools	Yes
Carmarthen	Allt Rhyd-y-groes	9 m. n. of Llandovery	153	Sessile oakwood	Yes
Pembroke	Skomer	14 m. w.s.w. of Haverfordwest	759	Offshore island	No

INDEX

In this index of place-names the county and map reference will be found in brackets between the place-names and the page number. The following abbreviations have been used: I. (Island), L. (Lake or Llyn), M. (Mountain) and R. (River).

285

Index

Index

Index

288

Index

Index

Index

Index

Index

Index

Index

Index

Index

Index

Index

Index

Index